PURCHASING POWER

# STUDIES IN GENDER AND HISTORY

General Editors: Franca Iacovetta and Karen Dubinsky

# Purchasing Power

## Women and the Rise of Canadian Consumer Culture

DONICA BELISLE

UNIVERSITY OF TORONTO PRESS
Toronto Buffalo London

ISBN 978-1-4426-3113-7 (cloth)     ISBN 978-1-4426-2587-7 (EPUB)
ISBN 978-1-4426-2911-0 (paper)     ISBN 978-1-4426-2586-0 (PDF)

Studies in Gender and History

**Library and Archives Canada Cataloguing in Publication**

Title: Purchasing power : women and the rise of Canadian consumer culture /
Donica Belisle.
Names: Belisle, Donica, 1976– author.
Series: Studies in gender and history ; 50.
Description: Series statement: Studies in gender and history ; 50 |
Includes bibliographical references and index.
Identifiers: Canadiana (print) 2019023699X | Canadiana (ebook) 2019023704X |
ISBN 9781442631137 (cloth) | ISBN 9781442629110 (paper) | ISBN
9781442625877 (EPUB) | ISBN 9781442625860 (PDF)
Subjects: LCSH: Consumption (Economics) – Canada – History. | LCSH:
Consumption (Economics) – Social aspects – Canada – History. | LCSH:
Consumption (Economics) – Political aspects – Canada – History. | LCSH:
Women consumers – Canada – History. | LCSH: Consumer behavior –
Canada – History. | LCSH: Women, White – Canada – Economic conditions. |
LCSH: Women, White – Canada – Social conditions.
Classification: LCC HC120.C6 B42 2020 | DDC 339.4/70820971 – dc23

University of Toronto Press acknowledges the financial assistance to its
publishing program of the Canada Council for the Arts and the Ontario Arts
Council, an Ontario government agency.

This book has been published with the help of a grant from the Federation
for the Humanities and Social Sciences, using funds provided by the Social
Sciences and Humanities Research Council of Canada.

Canada Council    Conseil des Arts
for the Arts      du Canada

ONTARIO ARTS COUNCIL
CONSEIL DES ARTS DE L'ONTARIO
an Ontario government agency
un organisme du gouvernement de l'Ontario

Funded by the    Financé par le
Government    gouvernement
of Canada    du Canada

MIX
Paper from
responsible sources
FSC® C016245

# Contents

*List of Illustrations*   vii

*Acknowledgments*   ix

Introduction – Consumer Culture in Historical Perspective   3

1 Temperance and the Rise of Sober Consumer Culture   18

2 Shopping for Victory: Consumer Citizenship in Wartime   43

3 Home Economics and the Training of the Consumer
Citizenry   73

4 Rural Consumer Citizens: Consumption in the
Countryside   98

5 For Whom Do We Dress? Feminism and Fashion   124

6 Challenging Capitalism? The Limits of Collective Buying   148

Conclusion – Empowerment and Exclusion: Consumption in
Canadian History   180

*Notes*   193

*Bibliography*   233

*Index*   249

# Illustrations

1.1 "What are They to Me?" article criticizing selfish, unpatriotic shopping 26

2.1 "Vision Your Sons, Mothers of Canada!" food service pledge advertisement 49

2.2 Poster advertising Canada Food Board recipe books 61

2.3 "An Army of Savers," illustration of a conservationist army 65

2.4 "Buy Fresh Fish," Canada Food Board poster 68

2.5 "Waste Not – Want Not," Canada Food Board poster 69

2.6 "Remember We Must Feed Daddy Too," Canada Food Board poster 71

3.1 Photograph of Antoinette Gérin-Lajoie and Madame Lacroix at a table decorated with Dupuis Frères products 86

4.1 "Product of Nova Scotia" label advertisement 113

4.2 Photograph of Mrs. J. MacGregor Smith presenting a basket of Alberta-made goods to Edmonton mayor D.K. Knott 115

5.1 Photograph of a bathing suit designed by Florine Phaneuf 139

6.1 Photograph of a young participant in a Co-operative Day Parade, Sydney Mines, Nova Scotia 155

6.2 Illustration of on overwhelmed consumer in need of guidance 159

6.3 Photograph of shoppers and their children waiting in line to enter the Housewives' League Sale 167

# Acknowledgments

Research for this book was funded by the Social Sciences and Research Council of Canada (SSHRC), specifically by Standard Research Grant 410-2011-1239. Thanks go to SSHRC, as well as to Athabasca University, which awarded a generous research incentive grant in 2009.

From the beginning the University of Toronto Press has been incredibly supportive. Thanks go to editor Len Husband, who has been integral to the book's success. Crucial, too, has been the support of Angela Wingfield, Robin Studniberg, Dallas Harrison, and Breanna Muir. Franca Iacovetta and the book's anonymous peer reviewers have also contributed generous insights. These have enhanced what follows.

The arguments of *Purchasing Power* were workshopped in several venues, including speakers' series at the University of Alberta (2012, 2013) and the University of Calgary (2012). Portions of the book appeared at the annual meeting of the Canadian Historical Association in Calgary (2016), Victoria (2013), Waterloo (2012), and Fredericton (2011) and at the following conferences: Dressing Global Bodies, University of Alberta (2016); Western Association of Canadian Studies, University of Manitoba (2015); Contesting Canada's Future, Trent University (2015); Canadian Studies Network, University of Prince Edward Island (2014); Sustainable Consumption Research and Action Initiative, Clark University (2013); Western Association of Women Historians, Denver (2016) and Berkeley (2012); Women and Food, Banff, Alberta (2012); Berkshire Conference on the History of Women, University of Massachusetts (2011); and Continuing the Conversations, Trent University (2011). Thanks go to all.

My research team and I have had the privilege of working with record keepers – and record creators – across the country. My gratitude goes to everyone at the provincial archives of British Columbia, Alberta, Saskatchewan, Manitoba, Ontario, Nova Scotia, and Newfoundland and to the many archivists at Bibliothèque et Archives nationales du Québec and Library and Archives Canada. Archivists at the Glenbow Museum and Archives, the University of Alberta, the University of Manitoba, Mount Allison University, the University of Guelph, and the Université de Montréal were instrumental in locating numerous records. Special mention must be made of Lindsay Murray of the Women's Institutes of Nova Scotia, who digitized the newsletters of that organization.

Colleagues at the University of Regina have been wonderful. I am grateful to Doreen Thompson and Christina Winter. Raymond Blake, Robin Ganev, Dawn Flood, Allison Fizzard, Yvonne Petry, Ian Germani, Ken Leyton-Brown, Philip Charrier, Allyson Stevenson, Jeff Loucks, Jason Demers, Rob Grodinsky, and others have also contributed. At Athabasca University, too, I enjoyed a stimulating intellectual environment, for which special thanks go to Marc Cels, Bob Barnetson, Nanci Langford, and Alvin Finkel.

Halfway through this project I gained the dubious distinction of becoming a "mid-career scholar." What this means, in practice, is that I had the pleasure of working with both senior and junior scholars. I would like to thank my mentors, Joan Sangster, Veronica Strong-Boag, Sarah Carter, and Beverly Lemire, whose brilliance has only been matched by their generosity. That many of the researchers who contributed to this book are now also highly accomplished intellectuals speaks not only to the time it has taken to complete this project but also to their own expertise. Thanks go to Meagan Beaton, Lisa Pasolli, Cedric Brousseau, Kristin Rodier, Kiera Mitchell, Brandi Adams, and Eric Schiffmann.

Several feminist colleagues and friends have been present from the start of this study to its finish. To Sharon Romeo, Chloe Taylor, Lianne McTavish, Siobhan Byrne, Jaymie Heilman, Vanessa Mathews, Jennifer Gordon, Bridget Klest, Kyla Madden, and Karyn Taylor: thank you. I would also like to thank my mother, Julie Belisle, and my sister, Kat Belisle. Robyn Braun, both as a friend and as an editor, has been key to this project. Thanks go also to Dasha Chernova, whose contributions enabled extra writing time.

This book was written in the (very) early morning hours of this past decade. I thank my partner, David Taylor, and our two incredible children, Leo and Norah, who were born as it took shape. I am grateful to Awasis Daycare, which continues to provide a top-notch care environment. Finally, David's love and support, not to mention his wit, have been vital to this project. *Purchasing Power* is dedicated to him.

# PURCHASING POWER

*Introduction*

# Consumer Culture in Historical Perspective

In 1922 a young wife in Toronto named Mary Quayle Innis wrote in her diary that she had gone "downtown early and did Simpson's, Eaton's and 10c store. Got groceries, etc."[1] For Innis, who was twenty-two at the time, this entry was typical. From the earliest days of her marriage in 1921 until her passing in 1972 she spent much time in Toronto's shops. Remembered today as a prominent intellectual, one who published fiction and non-fiction alike, Innis was also a committed wife, mother, and colleague.[2] It was in these roles that she returned time and again to the shops. She brought her children to see the holiday displays in department stores, ate with friends and family in the stores' restaurants, and attended events in the stores' meeting rooms. She went regularly to Eaton's, Simpson's, and similar shops to buy travel tickets, have pictures framed, and pick up necessities.[3] For this urban, middle class woman, as well as for thousands of her contemporaries, department stores were integral to everyday life.

Exploring the meanings of shopping and commodities within Canada's past, this book joins a growing number of works in recovering the history of Canadian consumer culture.[4] By looking at select wives' and mothers' consumer involvements between the 1890s and 1930s, I argue that consumer issues have been central to the Canadian experience. According to numerous wives and mothers before 1940, consumption was tied not only to survival but also to caregiving, status, identity, creativity, belonging, and liberation. Examining the links that these women made among these issues, this study offers new insights into Canadian consumer histories. It argues that although wives and mothers tended to exist outside both the formal political process and the formal labour market, many considered their consumer roles to be evidence of their political and economic participation. It reveals, too, that before the Second World War, consumer matters were complex, involving questions of morality, stratification, justice, and aesthetics simultaneously.

*Purchasing Power* makes contributions in three main areas: the history of Canadian consumer culture, the history of the Canadian political economy, and the history of Canadian identity. This book was born of a long-standing interest in the everyday lives of wives and mothers, particularly the efforts that many poured into budgeting and shopping as well as into fashion, decorating, and cooking. Many publications have, of course, explored these issues, demonstrating that from the early nineteenth century onward white settler women have taken responsibility for feeding and clothing their families, furnishing and cleaning their homes, doing their families' errands, and securing the goods and services that have enabled their families to thrive.[5] Historians have shown, too, that for well over two hundred years white settler women have drawn strength from their maternal and homemaker identities, even using such identities to launch social movements.[6] Scholars have further examined cosmetics and fashion history, revealing that since the late nineteenth century countless women in Canada, including white women and women of racialized and ethnic minority status, have deployed their consumer skills to cultivate "modern" identities.[7]

This study builds upon all of this research, but it also charts new paths. Whereas most publications focus on the political, the economic, or the cultural aspects of consumption, this book explores all three. It shows that consumption, far from having been a sliver of many Canadians' lives, actually constituted a major portion of their total life experiences. Shopping and commodities were crucial to wives' and mothers' economic and political participation as well as to their artistic expression and identity construction. This centrality of consumption, moreover, arose from their gendered positions within the Canadian political economy. Between the 1880s and 1930s, breadwinning was coded as masculine, and homemaking was coded as feminine.[8]

For many wives and mothers, therefore, consumption was a lifelong activity, one that enabled the survival and well-being of their families. For a few women, too, it offered opportunities for artistic experimentation. Finally, some women turned to consumer culture to construct status. In their attempts to portray themselves as modern, they denigrated other women. Race, nation, and class featured in such portrayals. Some Canadian women of this era suggested that non-white and poor women's consumer practices were the antithesis of bourgeois sophistication. As such, they were also the antithesis of Canadian nationhood.

This book deepens historical understandings of consumer culture. Yet it also has relevance today. According to the World Wildlife Fund, Canadians' consumption of the earth's resources is now approximately three and a half times the "global average." More than this, Canadians' current consumer levels are "4.3 times greater than the amount of biocapacity that the Earth can provide for each person." Only three countries consume more of the earth's resources per capita than does Canada: the United Arab Emirates, the United States of America, and Finland.[9] Certainly, consumers are not solely to blame for the planet's environmental problems, including the "destruction of ecosystems and biodiversity," "climate change," alterations to the biosphere, and "land-system change."[10] Industry and government also are responsible for emitting green house gases, damaging ecosystems, and creating pollutants. Indeed, of all the fossil fuels consumed in Canada, only one-third are purchased by consumers.[11] Moreover, consumers live in "a context that limits their capacity for choice," as the Consumers Council of Canada puts it. Housing patterns, city designs, resource availability, and work hours, among other things, prevent sustainable living.[12]

Our current unsustainable moment – what Juliet Schor and Craig Thompson call the "business-as-usual (BAU) economy" – hence derives from numerous factors.[13] Canadian historians have begun exploring these factors, with recent promising research devoted to the energy sector.[14] At the same time, histories of consumption remain important. Only by recognizing the sources of consumer desire does it become possible to understand why, in the face of planetary destruction, Canadians continue to pursue unsustainability. By demonstrating the historical rootedness of many Canadians' propensity to consume, I reveal that for well over a hundred years Canadians have turned to consumer activity to survive, construct identities, seek pleasure, demonstrate citizenship, and communicate status.

This book, then, offers six chapters on the history of women and consumption. The approach is limited in that it does not provide a comprehensive overview of all people in northern North America. At the same time it does enable insight into a range of topics simultaneously. With chapters on the temperance movement, consumer conservation, the home economics movement, rural life, consumer co-operation, and fashion, this study provides snapshots of issues prevalent in the late nineteenth and early twentieth centuries. Each of these topics in turn was selected after an extensive examination of archival materials relating to the club-women's movement, the home economics movement, and the co-operative movement. These three movements were selected for investigation because each was involved in consumption. Materials generated by the club-women's movement proved particularly salient, offering extended coverage of consumption, often written in the consumer's own words. By exploring these materials, I avoid the common historiographical problem, articulated so well by Joy Parr, of seeking insight into consumer history by looking at sources not generated directly by consumers. As Parr put it in an historiographical overview in 1999, "we know more about Mr Eaton than about Mr Eaton's customers, and are tempted to infer what Mr Eaton's customers thought from what Mr Eaton thought."[15]

This book draws theoretical inspiration from a number of scholars, including Pierre Bourdieu. In his classic text, *Distinction: A Social Critique of the Judgement of Taste* (1979), Bourdieu suggests that social status is constructed partially through consumption. After studying "a survey" that he had "carried out in 1963 and 1967–8 on a sample of 1,217 people" in France, he concluded that the "dominant" classes and the "dominated" classes had opposing aesthetics. For the former group, it is important to erase all signifiers of "nature" and its various labours and gratifications; instead, "subliminated tastes" and "restraint" are the hallmarks of taste.[16] In contrast, immediate gratification is central to the dominated's aesthetic. In terms of food, for example, "industrial workers" demonstrate preference for hearty meals, eaten in "convivial indulgence."[17] As these preferences make clear, the tastes of the dominant and the dominated class form in opposition to each other. In that the dominant seek to erase all indicators of "natural ... enjoyment," they are attempting to demonstrate their freedom from poverty and material need.[18] And in that the dominated seek to "liberate" themselves "by ... overturning conventions and proprieties," they are calling out the dominant classes for being disingenuous.[19]

Employing Bourdieu's argument that aesthetics are a means of, first, expressing moral values, second, articulating class conflict, and, third, constructing social hierarchies, the study demonstrates that many Canadian women between the 1890s and 1930s deployed notions of consumer taste to solidify their own privileges. Even while it relies upon Bourdieu to make this case, however, it also departs from him in that it examines race and ethnicity. Specifically, this book views racial and ethnic hierarchies as integral to determining social rank. As such, it can be characterized not as Marxist but as intersectionalist. This theoretical stance draws from Nira Yuval-Davis who, in *The Politics of Belonging: Intersectional Contestations* (2011), suggests that intersectionality recognizes the "differential situatedness of different social agents" and furthermore interrogates the relationship between such situatedness and the "social, economic and political projects" of agents. Ideally, and as Yuval-Davis points out, intersectional researchers should not ascribe simplistic viewpoints to people based on the latter's positions along "socio-economic grids of power" but should rather take such positionings into account within broader analyses. Of specific importance are "race, class and gender," but other positionings such as age, disability, and sexuality are also crucial. Whereas some intersectional theorists focus on the marginalized, others – including Yuval-Davis – apply intersectionality to everybody, including those in power. In this way they make it possible to see relationships among power, group identification, and marginality.[20]

If Yuval-Davis's writings inform the theoretical lens of this book, they also influence its approach to consumption. As is Bourdieu, Yuval-Davis is interested in social exclusion. She writes, "[The] question of belonging and the politics of belonging constitute some of the most difficult issues that are confronting all of us these days." Yuval-Davis is referring specifically to the twenty-first century, but her analyses have relevance for other periods. Her argument that "the inclusion or exclusion of particular people" is central to identity construction is helpful for decoding the meanings of consumption in Canada.[21] As the reader will see, patterns of inclusion and exclusion based on race, ethnicity, gender, and class were central to consumer issues in this country. By purchasing and using certain goods, as well as by casting judgments on those who did not, white Canadian women defined who – and who did not – belong.

They also defined who qualified as Canadian. In her article on white women's travels to the north from the early twentieth century through to the 1960s, historian Myra Rutherdale demonstrates that white Canadian women pointed to Indigenous people's clothes as indicators of assimilation or lack thereof, as the case may be.[22] Despite their reliance upon Inuit women's preparation of winter clothing for them, white women policed the boundaries of what they referred to as "Eskimo clothing" and "white man's clothing."[23] In this way, they "dichotomize[d] race through attire."[24] Yet if white women demonstrated preference for Euro-Canadian customs, so they sometimes disparaged Indigenous women who adopted Euro-Canadian styles. During the 1950s a white nurse named Donalda McKillop Copeland described an Inuit woman named Sheownarlook, who had just returned to her community after four years in the south: she "had become something of a woman of the world ... Her jet black hair was cropped short and curled, her cheeks were smeared with face powder and rouge and on her lips was a bright red colouring which contrasted oddly with her sallow skin." Sheownarlook was thus much different from her "tundra sisters," who wore "long plaits of hair" and had "faces quite untouched by beauty aids."[25] By using words such as *smeared* and *sallow* to describe Sheownarlook, Copeland suggested that she had failed to assimilate; indeed, according to Copeland, it was inauthentic for her to try. Inuit women's true identities required being "untouched." Due to their racial difference Inuit women could never become fully Canadian.

*Purchasing Power* offers further evidence of the ways in which white Canadians associated consumption with racial and national belonging. It complements other recent studies in this area, all of which point to the importance of the consumer realm for membership within a racialized polity. Laurie K. Bertram's recent inquiries into the fashion choices of Icelandic Canadian women are especially important. According to Bertram, when Icelandic immigrants arrived in Winnipeg in 1875, a "crowd of ... Winnipeggers gathered at the docks to demand a display of the new arrivals."[26] This event occurred because anglophone Canadians assumed that Icelanders were an exotic people, stating, for example: "they are short of stature, about four feet high, rather short and sturdy, long jet-black hair, a good deal like Eskimos!"[27] Thus, the Winnipeggers were hoping to see people with different appearances from their own. Not only does this incident point to the surveillance that anglophones directed towards newcomers, but also it highlights the importance of dress. Due to the discrimination that Icelandic Canadian women experienced, many new arrivals discarded their *skotthúfa*, or tasselled hats. They also modified their dresses to conform to Anglo-Canadian styles. When they could afford to do so, they purchased Anglo-Canadian clothing.[28] As Bertram argues, their reasons for doing so were complicated and included a genuine appreciation of such attire. Yet a desire to "dress Canadian" was also at play.[29] Bertram states: "cloth [was] an alterable terrain though which migrants pursued, altered, destroyed, and created images of themselves to negotiate life in Canada."[30]

Attending to how white Canadian women held up their own consumer practices as evidence of modernity, this book supports a growing body of research that connects consumption to white Canadian nationalism. Chapter 3, for example, reveals that many home economists argued that English Canadian dining and cooking customs were scientifically preferable to those of other ethnic and racialized groups. They conflated English Canadian customs with modernity and healthfulness, broadly speaking; they also attempted to convince non-English Canadians to adopt English Canadian ways. Thus, just as immigrant-reception workers in late 1940s Canada attempted to convince immigrant women to shop the "Canadian way" – which usually involved "pushing overflow-ing grocery carts down aisles with well-stocked shelves, or cook-ing meals in modern and well-appointed kitchens" (writes Franca Iacovetta) – so did earlier home economists suggest that English Canadian consumer practices should become the norm.[31] In this way, they normalized white practices as Canadian; they also mar-ginalized other groups.

This study further draws from the feminist materialist tradi-tion. Scholars in this framework have demonstrated that there has long existed within Western European and white-settler nations a strong connection between femininity and consumption.[32] This connection has stemmed from two circumstances: women's posi-tion as consumers in the European gendered division of labour, and women's position as ornamental objects within European heterosexual economies of desire.[33] The first circumstance became acute in Western Europe and European settler societies during the middle of the nineteenth century.[34] During this period the "breadwinner-homemaker household" emerged and then "ruled for a century."[35] This breadwinner-homemaker arrangement was a form of family in which the husband earned money and the wife poured her energy into unpaid "household labor to produce the la-bor-intensive triad of domestic comfort, nutrition, and health ser-vices."[36] To achieve this triad, housewives shopped for, purchased, processed, and displayed commodities. Canadian households con-formed to this trend. In 1911 only 13 per cent of the labour force was female, and in 1941 only 20 per cent was female.[37] After the Second World War, however, women's labour-force participation in Canada began to climb. Between 1953 and 1990 the percentage of women between the ages of twenty-five and fifty-four in the la-bour force rose from 24 per cent to 76 per cent. By 2014, 82 per cent of women in this age bracket were employed.[38]

During the 1850s through the 1940s large swathes of Canadian women performed unpaid labour in their homes, transforming the products of the marketplace into usable items. They were thus po-sitioned as consumers within the gendered division of labour. At the same time women were tied to consumption for another rea-son. As Ellen Willis put it nearly fifty years ago, "one of a woman's jobs in this society is to be an attractive sexual object, and clothes and make up are tools of the trade."[39] Since sexist discrimination prevented many women from achieving independence, some women transformed their bodies into objects of desire. In this way they were able to attract cisgendered men, who in turn provided them with financial security. Now, it is true that many women did not engage in consumerist body display, and those who did were not always seeking romantic partnerships. On this latter point, and as Nan Enstad and Kathy Peiss argue, many women used make-up and clothing to cultivate sophistication, which then served them well in attempts to pursue independence and pleasure.[40] As will be discussed in chapter 5, such considerations were also important in Canada. Yet two points must be remembered. First, whites tended to associate consumer artistry with femininity.[41] Second, women of this period faced major hurdles towards independence.[42] Thus, Willis's argument remains valid. If women adorned their bodies for many reasons, one of these was to entice those with greater power.

A further area of scholarly research upon which this study relies pertains to periodization. In his overview of global consumer historiography Frank Trentmann observes that a variety of "spatial and temporal pairings ... dominate research." In Anglo-American work three paradigms are prominent: "18th century global exchanges," "20th century consumerism," and "Americanization."[43] For the most part, Canadian historians are situated in the second paradigm, offering studies on shopping, consumer activism, and consumer motivation.[44] Such studies provide important insights. Yet by focusing on the late nineteenth and twentieth centuries, historians minimize trends in earlier periods.[45] They also risk reifying intellectual linkages among consumption, urbanization, industrialization, capitalism, and modernization. Histories of consumption that portray consumption as part of a broader construct of modernity tend to perpetuate Eurocentric assumptions about historical change. As Lynn Hunt argues, when historians draw upon older theoretical models of human history, they conflate "the idea of modernity itself" with "Western ... models of development."[46] This approach has been criticized by post-colonial and sustainability scholars alike. Among its problems are its inherent racism, its assumption of Western universality, and its equation of Western models of development with progress.[47]

Given these difficulties, it is crucial that historians avoid relying on well-worn tropes linking consumer activity to urbanization, industrialization, and capitalism. It is also important to avoid packaging these items together into a whole known as modernity. Once these phenomena are untangled, in fact, it becomes easier to explore each of them on their own terms. Consumer history is a case in point. When one views consumption as having its own unique history, a history that can be related to but is not necessarily dependent upon industrialization, urbanization, and capitalism, it becomes easier to explore. The thirty-four essays that comprise Trentmann's edited volume *The Oxford Handbook of the History of Consumption* offer an example. With studies ranging from "splendour and excess in Ming China" to "National Socialism and consumption," this collection illustrates how consumer history, uncoupled from the weight of modernity, can be written.[48]

Even as historians remove consumption from modernity, though, new issues arise. Once consumer histories are separated from industrialization, urbanization, and capitalism, how are historians supposed to define *consumption*? Is consumer history simply *material history* by another name? This book argues that it is not. Instead, it agrees with Trentmann that the word *consumption* can act as "a shorthand that refers to a whole bundle of goods that are obtained via different systems of provision and used for different purposes."[49] It is a concept, moreover, that both references "the acquisition, use, and waste of things" and encompasses the topics of "taste and desire."[50] Consumption studies, then, offer a way for researchers to explore the topics of seeking, desiring, acquiring, using, recycling, and disposing of material goods. This view of consumption opens up important conceptual spaces for interdisciplinary discussions of these issues. Such discussions, in turn, are crucially important given the growing burden of resource exhaustion on this planet.

A final area of inspiration is the emerging field of consumer-citizenship studies. Works in this area are as diverse as the topics they explore, but they are connected by the premise that consumption and citizenship are intertwined.[51] According to consumer-citizenship scholar James Davidson, links between consumption and citizenship were made as long as 2,500 years ago in Ancient Greece.[52] Most historians, however, concentrate on the period from 1700 to the present.[53] This era is relevant for sustainability because it saw an ideology of growth emerge in Western Europe, one that connected development with citizen betterment.[54] As political economist Adam Smith so famously put it in *The Wealth of Nations* (1776), "consumption is the sole end and purpose of all production."[55] Crucially important were the retailing and technological innovations of the nineteenth century. These innovations, as Matthew Hilton writes, "enabled cheap, mass-produced, and pre-packaged commodities to be sold to all."[56]

Canadian historians have not ignored the relationship between consumption and citizenship. In 1976 Veronica Strong-Boag pointed to the consumer interests of the National Council of Women of Canada (NCW), the largest Canadian women's group at the time. Before the First World War, the NCW had developed an image of the Canadian woman as a "heroic consumer"; its members debated the cost of living and food quality.[57] Other historians who have enquired into consumer activism are Joy Parr, Ruth Frager, Joan Sangster, and Julie Guard. Their separate studies reveal that between the 1910s and the 1950s a range of housewives took to the public realm to address consumer concerns.[58] The most extended historical analysis of Canadians' conflation of consumption and citizenship is Magda Fahrni's 2002 article on two consumer initiatives in post-war Montreal: a boycott against butchers and grocers, and a fight to "secure the legalization of margarine as a cheaper substitute for butter."[59] According to Fahrni, price control during the Second World War had created an expectation among consumers that price regulation would continue in the post-war years. When it did not, housewives mobilized. Their "public claims [as] consumers," says Fahrni, were indicative of "some of the things to which citizens thought they were entitled in victorious, welfare-state democracy."[60]

Exploring the consumer interests expressed by thousands of women between the 1890s and 1930s, this study extends the historical examination of consumption and citizenship in Canada. It shows that many white women before the Second World War thought of consumer citizenship in three predominant frames: rights, responsibilities, and belonging. These conceptions grew out of notions of material entitlements and duties that were inherent to citizens' roles within political communities. As such, they mirrored what became over the course of the twentieth century major understandings of citizenship itself. Citizenship, as Yuval-Davis argues, is difficult to define; it has "been contested and debated both in political and sociological theory."[61] Nonetheless, certain themes are stable within theoretical approaches to citizenship, particularly the notion that citizenship involves "not just rights but also duties and responsibilities."[62] At the same time, there exists within citizenship theory a controversy over how to define the communities to which citizens belong. Whereas liberal theorists tend to focus on the "contractual relationship between the person and the state," feminist and anti-racist writings demonstrate that conceptions of citizenship extend beyond the state itself.[63] Yuval-Davis writes: "People's citizenship, as a full membership of a political community with its rights and obligations, is usually multi-layered, composed of local, regional, national, cross and supranational political communities, as well as often more than one national community."[64]

Such definitions of citizenship help make sense of white Canadian women's approaches prior to the Second World War. Between the 1890s and 1930s, white women's groups engaged in behaviours that indicated that they too conceived of consumption in relation to citizenship. By way of an example, it is useful to look at the citizenships explored in chapter 2. During the First World War, a special consumer-oriented relationship developed between the federal government and Canada's women's groups. Within this relationship, consumption was defined as white and feminine. It was also perceived as something in which women could engage for the state. In this relationship consumption thus emerged as a citizenship responsibility, one that certain "embodied" consumer citizens – white cisgender women – could undertake.[65] By taking up the patriotic consumer mantle, white women proved their loyalty to their government and demonstrated their civic importance. Hence, although most white women could not vote federally until 1919, they could still demonstrate a limited form of citizenship by taking on wartime consumer initiatives.

The theme of consumer citizenship also receives extended investigation in each of this book's other chapters. At the same time, this book also argues that consumer citizenship must not be the only frame by which scholars approach consumption. As my analyses make clear, consumption has also been linked to social stratification, artistic expression, and liberation. So that researchers do not lose sight of these themes, they must continue to pursue a variety of interpretive frameworks.

Chapter 1 explores arguments about consumption made by Canadian members of the Women's Christian Temperance Union (WCTU). During the late nineteenth and early twentieth centuries, the WCTU was deeply involved in consumer issues. From wanting to eradicate one of Canada's most controversial commodities (alcohol) to trying to recast Canadian consumer culture in their own image, female temperance campaigners were invested in consumption. Exploring the arguments of WCTU members, this chapter shows that even as the WCTU worried about sin, it promoted a capitalist-oriented version of Christian consumer culture.

Chapter 2 turns towards consumer culture in wartime. It suggests that white women's groups used the opportunity of total war to define themselves within the public arena as consumer citizens.[66] Embracing the government's food-conservation and -substitution efforts, such groups as the NCW, the Fédération nationale Saint-Jean-Baptiste (FNSJB), the Young Women's Christian Association (YWCA), the Women's Institute (WI), and others campaigned on behalf of Canadian homemakers. Demonstrating that women mobilized their consumer roles to declare their support for the British Empire, this chapter reveals that the Great War represented a time when women turned their shopping responsibilities into national priorities.

Looking at the rise of home economics in Canadian universities, chapter 3 asks why Canadian home economics programs were developed and looks at the consumer-based content they promoted. American home economics curricula were based on the notion that homemakers were consumers; post-secondary Canadian home economics between 1900 and 1939 offered similar perspectives.[67] Examining the issues that home economics instructors promoted, this chapter suggests that Canadian home economics curricula encouraged students to imagine homemaking as a form of civic activism. In this way they cemented the notion that a woman served her country best by shopping.

Given that Canada was predominantly rural until the 1920s, the fourth chapter looks at consumption in the countryside. Exploring records created by the WI, the largest rural women's organization in Canada, it asks: how did rural white women view shopping, commodities, and material life? Demonstrating that the WI was concerned about shopping, product quality, and leisure, it also reveals that many rural women were ambivalent as to the roles of commodities in everyday life. Embracing the labour-saving and beautifying aspects of many consumer goods, but also promoting an ethos of thrift and pride, rural white Canadian women of diverse backgrounds nurtured a consumer philosophy of producerist consumerism.

In chapter 5 the issue of ambivalence is taken up more broadly. Rather than focusing on a specific group of women, this chapter takes one issue – fashion – and explores its portrayal in the anglophone and francophone women's press between 1890 and 1939. It suggests that fashion was a source of both confidence and consternation. Wearing the latest fashions could enhance one's status, but it also meant that much time, expense, and discomfort had to be endured. Exploring these and other matters, particularly the ways in which many white Canadian women held up fashion as a barometer of belonging, this chapter suggests that for many women, fashion was a way of declaring one's membership in the modern Canadian polity.

White Canadian women may have thought deeply about consumer issues, but they also entered the public realm as activists. Chapter 5 enquires into white women's attempts to reform the consumer marketplace between 1900 and 1939.[68] Exploring, first, women within the Canadian co-operative movement and, next, women's efforts to reform capitalist retail, this chapter argues that although many women initiated consumer projects, their efforts were short lived. Uphill battles involving cost, discrimination, and staffing eventually caused all of their plans to fold. In these ways they resembled the types of efforts made in Australia and the United States, wherein activist women demonstrated interest in reforming retail but lacked the resources to follow through.

The conclusion reviews the major findings of the book and reiterates its main argument: for many white wives and mothers in Canada before the Second World War, consumption was a multi-levelled initiative that sought liberation, morality, solidarity, pleasure, civic influence, and distinction. Following this discussion, the conclusion returns to the question of how best to approach consumer history.

*Purchasing Power* reveals the diversity of consumer issues that white Canadians confronted between the 1890s and the 1930s. At the same time, it recognizes its own limitations. So that further knowledge may be developed, it is crucial that scholars continue launching new investigations.[69] In this way they will provide further answers to the question of why, in the face of ongoing resource exhaustion, Canadians continue to pursue unsustainable rates of consumption. They will also provide new insights into why, despite so many Canadians' lip service to equality, there continues to exist widespread material disparities among all those who reside in northern North America.

*Chapter One*

# Temperance and the Rise of Sober Consumer Culture

Fans of the recent Home Box Office (HBO) television series *Boardwalk Empire* (2010–15) will be familiar with the Women's Christian Temperance Union (WCTU). On that show, set in the American Prohibition era, WCTU women are fiery anti-booze advocates, moralistic types who march down the streets shouting about alcohol.[1] Certainly there was a moment in time – the late nineteenth century – when such characterizations would have been apt. Yet the WCTU, in its long history, was known for much more than strident anti-alcoholism. Scholars have explored various aspects of that history, including its campaigns for women's suffrage.[2] This chapter, though, takes a different tack. In addition to promoting prohibition and women's rights, the Canadian union helped usher in what historian Erika Rappaport has termed a "sober consumer culture."[3] Specifically, between the 1890s and 1930s, the Canadian WCTU helped shift consumer spending away from alcohol and towards temperance-approved goods and services. These goods and services reflected the priorities of white wives and mothers.

This chapter uncovers the material desires underpinning temperance advocacy. In her study of the early nineteenth-century temperance movement in the United Kingdom, Rappaport notes that campaigners often held massive tea parties. These gatherings celebrated sobriety by offering "bread and cake, butter and cream, fruits, sugar, tea, and coffee" as well as "meaningful décor." Such parties encouraged attendees to associate temperance with conviviality, caffeine, and abundance.[4] English Canadian members of the WCTU did not hold parties of the same size and frequency, but they, too, associated sobriety with certain "material and gustatory" pleasures, including those driven by caffeine.[5] Moreover, like their British counterparts, Canadian WCTU members viewed mothers as central to the consumer order. According to the Canadian union, men had too much control over consumer spending. It was time to transfer that spending to women.

This chapter argues that female evangelicals helped create the consumer culture that defined English Canada during the twentieth century. First, I demonstrate that the temperance espoused by the WCTU was pro-capitalist and pro-consumption. Second, I show that the WCTU's capitalist and consumerist ideals were mother centred and domestic oriented. Third, I illustrate that the union's campaigns foreshadowed developments that came to characterize Canadian consumer culture generally. By calling for the integration of mothers and children into commercialized spaces, as well as by holding up coffee, tea, and dairy treats as substitutions for alcohol, the WCTU in its demands represented early desires for what would later become major components of Canadian consumer culture.

## A Brief History of the WCTU

Founded in the United States in 1874, the WCTU had claimed 150,000 American members by 1893.[6] Membership rolls north of the United States never reached that high; the number of people belonging to the WCTU in Canada peaked during the First World War when the union had 16,000 members.[7] Nevertheless, the WCTU was a strong presence in Canada. Asserting that Christian women were superior to both men and non-Christians, members of the Canadian WCTU ventured into politics, media, recreation, and law, arguing for reforms so that Canadians could live what the union saw as more fulfilling lives. Their primary focus was prohibition, but in their minds the notion of temperance had broader applicability. By avoiding spicy food, tobacco, narcotics, salacious media, dancing, flirtation, dark lighting, and sensuous clothing, individuals could liberate themselves from misery.[8] As the editor of the Ontario WCTU magazine put it, "the producing of good citizenship, for

this world, and the world that is to come, is the sole aim of the
W.C.T.U."[9]

The WCTU in Canada organized along local, regional, and national lines. By 1877 there was sufficient interest to form an Ontario
chapter. By 1885 there were unions in British Columbia, Manitoba,
Quebec, New Brunswick, Nova Scotia, and Prince Edward Island.
In 1899, activists announced the creation of a Dominion WCTU.[10]
Between 1885 and 1903, Ottawa members published the *Woman's
Journal*, a monthly that informed members of events and promoted
a sense of community.[11] After the *Woman's Journal* ceased publication, the Ontario WCTU began publishing a new organ called
the *Canadian White Ribbon Tidings*. Billed as the "Official Organ
of the Women's Christian Temperance Union in Canada," it had
ten thousand subscribers during the First World War. Meanwhile,
the WCTU's national office launched its own monthly journal,
the *White Ribbon Bulletin*, in 1910.[12] In 1920 the Ontario WCTU accepted the Dominion WCTU's offer to purchase the *Tidings* and
make it the WCTU's primary publication.[13] Until at least 1940 the
*Tidings* was published in London (Ontario), and until 1930 all of its
editors hailed from Ontario.[14]

As Sharon Cook notes, the union's publications projected
"an ongoing acceptance and proselytizing of the evangelical
creed."[15] The *Journal's* tagline was a biblical quotation, "And
who knoweth whether thou art come to the kingdom for a time
such as this" (Esther 4:14), which was a reference to the WCTU's
belief that modern life required salvation from sin.[16] The *Tidings'*
motto, for its part, was "For God, Home, and Native Land."[17]
In invoking religious language, neither journal was unique; indeed, *Woman's Century*, the official organ of the National Council of Women of Canada (NCW), also incorporated biblical text.[18]
Nevertheless, the WCTU's publications were distinct in that they
were aggressively evangelical. Discussions of scriptural passages appeared often, as did the belief that the devil walked the
earth. A 1913 article stated that "Cider" is "the Devil's Kindling
Tool."[19] Perhaps nothing more indicated the union's religious
outlook than its view of prayer as a tool of political activism.
In a typical passage in 1926 a Mrs. May R. Thornley wrote to
the *Tidings* to ask readers to pray for the ending of government
liquor control.[20]

## National Prohibition, National Prosperity

The pro-capitalist rhetoric of the WCTU was couched within a broader endorsement of capitalism. In articles and editorials, members made arguments for the benefits of prohibition not just for the economy generally but for Canada specifically. Well before prohibition was enacted in 1918, the WCTU was publishing statistics on how liquor hindered Canadian economic progress. In 1893 the *Journal* argued that "$32,678,633" annually was "wasted in drink," and another "$23,629,175" worth of grain was "wasted in breweries and distilleries." What's more, significant sums were wasted in the fuel and labour needed to produce alcohol, in the theft caused by alcohol-induced crimes, in the "productive service lost through ... drunkenness," and in the "productive services" needed to process "criminals" through the justice system. All told, Canada would be over eighty-two million dollars richer under prohibition.[21]

Nationalist sentiment was especially strong during the First World War. Along with other major women's groups such as the NCW, the WCTU supported not only the war effort but also the "Made in Canada" campaign that accompanied it.[22] Echoing the government's messaging to "Demand Canadian products" to "Keep Canadian workmen employed," the union endorsed economic patriotism as a crucial strategy of national development.[23] The WCTU was unique, however, in so far as it used guilt as a method of provoking women into nationalistic shopping.[24] In 1919 *Tidings* published a letter from the Canadian trade commissioner who stated, "As the women of Canada purchase about 90% of the commodities used in our domestic life, a realization by them of their power to remake and vitalize Canadian trade and finance is a first step towards ... safeguarding the national future." Indeed, "for every million dollars retained in Canada by a refusal to buy other than Canadian Goods, a year's continuous employment can be given to at least 1,000 people."[25]

Members thus frequently argued that without alcohol Canada would be more productive. Such rhetoric was linked to older, nineteenth-century arguments that the elimination of drunkenness would reduce workplace accidents and inspire Canadians to become more industrious.[26] It was also linked to a newer set of concerns, namely that money spent on liquor was diverted out of

communities. Throughout the 1920s the Canadian WCTU main-
tained the position that government control of liquor was ruining
every province's economy and would eventually destroy the nation's. Workers were spending too much money on booze, and the
workforce was becoming unmotivated. More than this, non-liquor
businesses, including grocers, shoemakers, and retailers, were suffering. Liquor manufacturers were growing rich, and, rather than
putting their money back into their communities, they were hoarding it or using it to influence politicians and governments. Thus
government sales led not only to working-class laziness but also to
stagnation and corruption.[27]

The WCTU kept up this rhetoric into the 1930s, even as movements against prohibition and government control made headway.
As many provinces rescinded total prohibition over the decade,
*Tidings* became apoplectic. Writers attacked not only the immorality of the situation but also the certain economic drain. According
to the magazine, prior to the 1929 stock market crash liquor-free
America was a shining example of how the eradication of alcohol
led to a healthier, happier, and richer society. If Canada reintro-
duced prohibition, prosperity would reign north of the border. "It
is safe to say that the economic depression would not have been
felt nearly so keenly in Canada had it not been for the enormous
sums invested in the liquor industry and the enormous sums spent
upon their products," said the WCTU in 1933.[28] Secondary-school
student Dorothy E. Clarke of Calgary, Alberta, agreed. As her
award-winning 1935 essay put it, "if we are going to found the
prosperity of the country, its commercial prosperity, its industrial
prosperity, upon an impregnable basis, we must cleanse the foun-
dations of the rot of alcohol."[29]

### Anti-alcohol, Pro-business

While some twentieth-century evangelicals viewed capitalism as
an indicator of corruption, WCTU members were fine with capitalism per se.[30] In their opinion, capitalism was not an enemy of a
moral life. Rather, drunkenness prevented the moral life that capitalism enabled. In the opinions of many members, a capitalist political economy that was managed by temperance forces was the
key to prosperity.

From its beginning, the *Journal* included advertising content, featuring, for example, Tarr's Bazaar in Ottawa, Dr. Chase's Nerve Food (for menstrual cramps), and Eaton's and Simpson's department stores in Toronto.[31] Certainly, the inclusion of advertising within the union's publications did not translate into a wholesale endorsement of capitalism. By 1900 every major Canadian press was almost completely dependent upon advertising revenue.[32] Nevertheless, through an analysis of the advertisements carried in its publications we can gain an idea of the kind of capitalist consumption the WCTU encouraged. The organization only carried advertising for products and brands that conveyed the values of the temperate consumer society for which it was fighting. By endorsing companies that promoted temperance, the WCTU created alliances with such corporations as Eaton's and Red Rose Tea and such brands as Shredded Wheat and Purity Flour, among others. Members sang the praises of these companies, arguing that their products would enrich buyers' lives. In so doing, the WCTU helped make these brands common household names. The advertisements also enacted the centrality of food corporations, particularly, within English Canadian diets.

Department stores received special attention. Major North American retailers indeed sought this attention as a way in which to prove their respectability, which was sometimes called into question as the result of the low wages they paid.[33] Members of the Canadian WCTU, who as wives and mothers were among department stores' primary customers, were receptive to such publicity. In 1899 the *Journal* applauded Wanamaker's of Philadelphia for not advertising on Sundays, and it called on other retailers to do the same.[34] Timothy Eaton and his colossal department store received even greater accolades. An avowed Methodist, Eaton prohibited his stores from selling alcohol or tobacco and made sure that his window display curtains were drawn on Sundays. Stated *Tidings* in 1932, "by his honesty, his energy, and consideration for others, he left an example which will inspire ambitious boys in many countries."[35] Other businesses that members saw fit to applaud were major magazines. In 1911 *Tidings* published an "Honor Roll of Magazines Not Advertising Liquors."[36] In subsequent years it dished out praise for the *Canadian Home Journal,* whose editor called upon readers to support the WCTU; the *Ladies' Home Journal* for having come out against Quebec liquor sales during US prohibition; and the *Saturday Evening Post* for banning cigarette advertising and removing all reference to tobacco in its "reading matter and pictures."[37]

The WCTU also entered into more direct endorsements. For example, in 1898 the *Woman's Journal* began carrying Happy Thought Soap advertisements that promised to "pay one cent [to the WCTU] for each ... wrapper returned to us by the President of the Dominion W.C.T.U."[38] The largest scheme of this type ever adopted by WCTU periodicals was launched by *Tidings* in 1908 when the editors announced a "With Our Advertisers" section. This section carried advertisements from specially selected businesses alongside letters and recipes from readers who admired the products. *Tidings* adopted this approach, noted Lottie McAlister, because its "prospect for healthy life lay in the adoption of some advertising scheme that should not only attract those who had goods to market, but prove of real value to them."[39] Until 1920 each issue of *Tidings* carried at least three pages of readers' letters, all of which endorsed the brands of the WCTU's biggest advertisers: Red Rose Tea, Christie Biscuits, Ingersoll Cream Cheese, Moffat Stoves, Purity Oats, Shredded Wheat, Canada Starch, and Epps Cocoa. *Tidings* also occasionally published glowing biographies, complete with photographs, of the owners of these businesses. One 1911 issue featured write-ups about the heads of Red Rose Tea, Chapman's Dry Goods House, the E.D. Smith fruit company, and Aylmer Cream. These men and their businesses were notable for their "courtesy," "reliability," and "'high standard,'" stated the journal.[40]

"With Our Advertisers" was significant to the financial health of the WCTU, but it also helped integrate capitalist consumer culture into the lives of readers by familiarizing them with particular companies and products.[41] In 1912, for example, a Sarnia correspondent reported on a special WCTU event that featured samples of "Triscuits, [Ingersoll] Cream Cheese, and Red Rose Tea." After the gathering "so many spoke of the tea as being particularly good, and the Triscuits and Ingersoll Cream Cheese were heartily appreciated."[42] Readers' recipes featuring advertised brands demonstrated how "With

Our Advertisers" encouraged the adoption of not only mass-marketed capitalist commodities but also their specific flavours and ingredients within English Canadian kitchens. One recipe sent by Mrs. D.M. Leitch, also of Sarnia, suggested that "Plain Breakfast Muffins" could be made with "2 cups Purity Flour" and "1 tablespoon St. Lawrence Sugar."[43] Moreover, since many of the editorials and letters featured in the "With Our Advertisers" section adopted folksy language, the social aspect of the section helped foster a sense of inclusion within a community identified by its temperance beliefs and its consumer habits. A typical column invited readers to peruse its "little talk" about "our regular firms," including letters by Mrs. Ewing of Sault Ste Marie, who "assures us that 'SHREDDED WHEAT is a daily food in our home,'" and by Miss Elvira Schaef of Hanover, who stated that "'I have been using SHREDDED WHEAT for three years and ... it is the best Breakfast food I have ever eaten.'"[44]

WCTU publications were also sites where the group could instruct its readers on the kind of consumer they ought not be. In 1921, *Tidings* editors were compelled to reprint a full-page article titled "'What Are They to Me?'" from the *Galt Daily Reporter*. Written in a gossipy style, the article had a tone similar to that of people talking about someone as she passes by: "Look at her. There she goes – her hat came from Chicago," "Her dress came from New York," "Her shoes came from Boston," "Her lingerie came from France," "Her stockings came from Philadelphia," and "Her corsets came from Newark." The article suggests that all of this is extraordinarily "thoughtless, selfish," and "foolish," for it meant that foreigners were growing rich while "Canadian men and women" grew impoverished (fig. 1.1).[45] According to *Tidings*, therefore, true Canadian womanhood depended not only upon purity but also upon civic-minded consumer spending.[46]

## Temperate Treats and Outings

The WCTU is often remembered for its fiery denunciations of booze, and it is true that the organization formed in opposition to alcohol. Nevertheless, its hostility to the liquor trade did not translate into a widespread suspicion of capitalist enterprise. Moreover, the WCTU recognized that alcohol offered certain attractions.

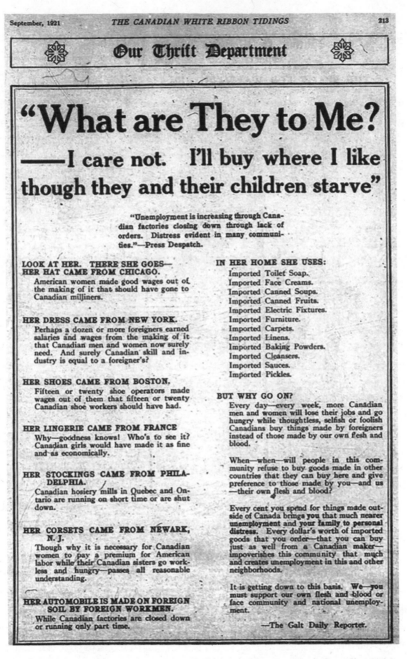

## Our Thrift Department

# "What are They to Me?
## ——I care not. I'll buy where I like though they and their children starve"

"Unemployment is increasing through Canadian factories closing down through lack of orders. Distress evident in many communities."—Press Despatch.

**LOOK AT HER. THERE SHE GOES— HER HAT CAME FROM CHICAGO.**

American women made good wages out of the making of it that should have gone to Canadian milliners.

**HER DRESS CAME FROM NEW YORK.**

Perhaps a dozen or more foreigners earned salaries and wages from the making of it that Canadian men and women now surely need. And surely Canadian skill and industry is equal to a foreigner's?

**HER SHOES CAME FROM BOSTON.**

Fifteen or twenty shoe operators made wages out of them that fifteen or twenty Canadian shoe workers should have had.

**HER LINGERIE CAME FROM FRANCE**

Why—goodness knows! Who's to see it? Canadian girls would have made it as fine and as economically.

**HER STOCKINGS CAME FROM PHILADELPHIA.**

Canadian hosiery mills in Quebec and Ontario are running on short time or are shut down.

**HER CORSETS CAME FROM NEWARK, N. J.**

Though why it is necessary for Canadian women to pay a premium for American labor while their Canadian sisters go workless and hungry—passes all reasonable understanding.

**HER AUTOMOBILE IS MADE ON FOREIGN SOIL BY FOREIGN WORKMEN.**

While Canadian factories are closed down or running only part time.

**IN HER HOME SHE USES:**

Imported Toilet Soap.
Imported Face Creams.
Imported Canned Soups.
Imported Canned Fruits.
Imported Electric Fixtures.
Imported Furniture.
Imported Carpets.
Imported Linens.
Imported Baking Powders.
Imported Cleansers.
Imported Sauces.
Imported Pickles.

**BUT WHY GO ON?**

Every day—every week, more Canadian men and women will lose their jobs and go hungry while thoughtless, selfish or foolish Canadians buy things made by foreigners instead of those made by our own flesh and blood.

When—when—will people in this community refuse to buy goods made in other countries that they can buy here and give preference to those made by you—and us —their own flesh and blood?

Every cent you spend for things made outside of Canada brings you that much nearer unemployment and your family to personal distress. Every dollar's worth of imported goods that you order—that you can buy just as well from a Canadian maker— impoverishes this community that much and creates unemployment in this and other neighborhoods.

It is getting down to this basis. We—you must support our own flesh and blood or face community and national unemployment.

—The Galt Daily Reporter.

1.1 Selfish, unpatriotic shopping. "What Are They to Me," *Canadian White Ribbon Tidings*, September 1921, 213; reprinted from the *Galt Daily Reporter*.

Conviviality, respite, and stimulation, particularly, accompanied its consumption. Thus the organization was careful to do more than simply call for prohibition. Instead, it offered alternatives to alcohol. In this way it attempted to transform Canada's consumer culture, switching it from one of inebriation to one of sobriety.

By examining the alternatives recommended by the WCTU, one can discern the rise in popularity of various consumer items, many of which remain with us today. Consumption of ice cream, water, fruit juice, milk, fruit cocktails, desserts, and coffee were particularly promoted by temperance. Campaigners also called for the replacement of saloons, beer rooms, and wet canteens with dry hotels, milk bars, tea houses, and coffee huts. I suggest that the WCTU was articulating a broader Canadian demand for such goods and services, as evidenced by the growth in popularity of most of these commodities and venues during the twentieth century. Whereas the taverns of the nineteenth century were masculine spaces, the growing popularity of dry establishments in the twentieth century indicates that not only men but also women and children wanted access to commercialized venues. This demand for family-friendly establishments indicates a shift in northern North American consumer culture away from male homosocial spaces and towards mixed gathering places.

From the time of its formation the Canadian WCTU perceived saloons especially as heinous. Not only did these establishments sell alcohol, but they were male social spaces. According to the union, the carousing and competitiveness that characterized them encouraged patrons to forget their domestic responsibilities. Particularly before Prohibition, the WCTU expended much time and effort towards eliminating saloons. After the war, and accompanying the repeal of prohibition laws, it re-engaged its anti-saloon campaign. A poem submitted by a Yorkton (Saskatchewan) member, Mrs. C.E. Baldwin, to *Tidings* in 1932 well expressed the WCTU's thoughts. Saloons were

A bar to manliness and wealth,
A door to want and broken health!
A bar to hope, a bar to prayer,
A door to darkness and despair!
A bar to honored, useful life,

A door to brawling, senseless strife
A bar to all that's true and brave,
A door to every drunkard's grave!
A bar to joy that home imparts,
A door to tears and aching hearts![47]

Saloons prevented prosperity and domesticity. They were the antithesis of a family-friendly, Christian-oriented public sphere.

Prior to Prohibition, saloons were situated in hotels. There they provided food and refreshments to travellers and created a space for conviviality. Given their significances, the WCTU made sure to promote dry accommodations and eating places. Hotel business, stated a New Brunswick contributor in 1891, was not dependent upon "selling liquor." "Elegant and comfortable" accommodations could just as easily be provided by "temperance hotels" as they could by hotels with bars. Indeed, women and temperance travellers, given the choice between a wet hotel and a dry one, would always choose the latter.[48] Recognizing that hoteliers worried about declining sales, the union reassured them that if they improved their food and furnishings, they would be able to recoup any lost profits.[49] Prior to Prohibition the WCTU informed readers of the location of temperance hotels, and into the 1920s it published reports on dry accommodations.[50] Whereas licensed hotels featured "ancient tobacco juice" on their verandas, "horrible [liquor] fumes" in the air, and "semi-intoxicated, blurry-eyed men" throughout the premises, temperance hotels were clean and safe. As another article put it, they were "the very essence of cleanliness."[51] Such comments demonstrated that temperance advocates viewed liquor and tobacco as literally and morally "dirty." In contrast, sanitary physical conditions were indicative of moral respectability.[52]

Members also appreciated dry hotels for their welcoming attitudes towards women. "People who have motored considerably in Ontario this summer," noted one 1919 contributor, "have been impressed by the change in the conduct and atmosphere of the rural hotel." Before Prohibition, "the train of evils" present in every hotel bar-room "repelled sensitive people," especially women. Now that alcohol was illegal, rural hotels had "become more comfortable and homelike."[53] Consequently, both women and respectable "farmers" could visit hotels. For this writer, as for temperance advocates generally, the banning of booze opened up new possibilities for women.

WCTU members further advocated dry restaurants. When, upon plebiscite, individual municipalities became dry, the union applauded restaurateurs' efforts in those districts. Visitors to the newly dry municipality of Blenheim (Ontario) in 1904, for example, did not need to "picnic on the campus," for there existed "two restaurants serving meals" in the town.[54] New shops were also opening. "The stores have taken the place of the hotels," one young girl in Blenheim noted, adding that "Ma was in the new one that started lately, and she thinks things are as cheap here now as in Toronto."[55] For the WCTU, social progress was denoted not only by the eradication of alcohol but also by the elimination of male-only spaces, the movement of white women into the public sphere, and the ability of women to spend money on their own freely chosen consumer items.

Canadian WCTU members were equally impressed by the efforts of their American counterparts in this regard. In 1893 a group of Ontario members travelled to Chicago to visit an establishment called the Coffee House, owned and managed by the American WCTU. With over a hundred employees, meeting rooms on the second floor, and women's accommodations on the upper floors, this institution served the city's female temperance population. On the House's white walls were painted scriptural passages; the all-female staff members were "neatly dressed in white"; and the tables were "covered with ... clean white cloth[s]." On Sundays, Christian services were held. Part hotel, part meeting space, and part restaurant, the premises were always packed. Most impressively, stated a *Journal* contributor, the meals and drinks were reasonably priced, with coffee and tea marked at "five cents a cup."[56]

In that the Coffee House was religious, female operated, and dry, it served as a peaceful antidote to the often male-only, raucous world of the saloon. The House reflected other temperance priorities as well. By calling itself a coffee house, it demonstrated its commitment to civic engagement. Since the middle of the seventeenth century people in the anglophone world had viewed coffee houses as sites for rational public debate.[57] At the same time, by serving tea, the House also indicated its support for women's empowerment. During the nineteenth century and especially in the United States tea was known as a feminine drink. Department stores offered tea rooms, where affluent women could enjoy a quiet meal and refreshment; independent tea rooms also opened in both rural and urban locations. Lavishly decorated with such "feminine details" as "ruffled curtains, doilies, cretonne, chintz, and carefully chosen knick-knacks," tea rooms were purposefully created for women's respite.[58]

Even as the WCTU worked to create spaces for temperate women, so did they attempt to offer alternatives to alcohol for all. Perhaps unfortunately for the movement, one of its most popular suggestions was milk. Although milk may seem a dull beverage, entirely unlike liquor in every way, it was, according to the WCTU, a "true elixir of life." An enthusiastic 1917 article explained that it had "sugar, minerals, oils and fats, albumens, starches, and water." This combination induced in milk consumers an energy and liveliness that could not be matched: milk is a "vital tonic" that "leaves not the slightest trace of harm behind." It was thus the perfect replacement for booze.[59]

So keen were some members that in 1937 Miss Laura Hughes of North Wiltshire, Prince Edward Island, opened three "milk bars." Such establishments were informal food outlets that sold milk by the glass and also offered other dairy drinks and treats. Their goal, according to Hughes, was to "get people drinking more milk and less beer."[60] After reading in *Tidings* about successful milk bars in England, Australia, and New Zealand, Hughes had decided to bring the trend to Canada. Partnering with her family business, the Hughes Drug Co., she opened a milk bar in North Wiltshire. The "site chosen already had gingerale and other drinks for sale; also magazines and newspapers." She added a "soda fountain" and a "'Milk Bar' sign." As a result of these efforts, business "increased."[61]

So heartened was Hughes that she next opened what she called an "Oasis Milk Bar" at a local "Exhibition." She also, upon noticing "an open-air booth being prepared to sell cigarettes and home-made beer" on "the street leading to the Exhibition," helped to convert that booth into a "Temperance Bar." After convincing the proprietor to sell milk and pastries, she "bought two gallons of good country buttermilk and four dozen homemade doughnuts," which she sold at the booth under a sign advertising "Doughnuts and Buttermilk, 5 cents." Foreshadowing the doughnut shops that came to dominate English Canada after the Second World War, this early pastry bar was a success.[62] Most notably, "sailors from two warships in port came and had two drinks each and came every day." Maybe, she said, "the Milk Bar saved them from going other places and getting alcohol." After the exhibition was over, she and the booth's proprietor planned to move the temperance bar indoors and "hope[d] to build up quite a trade."[63]

Milk was the favoured drink of the WCTU, but it did promote other beverages. Members in southern Ontario offered water fountains as a means to keep people out of taverns. By 1901 the Cornwall branch had raised funds for the installation of four drinking fountains in that town. To mark the fourth installation the WCTU held an evening ceremony featuring "refreshment booths," all "prettily decorated," in the town square.[64] As the fountain and beverage booths attest, the Cornwall union well recognized the role that saloons played in slaking thirst. The beverage ceremony, as well, demonstrated the WCTU's recognition of the social role played by saloons. The Cornwall WCTU hence presented temperance as an enjoyable alternative to the tavern.[65]

Fruit juice, too, was offered. Throughout its existence the WCTU recommended grape juice for Christian ceremonies.[66] During the late 1930s it also promoted fruit juice. This time the group's aim was to counter the cocktail craze. Illegal vendors had responded to booze shortages by creating mixed liquors, or "cocktails." By the 1930s cocktails had become a permanent fixture in drinking culture and were especially popular among women. "It has become one of the insignia of smartness," fretted the WCTU in 1932, "to pour into an empty stomach horrible concoctions of gin, vermouth, rum, brandy, sherry, and other forms of alcohol, and to spend as much in cocktails in a day as would feed a man for a week."[67] Instead people should drink fruit cocktails. "Take one quart of sweetened grape juice, juice of one lemon, one orange sliced fine, 1 quart of ginger ale, and a chunk of ice," instructed one WCTU article in 1935.[68] According campaigners, temperance could be both refreshing and delicious.[69]

Temperance foods were further recommended. In the WCTU press, editors published recipes that omitted alcoholic ingredients. In so doing, they encouraged readers to avoid using brandy, rum, wine, and malt as flavouring agents. In 1892, an article titled "Temperance Recipes" offered four pudding recipes, including ones called "Boiled Plum" and "Orange." Whereas typical puddings of this period included spirits, these were flavoured with fruit, spice, and sugar. The accompanying "sauce" omitted alcohol. "Flavour with lemon, or any extract desired, but never with wine," instructed the article.[70]

Just as the WCTU offered substitutions for food and drink that once contained alcohol, so it was inclined to offer substitutions for "salacious" media. Certainly the organization wanted to ban desultory imagery, but it also knew that its pursuit of Christian values would not be effective unless it promoted alternative entertainments. In fact, WCTU members frequently stated that "good literature" was the best weapon in the fight against intemperance.[71] Members worked tirelessly to distribute approved literature and other forms of media. In this work they were heartened by encouragement from religious leaders. Pastor R. Fulton Irwin of Thamesville (Ontario) stated, "I have for a long time been in the habit of ... getting into the most degraded homes the good literature that passes through my hands."[72]

Within WCTU-endorsed media, conversion themes were prominent. Before the First World War the union was committed to changing the ways of men in lumber camps, where, it suspected, the male culture encouraged drinking and prostitution. Thus the WCTU sent "comfort bags" with blankets, socks, and Christian media to the camps.[73] In 1901, members in Guelph were heartened to hear that a conversion novel sent to the French River lumber camp had encouraged one atheist to change his ways. Apparently he had "crushed" his foot in an accident, and during his convalescence had read the materials sent by the WCTU. One of these was a novel featuring "the story of a young man" who "ran away from home." Together with a "small Bible," the book "led" the worker "to God"; it also encouraged him to start attending "college in Woodstock."[74]

Of all the groups the WCTU attempted to reform, sojourning male labourers were the most heavily targeted. Members were aware that men of all classes patronized saloons, smoked, with-held money from wives, neglected their children, and behaved as sexual predators towards women and girls, but they were particu-larly concerned about the behaviours of men who worked away from home. For this reason they worked hard to change these men's consumer habits. Yet rather than simply condemning their carousing ways, they offered them some temperance alternatives.

Beginning in 1888 the WCTU in Canso (Nova Scotia) started "gathering funds" for a "suitable reading room and rest [house] for our sailors." It was "urgent," for "God, and Home and Human-ity" that the union build such amenities, for "frequently a fleet of fifty vessels and upward, carrying a complement of fifteen men each, anchors in our harbour for days, coming and going contin-uously through the summer." Given that the sailors had "very lit-tle to do," they usually went to "the saloons, which are scattered in every direction."[75] By 1892 the Canso WCTU was happy to re-port that it had built its "Sailor's Rest," which had been "formally opened" by the Reverend Joseph Angwin. The thirty-by-fifty-foot building was "well lighted," containing "magazines, daily and weekly papers, ... pens, ink, paper and envelopes, [and] games." Treats, including "ice-cream, cake, biscuit, sandwiches, hot coffee, syrups, nuts, confectionery, fruit," were always available. Through various donations the WCTU was able to hire a "young man ... to take charge of the building, keeping it open from 8 o'clock a.m. un-til 10 p.m." During the building's first three weeks over two hun-dred sailors registered.[76]

Into the interwar years the WCTU worked towards sailors' redemption. A 1912 report of the "Sailor's Department" of the Dominion union reveals the extent of such work. That year the On-tario WCTU handed out to sailors 99 "comfort bags" stocked with Christian reading material, candies, and hand-knit items; 581 pa-pers; and 99 "marked New Testaments." The Almonte union alone sent "a bale of goods valued at $93.10 to Deep Sea Mission," as well as "85 magazines and a large number of leaflets ... to Labrador Mission." Members made sure to always include a "motherly let-ter" to comfort the "boys at sea."[77] Indeed, in much of their work with the sailors the women adopted a maternalistic tone. Sailors were not immoral by nature; rather, they were "frank and gener-ous to a fault." This is why they became "ready victim[s] to the insidious temptations which are too often on every hand." It was the task of the WCTU to "offset the allurements of the saloon by [providing] music, reading and games, varying such with gospel temperance meetings ... pledge cards and literature." Sailors were open and impressionable; it was thus possible for the WCTU to turn them towards salvation.[78]

Soldiers were a final group targeted by the WCTU. By the start of the First World War the WCTU had been campaigning for over twenty years against soldiers' drinking. Thus when Canadian General Alderson revoked the Canadian Expeditionary Force's no-liquor policy in 1914, the union was incensed. Whereas the general was hoping to contain Canadian drinking by instituting "wet canteens," or structures offering beer rations and other diversions, the WCTU took a different view.[79] According to the Dominion organization's president, Mrs. Wright, the action represented "a most unjustifiable and uncalled for retrogression."[80] That December, as Tim Cook notes, the Ontario WCTU had "raised a petition of 66,186 names signed only by worrying mothers."[81] Mrs. Lottie McAlister, editor of the *Canadian White Ribbon Tidings*, explained her organization's position: "The most satanic aspect of the wet canteen is that mothers are giving sons – mere boys – who are pure but at an age when appetites are strong and need to be well guarded until the years of maturity give judgement and control, and the Government immediately debauches them [with] a wet canteen and a rum ration."[82]

Despite its ongoing efforts, the WCTU was never able to abolish drinking in the Canadian military. Thus, in 1917, it switched its efforts towards providing alternatives. That year, it announced a fundraiser to providing "FREE drinkables" in the "fighting areas."[83] In October 1917, the WCTU started a "Thimble and Trinket Fund, which "melted down" donated objects and used the proceeds to "flood the forward trenches with the harmless drinks our boys so need," particularly "Tea, Cocoa, Coffee and Lemonade."[84] That December the *Canadian White Ribbon Tidings* was also happy to feature a photograph of soldiers in France enjoying free victuals served by a YMCA coffee stand. According to the caption, "when the [soldiers] sighted the Y.M.C.A. Coffee Stall, a whoop of joy went up and the whole squad moved forward as one man." They appreciated the "friendly faces" behind the counter just as much as the "mugs of fragrant, steaming coffee," which "sent a thrill of life and warmth through their cold and exhausted bodies."[85] Adopting the position of the worrying mother, this caption well demonstrates both the concern members had for soldiers and their determination to provide non-alcoholic drinks at the front.

## More Money for Mother: Consumer Culture and Women's Rights

Recognizing the importance of offering substitutes for alcohol and salacious media, the WCTU suggested that temperance drinks, foods, reading materials, and venues could combat the evils of drink. Yet its attempts to change Canadian consumer habits were even farther reaching. In addition to supplanting immoral commodities, it sought to bring more domestic goods into individuals' lives. With the money saved on drink, members claimed, families could finally buy the clothing, furniture, and other goods they wanted. Through temperance, in other words, various home-centred consumer desires could be realized. As a WCTU article in 1932 put it, "no money has ever been spent upon alcohol that would not have been better spent upon the domestic, social, and educational needs of women and children."[86]

To understand the WCTU's emphasis on improving access to commodities, it is important to recognize the union's fierce mother-and-child-focused vision. Within the WCTU there existed a strong interest in improving mothers' living conditions. Since mothers had a relative (compared to men's) inability to access money, members fought hard to improve mothers' standards of living. As early as 1890 the *Woman's Journal* ran a front-page article titled "How Some Women Earn Money," noting that renting out rooms, selling produce and baked goods, working as cooks and nannies, doing others' ironing and laundry, arranging social events, and taking in mending were tried and true methods by which housewives could earn cash.[87] This article and others like it represented an early articulation of what later became a major objective of the twentieth-century feminist movement, namely women's economic independence.

For many members, indeed, it was unfair that while they toiled as hard – if not harder – than their husbands, they did not receive financial compensation. Asked one writer, rhetorically: "Is not the transformation of raw materials into food upon the table the same industry for which the 'chefs' in hotels and restaurants are paid[?] Is not the expenditure of vitality in bearing children and rearing them to maturity greater and more engrossing than day labor in shop or factory?"[88]

Wives and mothers in the WCTU wanted money. In fact, one of the main reasons the group wanted to ban alcohol was to free up money otherwise spent on liquor. A favourite story told by members, printed in the WCTU press in 1898, 1908, and 1932, was about a boy who looked for his shoes in a whiskey bottle. After catching the boy breaking a bottle in half and peering inside, his father asked him what he was doing. "Why," the boy answered, "I was looking for a pair of new shoes; I want a pair of new shoes awful bad – all the other chaps wear shoes." His father queried him as to why he thought shoes would be in the bottle. "Why, mother said so," was the response. "I asked her for some new shoes, and she said they had gone into the black bottle, and that lots of other things had gone into it, too – coats and hats, and bread and meat and things; and I thought if I broke it I'd find 'em all," he said.[89] As this tale indicates, WCTU members were angry that men's control of family finances enabled them to purchase whiskey, even as their own sons went without shoes as well as coats, hats, and food. Since housewives did not themselves earn money, the only answer to familial deprivation was temperance.

Families of male drinkers suffered when fathers spent their paycheques on booze. From a 1904 story that stated "popular bar-tenders ... impoverish families," to a 1934 piece that stated the families of alcoholics lived in "poverty and sorrow," the WCTU press argued that liquor impeded men's ability to be good providers.[90] Members' assumption that liquor stole money from families was also enshrined in a song called "Sing a Song of Whiskey." According to this ditty, those who sang whiskey's song had "a pocket without pence," and their wife's "purse [was] always empty." As well, while "starving little children, / And women lean and poor" were in "rags" and "beg[ging] from door to door," the "barman" and the "brewer" grew rich with "others' honey."[91] Prohibition, as this song revealed, was the only method by which women and children could escape poverty.

Members were quite specific about the kinds of material hardships that wives and children endured due to male drinking. When making these arguments, they categorized drinkers and their families into two social groups. The first can be considered "other" people; that is, non-WCTU members. These people were generally portrayed as pathetic, in the "pathos" sense of the term. They starred in fictional stories about drinkers who ended up destroying everything – and everyone – they loved. In 1905, a "true story" called "The Rum Mill's Grist," set in New York City, appeared in the *White Ribbon Tidings*. In this tale an alcoholic named Mr. Fischer was sober for eighteen months, during which time he made enough money to allow his wife, himself, and his two daughters to live in a "well-furnished flat." They had respectable clothes and money for groceries; the children were able to go school, where they excelled. Unfortunately, the husband "fell" back into drinking. He became a raging alcoholic and lost his job. In response his wife had to become a "janitress"; she also had to pawn all of the families' furniture and clothing. Her husband became violent, ripping his wife's clothes off her back and her wedding ring off her finger so that he could pawn them; he also sold his daughter's Bible. After the family's electricity bill was cut off, he grew so desperate that he purchased a gun, killed his wife, and shot himself. The story ends with the children going to an orphanage.[92]

In "The Rum Mill's Grist," the Fischer family loses everything. The moral, the spiritual, the corporeal, and the material were all victims of Fischer's alcoholism. Other stories repeated this theme. They also tended to detail the particular deprivations caused by alcoholism. Food and clothing were mentioned most frequently, with authors suggesting that wives and children went hungry and lived in rags.[93] Bread was an especially needed yet lacking item.[94] Inadequate housing was further put forth. According to a 1911 poem, many drinkers' families could not pay rent and they lived in "wretched tenements." Their experiences thus typified the living conditions of the poor as described by social reformers during this period.[95] In other articles, lack of heat and electricity were alcohol's casualties. And it was the children of drunkards who paid the most costs. Frequently they went without shoes and coats. Their education was also curtailed. Since their families could not afford "school fees," "pencil[s]," and "scribbler[s]," they had to drop out of school.[96]

Yet even as the union's members argued that male drinking created poverty, they also suggested that male drinking affected the budgets of all families. They portrayed society's most down-trodden as pathetic victims of drink, but they also made a related argument that removing booze from the budgets of all families – not just those of the poor– would improve their ability to afford needed things. In other words, just as booze caused poor families to live in insecurity and depravation, so did it impede the ability of more affluent families to improve their own quality of life.

Home ownership was especially important. Members pointed out that when people put former booze money towards housing, they could purchase their own homes. One article on this subject described the case of a shop clerk who was frustrated that his co-worker had been able to purchase "a home of his own," send "three children to school for four years," and loan someone one thousand dollars. In contrast, the shop clerk was "in debt." On closer inspection, it turned out that he paid for two beers daily; he also smoked and chewed tobacco and visited "bar-rooms" every Saturday. The moral of this story was that temperance could create upward mobility. That the WCTU intended all people to learn from this lesson, and not just poor "others," was evident in the article's last line: "Suppose, dear reader, you should figure up a little on *your* personal habits."[97]

If removing liquor and tobacco enabled people to buy homes, so would it allow them to fill such homes with attractive items. According to one piece, limiting the sale of liquor would "promote larger sales of ... pianos, and victrolas, good clothing and many home comforts."[98] Another article quoted the National Dry Goods Association of the United States. So profitable was prohibition, said this association, that the United States was diverting five billion dollars yearly into "other classes of commodities," including "home furnishings," "automobiles," "musical instruments, radio, travel, amusements, jewelry, insurance, education, books and magazines."[99]

If some temperance supporters wanted more home furnishings, others thought that wives' and children's wardrobes could use re-freshing. One writer noted that a year's worth of beer money could buy substantial amounts of groceries; more than this, it could enable families to buy "shoes for the children" and "a new dress for mother."[100] A similar argument appeared in 1924, when *Tidings* published a poem called "Curly's New Suit." Possibly authored by the late Egerton Ryerson Young, a Methodist author and missionary, it suggested that when the father of a boy named Curly stopped drinking, Curly was able to acquire a suit. His mother, meanwhile, purchased a "dandy dress." They were hence hardly recognizable, because when Curly's father spent the family's money on alcohol, both Curly and his mother lived in "dirt and rags."[101]

Items referred to as "comforts," too, could be purchased. Authors frequently noted that "little comforts," "comforts," and "comfort for the home" became available to families after husbands stopped spending money on alcohol.[102] Writers did not define what they meant by *comforts*, but they probably referred to small items of home décor, such as plants, blankets, curtains, and knick-knacks. During this period, home economists instructed housewives to make their homes attractive and comfortable, in part through the careful selection and arrangement of such objects.[103]

WCTU members' mother-centred spending vision similarly appeared in their oft-repeated assertion that banning booze would free up money for items that wives would appreciate. One 1921 *Tidings'* article suggested that "each woman voter should calculate, with pencil and pad, how many beautiful luxuries can be purchased with the price of a case of liquor."[104] As this quotation indicates, some WCTU wives may have watched resentfully as their husbands spent money on booze. Again, in 1926, the same journal noted, "Nothing could possibly supply the average Canadian family with more luxuries and comforts than the cutting out of liquor expenditure."[105] For this writer, "comforts and luxuries" – as opposed to necessities – were what the average Canadian family had to give up when the husband drank.

In their writings, members thus focused on items that wives desired. Such emphasis reflected their own positions within the gendered division of labour. Many working-class and rural women spent upwards of twelve hours or more daily on household chores; and, many affluent women were losing their servants to factory and service work. In response, women of both working and middle classes wanted to increase their household's goods.

According to a 1910 editorial, true social improvement hinged on the abilities of wives to own "modern conveniences and labor-saving appliances."[106] Another piece offered a variation upon this theme, noting that the vacuum cleaner was a blessing, for it "will largely relegate the traditional spring cleaning," with its "heavy all-over carpets," to the "memory of the oldest" person in the house.[107]

If labour-saving devices were desired, so were items of home décor. During the early twentieth century the women's temperance press frequently printed articles on how to furnish rooms, to turn one's veranda into a "sitting room," to select wallpaper, to arrange wall hangings, to set the Christmas table, to choose colours, to light one's home, and to arrange furniture.[108] Authors effectively taught readers the art of homemaking, noting that it was wives' responsibility to ensure their homes were "happy."[109] Stated one, "The furnishing of a home is a very important item in the health and happiness of family." Readers were to remember that wives had two goals: to create comfort, on the one hand, and beauty, on the other.[110]

For many in the WCTU, indeed, skilled homemaking signified womanhood. For them, a good wife and a good mother was one who could "make her home bright and happy."[111] Should anyone be in doubt about a woman's housekeeping skills, one could, as an 1899 poem suggested, take a "peeping" at her "back and unseen rooms." Her cellar should have "cleanly shelves and whitened walls," and her kitchen should have "cleanliness and sweetness."[112] A woman's true character, in other words, could be judged on how well she tended her private spaces. If these areas were kept washed and organized, then the woman could be considered virtuous. "God help the poor man" whose wife could not keep "a bright and happy" home, argued a 1905 piece, for "he is virtually homeless." Good wives and mothers created "refuge[s]," places where families could "retreat" from the "toils and troubles of the outer world."[113]

By the 1920s, older ideals of tidiness had blended with newer ideals of homemaking. Not only were good wives and mothers clean and cheerful, but they were also skilled decorators. A 1920 piece explained this dynamic. One should arrange the living room with an eye to both artistry and comfort. There should be a separate space for each member of the family: the husband should have a chair beside a "well-lighted table, where he could rest in peace"; the "bright-faced laddie" of the home should have a table furnished with "magazine[s]" and "book[s]" about either "athletics" or "art," whichever he is interested in; and the "girl" should be provided with "a pad or two of paper and a supply of pencils" by the fireplace. Such placements would pay off: the man and boy would stay home in the evening – avoiding the "saloon" – and the girl would feel nurtured. Moreover, by providing these "frillings," the mother's hand "shall help to draw out and intensify the seed, God-planted, that lies deep in every soul."[114] Through strategic placement of consumer goods, mothers could help family members achieve peace and creativity.

When one is considering the developing character of Canadian consumer culture, such sentiments are significant. For the WCTU it was not enough that men should stop spending on drink. It was important too that wives and mothers should take their families' earnings and spend them on goods. Doing so, the logic went, would enable women to communicate their respectability to others. It would also protect their families from sin and improve their well-being. Consumer goods, in other words, were integral to the WCTU's definition of modern Canadian living.

## Conclusion

According to a 1910 piece in the Canadian WCTU press, the meaning of life was "[t]o live content with small means; to seek elegance rather than luxury, and refinement rather than fashion."[115] While an emphasis on being content with small means does not suggest that the WCTU played a role in shaping Canadian consumer culture, the appreciation of elegance and refinement as a reflection of the spiritual does. WCTU members took this message to heart and sought to stage their homes in ways that reflected these values. Many wanted to purchase the commodities that signified this sensibility.

WCTU advocates put forth a vision that placed women and their consumer preferences at the centre, calling on men to devote money to their families. WCTU members wanted Canadians to be able to afford not only clothes, shoes, and school fees but also houses, furniture, musical instruments, "luxuries," and "comforts." Such accoutrements were necessary for fulfilment.

It can be concluded that the Canadian WCTU was a maternalistic consumer movement. It was not flashy but it did call for a political economy in which female consumers were empowered agents. The current political economy gave too much power to men; it also gave too much power to intemperate organizations. By supporting temperate businesses, the WCTU called for a new kind of capitalism, one that was sober and family oriented.

The story of the WCTU's consumer advocacy may not be as exciting as the stories of members' demonstrations against alcohol. It does however reveal the centrality of white Christian women's material desires. WCTU members recognized the importance of consumer goods in conveying respectability. More than this, they were keen to promote children's success, so that children could attain upward mobility.

Ultimately, the struggle fought by the union was intimate and feminist: members sought to take money out of the hands of husbands and to put it in the hands of wives. Money, the WCTU recognized, granted power, and it was time for men to give that power to women. The organization did not ask for much, but it did ask for better conditions for the Christian family. In so doing, it represented an early vote for the family-oriented consumer culture that came to characterize English Canada for much of the twentieth century.

*Chapter Two*

# Shopping for Victory: Consumer Citizenship in Wartime

Canada's declaration of war against Germany on 5 August 1914 was merely a formality. The United Kingdom had declared war a day earlier, and Canada, as a British dominion, was automatically involved. Until Germany capitulated in November 1918, Canadians sent unprecedented numbers of troops, munitions, money, and supplies overseas. They did so not only because the mother country bade them but because they were deeply patriotic.[1] As Prime Minister Sir Robert Borden put it in 1918, "the people of Canada entered this war from a profound conviction of duty to the Empire and to the civilized world."[2] At war's outbreak many Canadians had been enthusiastic, believing that war offered Canada opportunities to gain international prestige. And indeed Canada's impressive war machine, coupled with Borden's determination to gain more representation abroad, garnered the nation further independence in international affairs.

As part of its war effort, the Canadian state called upon its inhabitants to become patriotic consumers. Due to wartime conditions, the government used both force and persuasion to convince Canadians to adhere to a growing list of consumer regulations and guidelines, asking them to put aside their own private consumer desires and to use their buying and saving power in support of the Allies' quest for victory. Not only did the state ask Canadians to purchase Victory Loans, but it also called upon them to curtail their spending on fuel, to stop producing and purchasing war-marked foods, and to start purchasing food substitutes such as fish, margarine, and whole wheat flour.

The First World War was hence a key moment in the rise of the Canadian consumer nation. For reasons both political and economic the Canadian state began linking the concepts of consumer and citizen, and it did so in ways that were explicitly gendered. Within the state's new definition of consumer citizenship, women were cast as the nation's pre-eminent consumers; it became their responsibility to spend, save, cook, and garden their way to victory. Making links between their traditional roles as the family's food procurers and producers, on the one hand, and their growing roles as their household's shoppers and budgeters, on the other, pro-war women all over the country embraced the government's campaigns.

This chapter charts how individual women and women's groups took up and responded to government food-control initiatives in ways that secured their social position as politically important to the country. It provides an overview of how food became a tactic of war, and then moves to an analysis of how women were specifically targeted by food-control measures. Next, it shows how and why women's groups became ardent supporters of government conservation efforts. As part of this argument, it demonstrates that self-styled patriotic female consumers largely ignored the criticisms of low-income women who, out of necessity, practised thrift. As such, it concludes that the feminized consumer citizen constituted by the state and women's groups during this time was not only loyal to her state but also implicitly affluent.

### Food as a Strategy of War

When war broke out, food became a target. In 1914, the United Kingdom introduced a naval blockade against Germany, effectively preventing all of the UK's trading partners from shipping food to the Central Powers. Germany retaliated with submarine warfare. Initially the underwater campaign targeted the Allies, but in 1917 Germany began taking aim at commercial vessels from neutral nations. Although the move did render dire the Allies' food situation, it also prompted the United States, in April 1917, to declare war on Germany.

Following the declaration of war the United Kingdom called upon its empire and trading partners to step up trade. As the UK's largest grain supplier and as one of its most important pork and cheese providers, Canada featured in the Allies' entreaties. Throughout the war the British government leaned upon its North American dominion to increase food exports, particularly of wheat, barley, oats, rye, corn, butter, cheese, beef, pork, bacon, fat, and sugar. In response Canada more than tripled its exports. In 1914, as Stacey Barker writes, Canadian food exports were worth $250 million, but "by 1918 this had increased to $740 million."[3] Wheat exports grew especially, with annual exported bushels rising from 95.4 million in 1914 to 158.7 million in 1918.[4]

In response to both British and US developments Canada formalized its food control in 1917. Due to crop failures, shortages, and submarine attacks, in December 1916 the United Kingdom had created a food-control office, designed to regulate the UK's production and distribution of food.[5] The United States, too, began taking measures. One month after entering the war it created a food-administration office that concentrated on production and conservation.[6] Following the lead of the United States and the United Kingdom, in June 1917 Canada created a food-control office. Its powers were formidable. Under the 1914 War Measures Act, which authorized the Canadian government to create and enforce orders and regulations at will, Borden appointed oil magnate William J. Hanna as Canadian Food Controller. According to Order in Council 1460, Hanna had the right to create and enforce regulations on "the prices of any article of food and the storage, distribution, sale and delivery thereof"; "the consumption of food in hotels, restaurants, cafes, private houses, clubs and other places"; and "the manufacture, preparation, storage and transport of foods." On behalf of the federal government he also had the right to "purchase, requisition, store, sell and deliver food."[7]

Hanna's appointment allowed for the mobilization of war-marked foods for export to the United Kingdom. As part of this plan Hanna wanted to restrict Canadians' consumption of such foods and to improve the domestic availability of those foods not needed in Europe.[8] Soon, regulations curtailing consumption of war-marked foods came into force. Between June and December 1917, Hanna brought in twenty-eight Orders in Council, intervening in food production and circulation. He also introduced licensing to enforce these orders.

Even while they applauded such efforts, many commentators displayed frustration with what they saw as Hanna's disregard for inflation. Due to shortages, the cost of living in Canada was rising precipitously, just as it had in Europe, the United States, and Australia. In November 1918 an average weekly budget for a family of five was "$13.49 as compared with $12.10 in November 1917, and $7.96 in November 1914."[9] Food prices were steep, with the price of bacon rising by six cents a pound between 1917 and 1918, and lamb by ten cents a pound. Lard and butter prices nearly doubled, and egg prices increased by 60 per cent.[10]

Across the country, critics said that Hanna should spend more of his time regulating prices and less of it making food orders. They called on him to bring down prices on beef, pork, flour, and bread. *The Voice*, a labour paper in Winnipeg, noted that "flour in England sells for $7.00 a barrel – in Canada $11.20 to $12.00 per barrel," and that "bread in England is 9 cents for a 2-pound loaf" while "bread in Winnipeg is 8 cents a pound." From Hanna's perspective, though, it did not make sense to control prices on foods needed in Europe. Indeed, such a step would serve only to decrease the availability of such foods for shipment overseas.[11] In light of the disparities in food prices in England and Canada, the *Voice* endorsed the decision of the Winnipeg Women's League to ask "for the recall of Controller Hanna."[12] Possibly due to criticism, he resigned in 1918. In his place, Borden appointed Henry B. Thomson, another Conservative.

In March, Borden dissolved the Food Control Office and instituted a new entity called the Canada Food Board.[13] This board was authorized to make orders "prescribing the amount of any kind or kinds of food that may not be used or consumed or that may only be used at times to be specified" as well as "the amount of any kind or kinds of food that may be sold, consumed or used." In response to more outcries against inflation, the Canada Food Board made it illegal for wholesalers in "meats, lard, cheese, oleomargarine [and] eggs" to charge over "four per centum" of their cost price.[14]

Thomson also introduced a ban on hoarding meat, poultry, margarine, butter, lard, eggs, cheese, and tinned and powdered milk. Food-control efforts included campaigns and licensing schemes, as well as fines and jail time for those in contravention of these orders.

In addition, the government embarked on a publicity effort to restrict Canadians' spending on war-marked goods.[15] Its endeavours in this regard were massive, but they all expressed a common set of concerns regarding how women shopped, cooked, and ate. Notably, much of this propaganda portrayed Canadian consumers as affluent white women. In this way, middle- and upper-class white women were positioned as integral to the war effort.

In speeches, pamphlets, films, posters, cookbooks, advertisements, and other media, Canada's Food Controller and the Food Board urged Canadians to preserve and reuse their existing goods, to grow and preserve their own foods, and to employ substitutes. As Hanna put it in a letter distributed to "clergymen throughout the Dominion": "We have a large supply of wholesome substitutes, and these should be used more freely ... Poultry and fish should be used as far as possible instead of beef, bacon or ham. War cereals should be substituted ... for wheat flour. The use of cane sugar should be curtailed."[16] Food messages often contained detailed instructions on how to carry out food-conservation orders. The advice ranged from how to shop for and prepare food substitutes, to how to order wartime meals in restaurants, to how to grow war gardens.[17]

## Government Campaigns to Organize Women

The theme that women, in particular, were responsible for carrying out Canada's conservation orders was central to the government's campaigns. As the nation's shoppers, homemakers, and cooks, women had a duty to ensure that each Canadian household followed conservation guidelines. As Hanna said in 1917, women's "work is of vital importance" to the war. In his view, "the kitchen dress may become a uniform in which is given only less valuable service to the Empire and to humanity than is given by our men in the King's uniform."[18]

Throughout 1917, thrift and conservation campaigns gained speed in Canada and other Allied nations, and organized women's efforts grew apace, reaching their apex between August 1917 and December 1918. As Rutherdale notes, various wartime volunteer movements during this period were marked by "a frenetic drive to organize, speak, delegate, and direct."[19] During the summer of 1917 Hanna decided to follow the lead of the food controllers in the United States and the United Kingdom by organizing a conservation-pledge-card campaign. The idea was to have Canadians sign and post the cards in their windows. It was believed that these individuals, in signing the cards, recognized "the gravity of the food situation" and knew that "Great Britain and our Allies look to Canada to help shatter Germany's threat of starvation." Pledgers vowed to "carry out conscientiously the advice and directions of the food controller [so] that requisite foodstuffs may be released for export to the Canadian Divisions, the British forces and people and the Allied armies and nations." At the bottom of the card housewives were to provide their signature, address, and the number of people in their household.[20]

To launch the food service pledge campaign the women's auxiliary of the Organization of Resources Committee, in co-operation with the Food Controller, ran a series of advertisements in the *Toronto Daily Star* that visually depicted women as the saviours of the Allies, for they were helping to secure their food. In one of the advertisements a large group of women hold out plates of meat and bread; their recipient is a young male Canadian soldier, who is separated from them by water and is waving his hat (fig. 2.1). As this image makes clear, the women's auxiliary believed that women, as mothers and homemakers, were essential to the conservation campaign.[21]

From Victoria to Halifax, women met to co-ordinate thrift-pledge canvassing, with prominent women leading the charge. In Quebec City Mayoress Madame Lavigueur was the first to sign the pledge; the president of the local housewives' league, Madame Tanguay, was the second.[22] Pledge-card canvassing was staggered, with women in Victoria undertaking the work in November and women in most other cities doing so over the winter and the following spring. By the end of November 1917 more than one million cards had been distributed, 143,000 of which were in French.[23]

# Vision Your Sons, Mothers of Canada!

Vision them at early morning when through rising mists, there bursts a hurricane of fire---

See your valiant boys --- calm, grim, but cheerful --- "stand-to-arms" until the Hun's morning hate dies away.

Picture them at breakfast, the meal that must bring them the bodily sustenance to carry them through the strain of another day.

Then think of what might happen if, one morning, there was no breakfast---no food to be had, and the word went down the lines that Canada had failed them.

Vision all these things, and then---As Women of Canada—Mothers of Men—Answer this Call to Service.

Canada must send to Her Own, and to the Allies Fighting Forces, more wheat, more beef, more bacon, and more of such other foods as are nonperishable and easily exported.

Canada can do this, without depriving her own population of a fair share of any of these foods if You Women will but help.

All we ask of you is, that instead of buying so much white flour (if you do your own baking) you vary your baking by using one third oatmeal, corn, barley or rye flour. Or, if you buy your bread, that you order a certain proportion of brown bread each day.

Second, instead of using as much beef and bacon as formerly, you vary your family's diet, by substituting for beef and bacon such equally nutritious foods as fish, peas, lentils, potatoes, nuts, bananas, etc.

*Third, and this is most important —positively prevent the waste of a single ounce of food in your household.*

## They Must Be Fed

Statistics show that, everyday, in Canada, sufficient food is thrown into garbage cans, to feed the entire Canadian Overseas Army.

Travellers have often remarked that many a European family would live well upon the quantity and quality of food wasted in some Canadian homes.

*Such waste is shameful at any time; but in these times it is criminal.*

Our only hope is that with these truths before you, and in view of the vital issues at stake, we may count upon your earnest co-operation in stopping this appalling waste; and in substituting other foods for the wheat, beef and bacon that must be sent overseas.

Next week a Food Service Pledge and Window Card will be delivered to you. The Pledge is your Dedication to War Service. The Window Card your Emblem of Honour.

Women's Auxiliary, Organization of Resources Committee, In Co-operation with The Hon. W. J. Hanna, Food Controller.

# Sign the Food Service Pledge

2.1 Women as homemakers and the food conservation campaign. *Toronto Daily Star*, 11 September 1917, 10.

Immediately after the federal food-control office had been created, many club-women in Victoria began working on their own
thrift-pledge campaign. Inspired by British prime minister Lloyd
George, who had stated that "food is as essential to winning the
war as men and munitions," members of the Local Council of
Women of Victoria printed and distributed thrift-pledge cards.
Deploying military language, cards stated that each bearer promised to "enlist in the woman's army of economy" and "to make
household and personal economies my special duty and service to
my country." In a newspaper article about the campaign Mrs. G.L.
Foulkes provided its rationale: "it is up to us housekeepers to do
our 'bit' by economizing."[24]

In the fall of 1917 the Province of Ontario, together with the Food
Controller, hosted a food-conservation convention in Toronto.
Over three hundred women, from "every district of the province,"
attended and heard speeches from various provincial and national
dignitaries, including Hanna himself, on patriotism, conservation,
and winning the war. Such speeches, as a report on the conference
in *Everywoman's World* reveals, were full of gendered warmonger-
ing. According to a Mr. N.W. Rowell, for example, it was only the
Christian and "civilized" nations that had granted women their
elevated status. Thus, women were told that the threat of German
victory was even more dangerous for them than for men: they
would lose their increased status and would again become subject
to barbaric male tyranny.

Discourses about the threat to women's status spurred many
women to actions that were consistent with government efforts
at the time. Not only did women promise to return home from
government-organized conventions with a commitment to undertake conservationist campaigns, but they did so with increased
vehemence. They also voiced their support of two government strategic initiatives: the recently passed Wartime Elections Act, which
granted the right to vote to women with relatives serving overseas; and the formation of a Union government in order to usher in
conscription, which was a controversial bid by the Conservatives
and a few dissenting Liberals. As evinced by a conference resolution, attendees of the food-conservation convention wanted "the
Premier and the leader of the Opposition to unite in forming a
national Government so as to organize the country on non-partisan

lines, and thus best utilize all our resources and all our man and woman-power for the sole purpose of winning the war."[25]

For its part, the federal government convened special events to recognize and spark women's efforts. In March 1918 the War Committee of the Canadian Cabinet convened a "Women's War Conference" in Ottawa, to which it invited "women from all Provinces of the Dominion." Representatives of over fifteen major women's organizations attended, including the presidents of the NCW, the Fédération nationale Saint-Jean-Baptiste, the Imperial Orders of the Daughters of the Empire, and the Women's Christian Temperance Union. Maternal feminists including Nellie McClung, Irene Parlby, and Elizabeth Shortt were also present. In order to garner support among women for the government's war objectives, the conference included topics such as "increased agricultural production," "conservation of food," "the compilation of the national register," and "the further development of a spirit of service amongst the Canadian people."

The conference lasted for three days and featured speeches by prominent Cabinet ministers, as well as breakout sessions that included representatives from both the government and women's groups. After the conference, delegates emerged with a renewed sense of commitment to conservation, thrift, and economy. As the concluding messages from the conference put it, "we are convinced that as women we can best serve the state at this time by simplicity of life, and by concentrating energy on increased production and on thrift in all our ways, in order to meet the demands for food and money made upon us by the motherland and our allies."[26] By hosting conventions, provincial and federal governments recognized the war efforts made by women's groups and sought to have women reaffirm their commitment to implementing government initiatives when they returned to their communities.

Women's groups preened under state approval, so fervent were they to prove their civic worth. Upon receipt of this approval, some became even more committed to promoting the state's agenda. In 1917 *Woman's Century* printed an article about conservation called "Active National Service for Women," by Kathleen Bowker. The subtitle of the article noted that, "R.B. Bennett, Director-General of National Service Has Approved of This Page, and Accepted Our Offer of Co-operation in the Case of National Service."[27] Similarly, in 1918, the NCW was proud to report that a "letter was recently received from Ottawa expressing appreciation ... and satisfaction with [members'] efforts [on] food conservation."[28]

Some women activists also felt compelled to defend the government's actions around food control. In November 1917 the editors of *Woman's Century* reminded readers that inflation was not the fault of Hanna but that of the "people." The article asserted that "thrift and economy, with their concomitant reduced demand, are the best regulators of prices."[29] Other organized women voiced support for the Food Controller's various initiatives. Thus, when Hanna announced that "every citizen of Canada will be able [to] go about with a fish bulging out of every pocket," *Everywoman's World* printed an illustration of him carrying fish in his pockets and told him to "Keep it up!"[30] More general initiatives, too, were applauded: "Our newly-appointed Food Controller ... is calling for economy of food ... Mr. Hanna has accepted a difficult task, one which not only entitles him to forbearance, but to the utmost support from all sections of the community."[31] As such, women's groups promoted the government's agenda and showed support for public officials who were being criticized in the public arena. They chided those who put their own tastes and preferences above the needs of the war effort and admonished them to sacrifice for the good of the country and the Allies.

### Resisting Conservation: A Question of Class

Canadians' responses to federal food-control campaigns were lukewarm at best. Across the country, people ignored the government's attempts to restrict their consumption of beef, pork, sugar, and white flour. On Prince Edward Island people continued to bake white bread and to serve richly iced cakes, much as they had before the war.[32] *The Globe* in Toronto, meanwhile, scoffed at the Controllers' encouragement of beefless and wheatless meals, stating that the people of Toronto "refused to embrace vegetarianism even for one day."[33] *Maclean's* magazine, for its part, felt obliged to remind husbands to eat "frugal meals at home cheerfully." Such encouragement suggests that when housewives did purchase and cook according to the government orders, they faced resistance from their spouses.[34] Many housewives were indeed critical of conservation. In an article about the monthly meetings of the local chapters of the Quebec Homemakers Clubs, which included discussions about the latest instalments of the *Canadian Food Bulletin*, the author felt compelled to point out that "constructive and not destructive criticism is the object of the clubs."[35]

During the 1917 and 1918 pledge-card campaigns, pro-conservationist disdain towards non-conservationists became apparent. To the surprise of some canvassers, not all housewives in the Dominion relished the thought of cooking for victory. They also did not enjoy talking to canvassers about how to be better shoppers, cooks, and savers. Further, they did not appreciate having women show up on their doorsteps with literature about wartime thrift and with pledge cards to be signed.

Some women's frustration stemmed from the class disconnect that often became apparent between canvassers and housewives. Members of Local Councils of Women tended to be affluent, and council leaders especially were comfortable enough that they could attend daytime meetings and devote adequate leisure time to council activities.[36] For this reason they knew that they had to be fairly sensitive to the feelings of working-class housewives, especially when dealing with thrift. As Mrs. J.D. Gordon of Victoria told her canvassers, "discretion would have to be used ... in the case of approaching a woman on a small income with a large hungry family, who was quite aware of the advantages of food conservation from the state of her purse."[37] Indeed, many housewives were insulted by the implied presumption that they did not know how to be thrifty.

In November 1917 one aggrieved canvasser wrote to *Woman's Century* both to complain about non-compliant housewives and to shame readers into conservation submission. "Women! Have we done our duty?" she asked, continuing: "Not while there is one window without a pledge card therein. If the window lacks a card the fault lies at our door. We have not explained properly ... or we have failed in some way unless the dweller ... is of German sympathy. All that is required of the housewife is to save Beef, Bacon and Flour. She need not starve the family! It is no insinuation that she was thriftless before!"[38] According to this canvasser, housewives who did not sign pledge cards either were Germany sympathizers or held biased perceptions against the canvassers and cards. Either way, the writer assumed them to be ignorant and in need of correction.

Dissenting voices were also featured in various publications. For example, *Woman's Century*, a primarily nationalist, pro-war publication, did print articles with opposing opinions, including those of Francis Marion Beynon, an avowed Winnipeg pacifist, and Violet McNaughton, a Saskatchewan populist who often spoke out against urban, central-Canadian views.[39] Perhaps it was the commitment of the editors of *Woman's Century* to showcasing a variety of perspectives that led to the publication of a piece submitted by contributor Margaret Graham Horton in 1918. Titled "Pledge Card for the Deserving Rich," the piece poked fun at the thrift campaign and drew attention to the clear class disconnect that frequently separated canvassers and low-income housewives. "Will you be good enough to print this personal pledge card for our perplexed food controller?" Horton asked. Her card included six items:

1  I hereby pledge myself not to wear fox or any other kind of furs in July and August, nor the $4,100 Russian sable muff and stole listed in one of this season's catalogues.
2  ... I promise to assist the canners of [peas and tomatoes] to conserve the supply of tin ... by refraining from smoking any cigarettes sold in tin boxes.
3  I promise not to attend horse races.
4  I promise not to add my name to the 25,000 motor car licences issued this year in Ontario alone ...
5  I promise not to blame Providence every time food prices shoot skyward.
6  Finally, I will not insult the poor by urging them to practise any further food economy.

At the end of her article Horton included a postscript: "Copies of my pamphlet on 'How the Worthy Rich can Live on Three Meals a Day,' showing how the omission of afternoon teas, late suppers, superfluous sweets ... will conserve many thousand calories of food energy ... may be had on application."[40] As Horton's satirical pledge card and pamphlet indicate, some politically engaged women were insulted by the suggestion that housewives should do all they could to scrimp and save so as to win the war.

Resistance to conservation measures pivoted on a critique of the continued indulgences of the upper and middle classes. If resources were indeed scarce, then the nation's affluent should not be wearing expensive clothes, smoking cigarettes sold in tins, attending horse races, buying cars, and eating "superfluous" foods. Asking individual housewives, who were already very thrifty, to sign conservation pledges seemed to shift the burden of conservation onto individual women; it also sidestepped broader political issues around resource mobilization.

Indeed, if it were so important that the Dominion conserve tin, fuel, and food, then perhaps the government should start looking towards the consumption of these resources by the rich, rather than by the poor. Although there is a strong moralistic tone to Horton's article – in that she castigates as extravagant all those who attend horse races and eat unnecessary foods – there also exists a class-motivated sense of outrage against the Food Controller's attempts to mobilize the nation's housewives in support of thrift. This outrage was levied in a context of implored thrift while those with power and privilege ignored both other forms of consumer excess and the burden of inflation faced by housewives.

Concurrent with the class-motivated sense of outrage against the pledge campaigns in 1917 and 1918 were other forms of criticism against conservation tactics. "One argument against the Food Pledge Cards," stated a frustrated canvasser, was "that they were weak and childish." Other people assumed that the cards were signals for the police to enter people's homes and seize "the goods you have canned." In other words, some people refused to sign because they would, in effect, be publicizing their own conservation work; in the event of a shortage, therefore, the government might requisition their stores. Others charged that the pledge cards were too costly for the government to print and that canvassers, moreover, were being paid to distribute them.[41] As these critiques of the pledge cards make clear, not all Canadians shared the enthusiasm for conservation, which they charged was infantilizing, expensive, and invaded the privacy of Canadians. In this sense, food and eating habits were positioned as a private matter into which the state should not interfere.

### Uptake of the Conservation Effort by Women's Groups

Major volunteer and non-profit organizations such as the Red Cross, the Rotarians, and the Canadian Club were vocal supporters of conservation.[42] Yet this support paled in comparison to that of the Dominion's major women's organizations, who donated unparalleled amounts of time and energy to food control. Canada's largest women's group, the National Council of Women of Canada – which had four hundred thousand members during the war – was particularly vehement. The Women's Christian Temperance Union, the Girl Guides, the Women's Institute, the Fédération nationale Saint-Jean-Baptiste, the Canadian Suffrage Association, the Canadian National Association of Trained Nurses, the Win-the-War League, the National Equal Franchise League, the Canadian Women's Press Club, and the Young Women's Christian Association were other important allies. By examining the tactics of these groups, it is possible to discern the motivations shaping their support of conservation.

Via debates over the proper role and responsibility of the Food Controllers, food was positioned as a public matter that required oversight and control. While some Canadians ignored and criticized the food-control orders, others criticized the Food Controllers themselves for overspending and for failing to intervene to curtail food prices. Canadians across the country believed that price control should have been the Controllers' mandate.[43] For example, Dr. Bessie Brighouse of the Burnaby Women's Forum stated, "No woman should be asked to conserve the food until [profiteering] is abolished."[44] Anne Anderson Perry of Winnipeg was similarly aggrieved. After the war she published a polemic against the food-control experiment. In her view, the Food Controller had not been a controller at all but a "Producter of the Profiteers" and an "Oppressor of the Poor." She opined that while he may have fulfilled his promises to the Allies, he did not bring down prices, and thus he did an injustice to his own people. Despite concerns levied on the grounds of class, privacy, and state responsibility, throughout the war women's groups showed strong support for the government and its conservation measures.

Faced with opposition to food conservation and the pledge campaign, some organized Canadian women grew exasperated and admonished women to become their own controllers. As one contributor to *Woman's Century* somewhat wistfully described, "a Food Controller might dictate, but it would be an impossible task for him to enforce his mandate by getting into our kitchens or our dining rooms no matter what sized staff he could employ as food

police."[45] Believing that many Canadians were either too ignorant, greedy, or wilful to follow conservation orders, they began to
call upon all Canadians – and all Canadian women specifically –
to self-regulate their food habits. "It is impossible to police all
the homes in the Dominion," stated campaigner Isabel M. Ross,
"but every woman can be her own food controller and if she takes
the regulations issued for public eating houses and makes them
part ... [of] her menage, she is accepting them in the proper spirit
and running her household on the true constitutional basis of
food control."[46] By making such declarations, these campaigners
demonstrated their adherence to the rising tide of liberal govern-
mentality sweeping the country, in which the state and its citizens
tacitly agreed to support each other's endeavours. This agreement
was contingent on citizens self-regulating to evade coercion.

The discourse of organized women also demonstrated that their
sympathy lay with their national government. One campaigner
said, "The responsibility of enforcement rests upon ourselves ...
and we can confidently hope that the women of Canada will give
the utmost support to Mr. Hanna ... in encouraging and fostering
that spirit of endurance and service based on the determination
to win the war at all costs."[47] As this passage indicates, organizers
believed they had a unique responsibility to act and consume in
such a way that served the government and supported the war
effort. In fact, some women took it upon themselves to act as
self-appointed volunteer agents of the government.

Various women's groups performed vigilante surveillance by
spying on restaurants and individual households to ensure that
conservation orders were being observed. In Montreal in 1918
a group of women who called themselves the Women's Food
Economy Branch of the Canada Food Board announced that they
were going to create a "vigilance committee" that would "receive
and report [to the board] all complaints of food laws violated."[48]
And in Regina, as one reporter announced, the "L.C.W. members ... mean to see that there is some actual conserving done."
Thus, "where any extravagance or waste or luxury shows itself
publicly, the Regina L.C.W. members, and there are one thousand
of them, mean to discountenance it." Having learned that "elaborate refreshments are still being served in many of the homes of
the city, and that as yet every effort is not being made to conserve

certain food stuffs," the Local Council of Women "most earnestly call[s] upon the women of Regina to do all in their power to conserve all white flour and sugar."[49]

Whereas some campaigners felt that surveillance would help prod recalcitrant restaurants and households to follow food orders, others suggested that stronger food laws were the only way to enforce compliance. Prior to the Food Controller's eventual creation of several food regulations, an August 1917 article in *Woman's Century* called on Hanna to be as strict as possible. "It would seem highly desirable that the Food Controller should use autocratic power [and] dictate rather than appeal," it stated. The anonymous author "would like to see him prohibit the sale of ice-cream" so as to boost butter production. She also called on the legalization of margarine, the reduction of sugar in candy making, and the ending of "the use of food-stuffs in the manufacture of alcoholic beverages." Save for the banning of ice cream, all of her recommendations were eventually legislated, indicating that Hanna's laws were not entirely his own ideas but rather ones supported by other Canadians, as well.[50]

Following the institution of numerous food regulations to which many Canadians did not adhere, female conservation campaigners began to suggest further measures. In February of 1918 a *Woman's Century* editorial made the bold assertion that just as conscription had been necessary to boost the military, so too were "compulsory food rations" in order to feed the soldiers. As the author stated, legal measures had been taken to reach "indifferent men," and it was now time to rein in the "haphazard housekeepers." Indeed, "there must be forceful leadership and law in this matter!"[51] At the 1918 annual meeting of the Saskatchewan Equal Franchise Board, members passed a resolution that called for food to be "Conserved by Law." The board stated: "Whereas dependence on the efforts of patriotic individual members of our committees has proven a most dilatory and unsatisfactory method of dealing with the question of food conservation, ... be it resolved that the board memorialize the federal government with a view to securing the conservation of necessary supplies for our troops by legislation."[52] For the Saskatchewan Equal Franchise Board, as for the editors of *Woman's Century*, food control was too important a matter to be left in the hands of unpredictable and ignorant individuals. Despite the lifting of all food orders and dissolution of the Canada Food Board in 1919, the way in which women responded to conservation measures resulted in lasting implications for women, their role as consumers, and their place in the citizenry. Conservation measures provided the conditions for the calls for restraint on moral and patriotic grounds. Tactics and campaigns of women's organizations often reinforced class-based divisions between women and showed that the primary concern for affluent organized women was government and country. These women charged that housewives who did not support conservation were either ignorant or treasonous.

As the war entered its second year, thrift and creativity became common themes within the publications of women's groups, reflecting growing concerns over shortages and high prices. One of the first Canadian references to food consumption during the First World War appeared in *Woman's Century*, the official magazine of the NCW. Edited by a group of reform-minded women in Toronto, the magazine had 21,600 subscribers. In 1915 the magazine ran an article called "The Best Foods to Buy during the War" which was published in the context of the rising cost of items that were becoming scarce in Europe, particularly beef, pork, white flour, and sugar. The article recommended substitutions that would allow consumers both to support the war effort and to avoid high prices. The author, Dr John McCollough, stated that women should replace beef and pork with "dried peas and beans." They could make bread from "oatmeal, cornmeal, and whole wheat," and they could substitute "maple syrup and honey" for sugar."[53] Women were encouraged to be creative in their shopping and in their kitchens and to do so with an overall view to serving their country and supporting the war.

Of all the publications of the women's groups, *Woman's Century* was most vocal in its support for conservation. Beginning in 1916, it ran articles that informed readers of the government's calls for production and economy, as well as articles that endorsed such calls. "Canada is following the lead of the motherland by the opening of a Dominion-wide campaign of 'thrift and production,'" announced editor-in-chief Jessie Campbell-MacIver. In this campaign, women were key in so far as they were "in charge of the domestic spending departments and [were] by far the biggest

buyers in the country." By co-operating in the state's efforts to produce and conserve, women "will not only have ensured victory in
battle but the future prosperity of the Dominion."[54] Through this
editorial Campbell-MacIver articulated a specific vision of wom-
en's consumer citizenship.

Interest in new approaches to household management also
fuelled some women's conservation work. Popular women's magazines frequently carried recipes and gardening advice, as well as
tips and tricks to stretch budgets and organize households. Much
of the printed materials emerging from the Food Control Office and
the Food Board, and women's campaigns resembled this literature.
The Food Board's recipe books, for example, had lavishly illustrated covers and straightforward titles, guaranteeing to spark interest in the contents (fig. 2.2).[55] A chatty article, "Mrs. Buchanan of
Ravenna," in *Everywoman's World* may have also proved inspiring.
"Dear Friends," this charismatic homemaker wrote, "I have been
asked to write out a few recipes for your benefit, and proceed to do
so, but would just like to state that I am not used to cooking by recipe. I just use my judgment, that is, knowledge born of experience."
In a subsection called "My Pet Recipes" she wrote in a folksy manner
about how to make soup, war breads, cookies, cakes, and cheese.[56]

During this period Christian doctrine equated material pleasure
with the sins of greed, lust, and pride. Thus, living austerely was
necessary for a holy life.[57] In July 1917 *La Bonne Parole*, the monthly
magazine of the primarily Catholic women's organization the
Fédération nationale Saint-Jean-Baptiste, published an article titled
"La vie en temps de guerre." According to the article, which had
been reprinted from a journal called *L'Echo*, acting "sérieusement,"
"virilement," and "chrétiennement" were necessary for victory.
Rather than spending on needless amusements, people needed to
slow down, work hard, and pray for peace.[58] Anglophone publications, too, linked austerity with virtue. According to the Victoria
Local Council of Women, "overeating" was a "sin" at all times, but
especially in wartime when "our dear ones [are] at the front."[59]

Not only was excess in eating inappropriate, so too was excess
in fashion. In the spring of 1916 Alberta Deards of the Montreal
Plain Clothes League had written to *Woman's Century*. She wanted
to persuade readers to adhere to the league's guidelines on clothing in a time of war. "Mrs. and Miss Canada have, on the whole,

2.2 Glossy Food Board recipe books. "Canada Food Board Recipe Books," poster, 1918. Courtesy of Toronto Public Library.

been generous in the matter of their contributions to war funds,"
she wrote, "but even the best of us ... cannot, in the face of what is
taking place in Europe, rest content in any self-satisfied state of com-
placency." And indeed, despite everyone's war efforts, "the hunt
after pleasure and distraction does not seem to be one whit less ...
the crowds of fashionably and expensively dressed women do not
diminish in our streets." Rather than spending money on "fine
clothes," Deards urged women to spend "on raw materials for Red
Cross work, on flour, milk etc., for the starving Belgians, on field
comforts for the boys in the trenches." In this way they would make
"luxury and extravagance an offence to all right-thinking people."[60]
Deards's article illustrates the conditions in which some women
would become receptive, a year later, to state attempts to control
spending in the service of war when the Food Control Office was
created. Already suspicious of luxury, and supportive of the Allies,
Canadians such as Deards would have taken seriously the messages
of self-sacrifice embedded within federal conservation campaigns.

Deards was subtle, but other *Woman's Century* writers drew
explicit links between luxury and evil. In 1917 the organ published
a piece by Louise Morris, titled "Extravagances and the War," which
resembled a sermon. According to Morris, the war was a blessing
in disguise, for it was curing North America of "the bacillus of
extravagance and the microbe of wilful waste." Morris was happy
that wartime inflation would end conspicuous consumption. No
more could "Mr. and Mrs. Middle-Class" afford the same goods
as did "Mr. and Mrs. Idle Rich," nor could they purchase "flowers and favours" at "bridge parties"; "the best of smokes"; "good
clothes, fine cooking, first class club[s]"; "fashionable schools";
"extravagant dress"; "electric lights"; the "telephone"; ostenta-
tious bathrooms; lavish jewellery; expensive motor cars; jewelled
collars for pet dogs; and, finally, "expensive theatre seats, taxicabs,
restaurants." Now that the war had come, the "super-civilization
that was settling down on us ... is lifting and under it all we see
coming forth real men, real women." They are "real," according
to Morris, because "nursing, cooking, knitting are once more in
evidence amongst our women," and "charity, patriotism, kindly
feeling are now uppermost in the minds of our men."[61]

According to Brown and Cook, during the First World War the
Protestant churches suggested that "the war provided the seedbed

for social reform."[62] Morris's article demonstrates that churches and many individuals viewed the war as "a pathway to political and social 'regeneration,'" as historian Joan Sangster described this movement.[63] Prior to the war Morris had been bothered by what she saw as class destabilization, and especially by the non-elite's use of goods to claim status. She cherished a conservative view of Canadian life, one in which people stayed inside their ascribed class positions. In her view, the distant past was an age of purity, one to be sought again. She hence welcomed the message of "simplicity and charity" that the war had brought.[64] Compared to many other women's writings, Morris' rhetoric was more religious. Nonetheless, its appearance in *Woman's Century* does indicate that some Canadians were prepared to embrace the government's messaging on conservation.

Other *Woman's Century* articles struck similar notes between austerity and morality. Another article in the same issue that ran "Extravagances and the War," called "Luxury and Womanhood," by E. Blakely, drew similar connections between extravagance and ignorance. Blakely begins the piece with a "Fore note," which describes terrible suffering at the front: "some [nuns] were taken, their hands and breasts cut off, their bodies thrown in a well." At the end of this note she asks rhetorically, "Can we indulge in luxury?" Indeed, rather than spending money on "upholstered motor cars," Canadians should think of the "men [lying and] writing in unutterable agony for hours in an advance dressing station" due to "insufficient motor ambulances." With these thoughts Canadians would be well inspired to start "lending money to the War Loan." Similarly, instead of spending money on blouses and wasting time making lingerie, Canadian women could buy wool and make warm clothes for soldiers and "British prisoners." Finally, by making their own hats instead of buying ones from Milan, Canadian women could "leave the Milanese free to pursue the battle for Christian Liberty."[65]

Until the end of the war the inducement of guilt remained a theme within women's calls for thrift. In March 1917 *La Bonne Parole* printed another article on simple living in wartime, which had originally appeared in *Extraits de la Revue Hebdomadaire*. The author expressed outrage that even though young French men were dying, young French women were wearing expensive, short, and showy dresses. Though this article was explicitly about France, its appearance in *La Bonne Parole* suggests that some French Canadian women, too, believed its messages of restraint and gravity to be relevant. Striking the same note as "La vie en temps de guerre," the article suggested it was time for everyone in France (and Canada, presumably), including civilians, to behave with modesty, seriousness, and chastity.[66]

In English Canada, meanwhile, writers continued to chastise readers both for living extravagantly and for ignoring the needs of soldiers and civilians overseas. In 1917 a contributor to *Woman's Century* asked readers if they would "stand behind our boys at the front ... or let them go to their long rest under-nourished to our everlasting shame." By saving flour, women could help feed the troops. They could also help out the "Spartan" women in England who "stand in hundreds, watching their wounded stretcher cases pass through Euston station."[67] For many women, then, thrift and morality were inextricably linked. To be thrifty was to be moral, not only because luxury was a sin but also because it was selfish to enjoy material pleasures while others were dying. The occasion of war provided an excuse to proselytize on the virtues of modesty and generosity.

Organized Canadian women frequently employed military metaphors to describe their activities, illustrating the citizenship imperative in them. Here, again, they took their cue from Hanna. According to the Controller, conservation "is real, actual military service, for without food supplies our armies cannot fight this war ... nor can the Allied nations hold their battle lines."[68] *Woman's Century* writers frequently picked up on this theme. In a 1918 piece an anonymous contributor reminded readers that we "are asked to join a great conservation army that will have as its aim sufficient food for the fighting men and for the allies."[69] It was, however, during the thrift campaigns that the army metaphor came most fully into its own.

In September 1917, *Everywoman's World* published an article called "An Army of Savers," with the subtitle "Canada Is Calling for Another Army – Women's Battalions Must be Raised in Every District for That Army." Accompanying the article is an illustration of a woman standing with a gardening shovel, which she is holding as if it were a rifle; her troops consist of the foods she is using in her conservationist battle (fig. 2.3). Subtly suggesting that female pledge canvassers were sergeants in women's conservationist army, this article made obvious connections between thrift and national service. It stated: "The call to-day is for Men, Munitions and Food. Women have helped recruiting and have helped in the

SEPTEMBER 1917                                      EVERYWOMAN'S WORLD    PAGE 25

# AN ARMY OF SAVERS
### Canada is Calling for Another Army—Women's Battalions Must be Raised in Every District for that Army

2.3 Woman as grower and her troops in the conservationist battle. Katherine M. Caldwell, "An Army of Savers," *Everywoman's World*, September 1917, 25.

making of munitions. But our greatest opportunity has now been given us; we are called upon to regulate the nation's meals ... Here it is – Women's Big Duty."[70] In casting themselves as an army of savers, Canadian women activists attempted to demonstrate their value to the war effort and legitimate their importance within the Dominion. In so doing, they also presented a specific iteration of femininity premised on a patriotic form of homemaking. Realizing that they could enhance their claims to citizenship by performing a gendered form of patriotism, they mobilized their traditional gender roles in the service of both citizenship and war.

Women's portrayals of themselves as members of conservationist armies also connected the concepts of femininity, citizenship, and domestic consumption. The figure of the battle-ready female "saver" represented modern femininity; her wise buying decisions were for the good of the Dominion and the Empire. At the same time, in her thrift she relied on pre-industrial and rural practices such as gardening and canning. As one writer said in *Woman's Century*, "our great-grandmothers, grandmothers and mothers were accustomed to preserve food by means of sugar, salt, vinegar, spices and drying to insure a plentiful store for the coming winter. That is practically what must be done now."[71]

Morality, however, was not the only justification trotted out by women campaigning for thrift. Loyalty to empire was another

reason, and the calls for thrift and conservation ushered in a patriotic consumerism performed by women. This form of consumerism also bolstered women's position during and after the war.
By becoming responsible purchasers, women could demonstrate
their patriotism. They could also illustrate their strategic economic
importance, as well as demonstrate their pivotal roles within their
nation and empire. As the war continued, women's groups continued to link notions of patriotic obligation and consumerism in
such a way that secured women's positions as socially, militaris-
tically, and politically relevant. For example, Mrs. Edwin Long
argued that because women were the "purchasing agents for
Canadian homes," it was their wise spending and saving decisions
that would help Canada in its fight for victory.[72]

Just as women who believed that luxury was sinful castigated
those whom they saw as spendthrift, so too women who pro-
pounded patriotism and victory criticized and condemned all who
were not abiding by their government's calls to economize and
conserve. Patriotic obligation, actualized at the site of the kitchen,
was a central focus of conservationist literature. A booklet called
"Win-the-War Suggestions and Recipes," published by the wom-
en's auxiliary of the Ontario Win-the-War League, was typically
didactic of the kitchen as a location where women must demonstrate their patriotism. "This is not a cookery book," the introduction begins; rather, it is "a few recipes and some sketchy hints to
help those who want to do more towards economizing our food
supply ... Economy is one of the most important factors in the successful carrying on of the war, though only one woman in a thousand or so seems to be in the least conscious of the fact."

Over the next ten pages, and interspersed among passages about
cooking without beef, baking with brown flour, canning vegetables,
making soup, and other tips on how to prepare food in wartime,
appears a series of patronizing remarks regarding women who do
not follow food orders. To cite just a few: "Women *must* sacrifice
their vanity, their mean self-indulgence and criminal selfishness on
the altar of their country's safety. They must do it in order to back
up all those who are suffering ... at the front." Furthermore, while
soldiers are suffering, "all the stores are crammed with ignoble
women spending precious money [on] 'nice clothes.'" And "men
can't give [to the war effort] if all they earn is squandered or care-
lessly wasted by their womankind."[73] Clearly, winning the war

was more important than the development of any kind of rapport with the housewives who might have decided to read the booklet.

Women's groups devised, in addition to general calls for thrift, specific conservation programs. The Montreal Women's Club and the Ottawa Women's Canadian Club, for example, called upon women and children to grow "Thrift Gardens" and "Patriotic Plots." In this way, as Mrs. J.A. Wilson of Ottawa put it, they could prove their patriotism and "lessen the excess of demand over supply."[74]

The Montreal Women's Club also announced that, as it was wartime, they had "eliminated all unnecessary expenditure." Their "hospitality committee," however, did continue to serve tea at "five o'clock on business days."[75] In Halifax, members of the Local Council of Women created a "Frugality Committee." Inspired by one of the member's circulation of "a poster which is being used in England advocating greater production and more thrift," the committee dedicated itself to collecting "rags, papers, and magazines, for the good of their funds," as well as gathering leather gloves to "line trench-coats for the soldiers."[76]

Women's conservation efforts were broadly shaped by discourses that linked women's consumption, cooking, and food production to proper femininity, citizenship, and national duty. Activists tethered women's daily food preparation to ideas of patriotism to prove that not only were they supporting the war effort, but they too were undertaking military duty. Politicized women responded to government pressure and campaigns for conservatism by casting women's consumption choices as socially, economically, and politically significant. For example, activists answered Hanna's plea for "women of all Canada to realize the situation now confronting us" (namely, the threat of German victory) and to conserve "wheat, beef and bacon supplies for contribution to the needs of Great Britain and her Allies," by framing Canadian women as virtuous consumers, conservers, producers, and savers.[77]

One Canada Food Board poster featured an image of a well-dressed, attractive woman smiling at some fish for sale; the not-so-subtle message was that well-adjusted Canadian women happily bought fish in lieu of beef and pork (fig. 2.4).[78] She was hence a role model for all Canadian housewives. Another poster portrayed two women happily canning vegetables (fig. 2.5).[79] By contrast, the Food Board never singled out men as either shoppers or cooks.

2.4 "Buy Fresh Fish," Canada Food Board, 1918.

2.5 "Waste Not – Want Not," Canada Food Board, 1918.

While Canada's Food Controllers sought to have women conserve, by distributing images of women happily following conservation orders, they also used shame to motivate compliance. A
1918 poster released by the Canada Food Board played upon these
themes, though it substituted women's sons for husbands (fig. 2.6).
In it a woman sits at a table, holding a child in her lap, and says,
"Remember we must feed Daddy too." On the wall is an illustration of a man, presumably her husband, wearing fatigues and aim-
ing a rifle. In this case, the mother is eating a very simple soup
and is thus denying her and her child's desire for extravagance. As
Joan Sangster notes, the general "iconography" of Canadian men
and women during the First World War "revealed man as the 'just
warrior' and woman as the moral mother, sacrificing her sons to
the cause."[80] Not only has the woman in the poster sacrificed her
husband to the war effort, but also she is helping soldiers get the
food they need. Women who did not make such sacrifices were
positioned as selfish and unpatriotic.[81] Characterizing themselves
as virtuous women and patriotic purchasers, organized Canadian
women sought to prove their economic and political importance to
their nation and their empire.

### State Recognition and the Status of Women

By exploring the state's intervention into consumption during the
First World War, this chapter reveals that conservation measures
provided the conditions for the emergence of a nationalist, feminized consumer citizenship. In examining the reasons compelling many women to support their government's new consumer
order, it becomes apparent that the messages of thrift and conservation tied in well to many women's existing approaches to household management. Thus the government's calls for conservation
appealed to some women's pride and interest in running their
homes along economical lines. Campaigns for conservation, too,
appealed to some women's creativity. By purchasing new foods
and trying new recipes, women could expand their cooking reper-
toire as well as share with each other their various food journeys.
Yet calls for conservation targeted not only women as individuals but also women in organizations who galvanized this political
moment to secure the status of women amongst the citizenry.

2.6 "Remember We Must Feed Daddy Too," Canada Food Board, 1918.

While individual Canadians' responses to conservation were mixed, Canada's largest women's organizations were enthusiastic. Creating conservation committees, canvassing neighbourhoods, developing and cooking war recipes, organizing pledge drives, and spying on restaurants and households, these groups demonstrated their support for their state. In the process they both became and represented themselves as patriotic consumer citizens.

This iteration of patriotic national consumerism was unique to the social and political contexts of the First World War. By taking up the Canadian state's call for conservation, Canadian women evinced their citizenship. Already participating in the war effort through raising funds, knitting materials for soldiers, sending parcels overseas, organizing social events for soldiers, tending veterans' wounds, and other initiatives, many women's organizations acquired another arrow in their quiver, conservation.[82] And since conservation touched on the activities – food acquisition and preparation – of most housewives, it became a particularly powerful one. As Jacobs states in reference to the US context, the First World War conservation movement "elevated ordinary household concerns into a vital national cause and imbued it with patriotic fervor."[83]

*Chapter Three*

# Home Economics and the Training of the Consumer Citizenry

Perhaps no more suitable training ground existed for the cultivation of consumer citizens than the discipline of home economics. Frequently associated today with the teaching of sewing and cooking, home economics during the first half of the twentieth century also taught pupils how to consume. Prior to the Second World War, budgeting, shopping, and maintaining commodities were central to home economics, as was the idea that to be a good housewife one had to be both a producer and a consumer. This chapter explores the history of post-secondary home economics education in Canada, focusing on the consumer components of its programming. It suggests that home economics offered a rich area of activity for middle-class female educators who were concerned about the role of consumption within the lives of Canadian women. Instructors encouraged their female students to become modern shoppers by providing them with information on proper financial management and teaching them how to shop for, select, and maintain commodities. As such, home economics and its curriculum encouraged girls and women to consider themselves professional consumers.

Examining Canadian home economists' treatment of consumer issues between the 1890s and 1930s, I argue that capitalist commodity distribution was central to Canadian post-secondary home economics education during the first half of the twentieth century. The chapter provides original evidence that in Canada, as in the United States, the discipline of domestic science was renamed *home economics* due to the extent to which consumer issues preoccupied those who were developing and administering the programs.[1]

By analysing curricula from the archives of various universities, I show that prior to the Second World War, budgeting, shopping, decorating, and commodity selection dominated Canadian home economics curricula and that, as such, these curricula allowed for the constitution of consumption habits and capacities, in addition to production habits and capacities. By teaching women how to shop, in addition to teaching them how to sew and cook, domestic scientists positioned themselves as elevating the economic status of women and enhancing the well-being of the nation. In so doing, they also justified their own position as consumer experts.

This chapter first explains its archive and then reviews the history of home economics in Canada from 1900 to the beginning of the Second World War. In this section it surveys some debates about whether and to what extent consumer culture changed at the time. Ultimately, however, it does not enter into such debates, focusing instead on assumptions made by home economists about supposed changes to consumer activity. This section also accounts for the development of home economics as an academic discipline during this time. The bulk of the chapter is then devoted to a consideration of the teaching of consumption in home economics curricula, a process that included both extensive training and the cultivation of ties with capitalist enterprise. One of the events organized by home economists in Alberta was the Home Economics Week of 1932, and I use this event to highlight the capitalist-friendly consumer ethos that informed the movement. Finally, the chapter considers the art and science of both cooking and dressing as they were taught in home economics programs. In this way, it shows that they were infused with a Euro-Canadian sensibility that cast white bourgeois womanhood as an ideal towards which consumers of all backgrounds should aspire.

## The Archive

This chapter's findings are drawn from the curricula of post-secondary home economics programs that were offered between 1900 and 1939 at six universities across the country: Mount Allison University in Sackville, New Brunswick; the École Ménagère Provinciale in Montreal; the University of Toronto; MacDonald College in Guelph, Ontario; the Agricultural College at the University of Manitoba in Winnipeg; and the University of Alberta in Edmonton. These programs were among the earliest in Canada to offer domestic science and, later, home economics training. They also have extensive archival records available.

Post-secondary home economics programming constitutes a valuable source for research into home economists' treatment of consumer issues. It is difficult to locate the records of home economists prior to 1939 since Canadian home economists did not come together as a national organization until that time.[2] Significant holdings in these areas have not yet been identified, though some of the groups, including the Alberta Home Economics Association, did leave archival records.[3] Therefore, the collections of materials on home economics prior to the Second World War held by university archives across Canada are a significant source of information. An examination of such records offers insights into the consumer issues that Canadian home economists identified as important during the first half of the twentieth century. They also reveal a shift in how household management was taught and the consumer subject therein cultivated. Moreover, since many post-secondary home economics courses during this period were intended to train public home economics teachers, the curricula also illuminate the topics that would be taught in schools to young pupils.

## Canadian Home Economics Education

During the 1890s, leading female educators in the United States began to argue that shopping had become more complicated.[4] According to Goldstein, this increased complexity was precipitated by major structural shifts, including industrialization and urbanization. Prior to these events, more people had lived outside of cities and were reliant on their own production capacities; housewives often made their own soap, bread, preserves, and bed and table coverings, as well as clothing. By the end of the nineteenth century, however, people were living mostly in cities and buying their household items in the marketplace. Packaged cereals, meats, and other household items – such as toys, furniture, and décor – were increasingly available and affordable. More expensive consumer goods, such as "gas and electric appliances," were also becoming available. As Goldstein argues, modern appliances "started to transform the homes of the urban elite."[5]

Nevertheless, the argument that urbanization and industrialization fundamentally altered consumption habits has been contested. Canadian historian Douglas McCalla has recently taken issue with the idea that nineteenth-century rural folk were not consumers. He argues that historians have a tendency to create "stories of dramatic change in consumption" that are characterized by two contrasting periods. The first is a stable, simplistic era in which "autonomous, independent families" survive largely through the means of their own production. The second is a highly complex era in which "families and communities" are "subordinated to the market and to capitalism."[6] According to McCalla, a wide range of Canadian authors have fallen prey to this "mythology" and have portrayed nineteenth-century Canadians as having "Crusoe-like self-sufficiency."[7]

McCalla's argument helps scholars recognize that many rural people in the nineteenth century had access to commercially produced foodstuffs, medicine, hardware, reading materials, and textiles.[8] However, regardless of the degree to which consumption habits actually shifted at the turn to the twentieth century, the development of the home economics movement was influenced by the *belief* in such a shift. In Canada, arguments in favour of the development of home economics as a discipline were premised on the notion that industrialization and urbanization were making the consumption of commercially produced goods increasingly significant.[9]

What is more, home economists themselves, in both the United States and Canada, subscribed to a broad narrative of social decline that often accompanied narratives of industrialization and urbanization. America's earliest home economists, as Goldstein puts it, were "worried that the expanding working-class population and the continued influx of immigrants into white Anglo-Saxon culture would result in social fragmentation." They also "feared that values associated with industry – individualism and personal isolation – would undermine the home as a place of refuge and destabilize it as a cornerstone of civilization."[10] In response, home economists tended to fetishize the promises of perfection held out by science and engineering. As part of this process they taught housewives to use reason and efficiency to "navigate the new world of consumption." By training them in the new science of consumption, home economists set themselves up as consumer experts, ones that women of all ethnicities and classes could emulate.[11] As this chapter will soon demonstrate, Canadian commentators also tied social decline to changes in housewives' consumption habits. Such messages thus animated not only American but also Canadian consumer pedagogy.

In both the United States and Canada, the institution of nation-wide home economics curricula relied on the prior institutionalization of the domestic sciences as an academic discipline. Supporters of domestic science at the elementary and secondary levels of schooling usually justified domestic science instruction on the basis of training. Specifically, educators said that girls needed to be trained to become skilled wives and mothers. Also, working-class girls required training in order to become domestic servants.[12]

At the post-secondary level, in contrast, supporters more often justified the demands for domestic science by stating it was necessary to train aspiring teachers in domestic science so that they could then offer correct instruction to their pupils.[13] Indeed, post-secondary domestic science curricula in Canada originated in response to this demand. By 1898 in Ottawa and Toronto the Young Women's Christian Association (YWCA) was offering courses for teachers on the subjects of cooking, household science, home nursing, laundry, and sewing. Two years later the Lillian Massey Normal School of Domestic Science and Art opened in Toronto.[14] Also in 1900 the Normal School of Domestic Science and Art opened in Hamilton.[15] Three years later this school was moved to Guelph and renamed the MacDonald Institute. It remained a leader in post-secondary home economics education well into the twentieth century.[16] By the time of the First World War, the University of Toronto, McGill University, Acadia University, the Truro School of Domestic Science (Nova Scotia), Mount Allison University, and the University of Manitoba all offered domestic science teacher training.[17] By the mid-1920s, domestic science teacher preparation was also available at the University of Saskatchewan, the University of Alberta, and the École Ménagère Provinciale in Montreal.[18]

Teacher training may have been the impetus for the delivery of post-secondary domestic science, but such curricula soon became

academic programs in their own right. In a broader context of male
hostility to women in the academy, domestic science programs in
early twentieth-century Canadian universities became havens for
female students.[19] However, even while home economics programs
expanded, they still remained small components of Canadian
post-secondary education. By the interwar period, household
science represented approximately 2 per cent of total Canadian
university enrolments. Moreover, women themselves comprised
a minority of the total Canadian post-secondary student body. In
1935 they represented 22 per cent of university enrolments, even
though they dominated certain areas. These included arts, household science, nursing, fine and applied arts, and education.[20] Many
of these programs fit women's traditional roles as caregivers, but
they also gave women opportunities to develop new skills.

Segregated within domestic science, female professors developed research programs that incorporated chemistry, political
economy, and business management.[21] These programs hence
served as a means for some women to secure their place in
male-dominated academic settings. At the same time, the development of the domestic sciences as an academic discipline served to
disseminate particular curricula. These teachings included materials suggesting that the proper place of girls and women was in the
home.[22] They also included, as this chapter will now demonstrate,
the notion that to be a proper Canadian citizen, girls and women
had to become expert consumers.

## Consumer Issues in the Home Economics Curriculum

During the early twentieth century, Canadian post-secondary
domestic science instructors turned their attention to consumer
issues. Within the MacDonald Institute's archival collection is
American author Ellen Richardson's classic, *Woman Who Spends*
(1904), which was a guide to intelligent, thrifty, and responsible
purchasing. "The emergence of women from the sphere of production into that of consumption," stated the introduction, opened "a
new vista for thoughtful women." Through consumption, women
could now influence "social conditions," and the book was written
"as an appeal to the conscience of the women of the land to think
on these things."[23]

The MacDonald Institute's holdings also include a "Lesson Paper" in "Household Management," authored by Professor of Home Economics Bertha M. Terrill and published by the American School of Household Economics in 1905. According to Terrill, production and consumption used to be equally performed in the home. However, "to-day, [the] shop and factory have taken most of the productions and developed them one by one," with the result that homemakers bought rather than made "dress goods and cloth," "carpets, bedding candles and soap." Women had thus become "the main directors" of home "expenditures," and it was crucial that they learned how to become better consumers. If they wanted to perform well as housewives, they had to start running their home as if it were a business. This meant knowing "where to economize and where to lavish," and being forever "on the alert for the small wastes."[24]

The Richardson and Terrill books reveal the role of consumption within home economics theory at the turn of the twentieth century. According to these authors, responsible purchasing – purchasing that benefited both home and nation – was the homemaker's chief task. They also implied that to make good homes, housewives were obliged to purchase certain amounts and kinds of goods. It is impossible to know whether the institute's staff taught this book, but final examinations for the 1904–5 academic year reveal that Guelph's instructors told students that home management required the purchasing of certain consumer items and the maintenance of specific living standards. In the final examination for the Household Administration course, students had to answer essay questions not only on "household duties" and labour-saving efficiencies but also on budgeting. After asking, "Why is a system of keeping household accounts desirable?" one essay question specifically instructed students to list and justify each item they would include in their accounts. The same test also asked: "What is considered by some authorities as an ideal percent of income to allow for rent, food, clothing?" "What provision is made for the remainder of the income?" And, "In what direction is there usually the greatest amount of wastefulness, and why?"[25]

Students in the teachers' training program at the École Ménagère Provinciale in Montreal were given similar lessons. Along with taking courses on laundry care, health and hygiene, infant care, physics, teaching methods, and chemistry, they could take a course in *economie domestique*. This course offered instruction in heating, lighting, and furniture maintenance. It also provided lessons in such consumer areas as home decorating, family budgeting, and responsible purchasing.[26]

Over the next few years, budgeting, decorating, and purchasing issues continued to appear within the Canadian domestic science curricula. Theoretical issues began to appear as well. Students in the Household Administration class at the MacDonald Institute in 1905–6 had to answer this final exam question: "What is meant by the terms Production and Consumption, as applied to the study of Home Economics?" They also had to explain how they would "divide an income of $1500 per year," as did the students who had taken the course one year ahead of them. Students had to further provide detailed answers to questions about particular consumer goods. "Give some general rules for distinguishing linen from cotton and selecting towelling, table linen and sheeting," instructed one. Another asked, "How is a side of beef cut up in the Guelph market?" Such questions indicate the importance of buying and shopping to domestic science instructors' conceptions of proper homemaking. They also reveal the presence of middle-class values within educational curricula. By asking students how and why they would select particular goods, instructors were in effect encouraging students to believe that towels, table linens, sheets, and beef were indispensable to modern Canadian life.

The 1910s saw the expansion of lessons about standards of consumption. Domestic science courses and programs at the Manitoba Agricultural College, the École Ménagère Provinciale, the Lillian Massey School of Household Sciences, and the MacDonald Institute all imparted to students the importance of consumption to the national economy. Students were taught that ideal Canadian homes included jewellery, brass fixtures, silverware, wood and upholstered furniture, china, linens, wallpaper, and rugs. Such items, students were told, were to be well cared for because clean and gleaming possessions were a mark of a woman's respectability and capability.

Lessons in shopping and cleaning taught students that women's modern roles involved not only consumption but also the importance of the ownership and display of particular consumer commodities. A March 1912 exam in a House Furnishing class taught by Mrs. Charlton Salisbury at Manitoba Agricultural College, for example, included the following question: "What color and material for floor covering and curtains would you suggest for a bedroom with golden oak furniture, walls decorated with pale blue and white paper ... cost to be moderate?" The same exam also asked students to "draw a plan of dining room, kitchen and pantry showing relative location and best arrangement of windows, doors and furniture."[27] As well, several schools during this period began building model rooms and even model homes, in which students could practise the art and science of homemaking. At the École Ménagère Provinciale, for example, there was a mock dining room, in which students learned how to set tables using proper linens and tableware. This dining room included simple but genteel-looking furnishings, such as a wood dining set, a fireplace adorned with decorations, a chandelier, and artworks.[28] The University of Toronto had a similar though more elaborate room.[29]

During the 1920s, attention to consumer issues in Canadian domestic science theory and curricula intensified. For example, at Mount Allison University during this decade, home economics courses included home management, sewing, cooking, and interior decorating – a relatively new subject. Interior decorating courses included topics such as "Color Theory, Block Printing, China Painting," and "Costume and Design."[30] The University of Toronto offered a similar course in the late 1920s called Art and Design in the Home, which was a required component of the bachelor of science degree with a concentration in the Household Science program.[31]

Interior decorating courses served multiple purposes. Not only were students trained for work in department stores and in other furnishing industries, but the courses imparted particular expectations about the commodities necessary to create comfortable and nourishing homes. Consider, for example, a notebook kept by University of Toronto student Harriet Clarke as part of her 1929 interior design course studies. The notebook is filled with pictures that had been cut and pasted from home design features in magazines, with each picture demonstrating an aspect of interior design. All the pictures in this scrapbook reflect upper- and middle-class income levels; such imagery is consistent with most house and furnishing advice contained in mass-distributed magazines. In her example of a house that "fits in with its surroundings," Clark clipped a country mansion nestled in a hilly area. Other pictures included hallways, living rooms, and dining rooms. A striking page from a magazine showed a large urban house, with a handwritten caption, "Beauty is simplicity." Under another picture of a large house surrounded by lush gardens Clark had written, "Home ownership develops pride in your home." As these notations indicate, her home economics teacher had encouraged pupils to see home ownership, together with lavish home maintenance, as appropriate, modern behaviour.[32] Such courses also trained future interior designers in principles of upper-class decorating that would continue to be reproduced in the homes of their affluent clients, whose income bracket would more likely enable them to outsource interior design than would middle- or low-income brackets.

Other post-secondary domestic science offerings during this period similarly offered a widening field of consumption. Junior-level courses in the Department of Household Economics at the University of Alberta in the 1922–3 academic year included standard classes such as sewing, home nursing, foods, and cookery. A class on textiles, in which students learned about the "manufacture of fabrics and the influence of these on selection," was also provided. The junior-level Household Management course taught students about "materials found in the home, principles involved in their care, the house, its equipment and furnishing," and "labor-saving devices." Economics of the Household was offered to senior-level students. Students would learn how to approach "the home as a business; the income and its expenditure; standards of living, budgets; household and personal accounts."[33] Ostensibly, courses on textiles, household management, and household economics imparted practical information that students could apply in their future positions as employees, consultants, or homemakers. Yet these courses also served to inculcate middle-class consumer values. By teaching students that ideal homes should have particular furnishings and equipment, encouraging them to spend money on particular items, and demonstrating that consumer culture was integral to modern adult femininity, they trained female students to be consumer citizens.

Special tie-ins between domestic science curricula and industry, meanwhile, began during the 1910s. Antoinette Gérin-Lajoie, the director of the École Ménagère Provinciale, collected an enormous range of advertisements, which are now housed in her archival papers.[34] These include brochures from companies such as Clover Leaf, Peek Frean, Dixie, Heinz, Jello, Cowan's Cocoa – all of which contain recipes, corporate information, and nutritional advice. It is unknown whether she used these materials within her classrooms, but the fact that she not only collected but also saved these mail-outs does indicate her willingness to stay abreast of new products. As she was the director of the École Ménagère Provinciale, this interest would have influenced post-secondary domestic science training in Montreal, in the sense that it may have promoted an openness towards commercialism within cooking classes.

Linkages between domestic science curricula and industry also occurred in the form of field trips. Students in domestic science at the Université de Montréal during this decade went on *"visites educatives"* to a range of corporations, many of them producers and distributors of domestic goods. These included Kraft Foods, Purity Ice Cream, St Lawrence Sugar, Compagnie Viau, Steinberg's grocery, Eaton's restaurant and groceteria, Atlantic and Pacific grocery, Franco-Canadian Dyers, Doric Textiles, Dominion Spinners, Draper Mills, Acadian Bobinet, Dominion Textiles, Chez Clermont (furriers), and Birks Jewellers.[35] By making such expeditions, instructors were providing lessons about the quality, content, and prices of foods, textiles, furs, and jewellery.

Given that female domestic science graduates often obtained employment in advertising firms, the kitchens of department stores, and restaurants, it is possible that such field trips were to familiarize students with employment opportunities.[36] Yet these trips also fostered links between homemakers, publicists, and commerce. To enterprise, class field trips made for good public relations; thus, representatives showed the best side of the company to students. Indeed, in suggesting that students should learn about industry's offerings, domestic science instructors were solidifying the notion that proper homemaking during this period involved not only purchasing particular household goods but also being knowledgeable about, and possibly receptive towards, the domestic offerings of industrial capitalism.

Domestic science instruction during the early twentieth century further featured branded goods. In a 1916 edition of *Woman's Century*, the Moffat Stove Company of Weston reported that the "kitchens at the Toronto Technical School Domestic Science Class are all furnished with [Moffat's] closed top gas ranges."[37] While it is unknown whether these stoves were donated or purchased, their installation represented a public relations coup for the company. Not only did it suggest that the stoves were of high enough quality to stand up to classroom use, but it also ensured that hundreds of young women would become acquainted with cooking on Moffat stoves – a trained consumer base that might then purchase a Moffat stove upon entry into married life.

Students at the MacDonald Institute also worked with brand-name goods. These included a Canuck bread mixer, in use for several years by 1918. As one instructor had stated in a letter to the E.T. Wright kitchen appliances company, the institute found the quality of the mixer to be excellent and indeed had chosen it because the school used "Canadian made" goods whenever possible.[38] As well, when the institute sent some of its students to work in a cooking demonstration at the 1918 Canadian National Exhibition in Toronto, it accepted the McClary Stove Company's offer to use its ranges and other appliances in the exhibition. By making this offer, the company likely reasoned that it would garner product exposure from both exhibition visitors and students who would begin to imagine McClary products as appropriate for their homes.

Close relationships between industry and domestic science programs continued into the 1920s. In Guelph the MacDonald Institute received so many requests from businesses asking them to endorse their products that it adopted a no-publicity policy. The institute did, however, welcome donations of equipment and materials. As one letter from the school to the Nineteen Hundred Washer Company put it, "we do not do publicity work of any kind, but we shall be glad to try out one of your laundry outfits, thus giving our students every opportunity to judge [the appliances] for themselves."[39] The institute received many donations during the 1920s, including items from Duro Aluminum Ware and Gunns Cooking Oils and Shortenings. As well, Eaton's donated an Acme stove.[40]

During this period, students of the institute further tested labour-saving devices. Presumably, these tests were used to train future homemakers in the practice of selecting and using such equipment, as well as to provide hands-on experience with various devices to those students wishing to enter sales, merchandising, or advertising positions. When such tests were conducted under the auspices of domestic science programs, however, they served a pedagogical function. Specifically, they encouraged students to perceive labour-saving devices as essential to home management. Rather than encouraging students to ask whether they needed such devices in the first place, they encouraged them instead to pick and choose from among them. In this way they made labour-saving devices – and the corporations that produced them – appear as natural and desirable components of Canadian homes.

During the 1930s, domestic science programs continued to welcome industry's involvement. Not only did institutes rely on donations from various businesses, but domestic science experts genuinely believed that industry was an essential partner in home economics. Given that employers largely considered women responsible for household shopping, decorating, cooking, and cleaning, women were positioned as suited to jobs in sales, buying, cooking, and advertising. Domestic scientists nurtured this belief, and indeed many domestic science programs prepared graduates for careers in dietetics, merchandising, and publicity. At the same time, domestic scientists believed that homemakers should become expert consumers. As part of their training, homemakers were not only to learn about what products were available for purchase but also how to assess the products in question. Examinations held at the MacDonald Institute during the 1930s succinctly illustrate this aspect of home economics theory. For example, an exam from a 1936–7 course in Household Management included the following instructions: "In buying any electrical appliance, give the four points of information you would look for on the name plate to insure good service."[41]

Home economics programs in French Canada also relied on industry support. In the fall of 1932 the Dupuis Frères department store of Montreal donated table linens, candles, dishes, and cutlery to the École Ménagère Provinciale so that students could practise preparing formal Christmas-dinner tables. A photograph featuring the school's long-time director, Antoinette Gérin-Lajoie, and senior instructor, Madame Lacroix, at a table decorated with

3.1 Antoinette Gérin-Lajoie and Madame Lacroix at a table decorated with
Dupuis Frères products, in *La Revue Culinaire*, 15 January 1933, 14.

Dupuis Frères products appeared in the next issue of Montreal's *La
Revue Culinaire* (fig. 3.1). The caption of the photograph noted that
the table had been *"dressée par la* Maison Dupuis Frères." By printing this photograph and caption, *La Revue Culinaire* thus provided
subtle advertising for the department store, suggesting the department store was both generous and respectable. The willingness of
Gérin-Lajoie and Lacroix, whose senior positions within the school
affirmed their respectability and consumer expertise, to pose with
the table functioned as a virtual endorsement of the company and
its products.[42]

Field trips to local businesses also continued. In 1932 the
MacDonald Institute asked the president of the Ontario Agricultural
College to approve a "Marketing" trip to Toronto. Senior students,
together with those in the "homemaker" stream, would visit, on
the Friday, the Royal Winter Fair. Here they would learn about
the "quality and varieties" of "fruits, vegetables, dressed meat,
dressed poultry, [and] butter." The next morning they would go
to the Canadian Terminal Warehouse to learn about storage. In the

afternoon they would visit either Simpson's or Eaton's, where they would become acquainted with "telephone orders, mail orders, packaging and delivery rooms, advertising, exchange department, methods of payment, charge, D.A., etc.," and the "Research Department." They would also learn about "what the retailer would like to expect from the consumer" in terms of "shopping habits" and "consumer education." Finally, on the Sunday they would go to the Consumer's Gas Company, where they would see a demonstration on "selection and use of gas ranges and appliances" and "refrigerators."[43]

It is unknown whether the college president granted permission for the trip, but the fact that a weekend trip was organized around various modes of shopping and consumption demonstrates that instructors at the MacDonald Institute positioned intelligent consumption as a skill necessary for contemporary young women. By learning about the merchandise for sale, as well as about how to purchase and behave according to retailers' wishes, women could become better homemakers and consequently better members of the Canadian polity. On a broader level, the field trip would have shown that consumer goods purchased from mass retailers entailed the proper manner of reproducing Canadian life. Rather than teaching students to question whether such goods and businesses made positive contributions to modern existence, home economics instructors in Guelph taught students to visit capitalist goods distributors and to pick and choose amongst the available commodities.

In Nova Scotia, Mount St Bernard College, affiliated with St Francis Xavier University, offered students the opportunity to spend time in a "Practice House," where they would "reside for six week periods, while taking the Home Management Course."[44] This house was likely similar to the practice house that existed at the Saint John Home Service School in New Brunswick. Furnished by "ten different businesses," it offered instruction to women seeking domestic service training under the Dominion-Provincial Youth Training Program. Within these houses, students learned how to clean, sew and mend, use electric appliances, and do laundry, as well as prepare meals.[45] Also during the 1930s the University of Toronto offered to home economics students courses in "Foods," "Household Science," "Textile Chemistry," "Dietetics," and "Economics of the Household." In as much as this latter course focused on "the economics of spending," it was especially consumer oriented.[46]

Between 1900 and 1939, Canadian post-secondary home economics education was hence deeply steeped in consumer issues. Since its earliest inception, issues of budgeting and shopping had infused the curricula. So too had lessons on how to shop for, choose, and maintain household goods. Moreover, implicit lessons about the bourgeois nature of modernity were subsumed within all these curricula. To be a modern Canadian citizen was to have the furniture, textiles, and décor featured in university home economics classes. More than this, one also had to cultivate a mutually beneficial relationship with the consumer marketplace. By using branded goods in the classroom and by taking field trips to department stores and manufacturers, students not only learned about the range of goods available for purchase but also were trained to be discerning in their selection of products for the home. Despite the evidence of consumer issues within Canadian home economics curricula, however, instructors rarely left detailed records as to the specific topics discussed within the classroom.[47] For this reason it is fortunate that detailed records were kept from the 1932 Home Economics Week held in Edmonton, Alberta.

### Spotlight on Consumer Pedagogy: Edmonton, 1932

Home Economics Week consisted of several women's groups coming together to celebrate the power of the female consumer. The event was organized by the Alberta Women's Institutes (WIs) and the Alberta Home Economics Association, with more limited involvement from the Edmonton Creche Society and the Edmonton Junior League. In addition to these community groups, members of the Faculty of Household Science at the University of Alberta helped to arrange the event. Organizers obtained sponsorships from the city's major department stores including the Hudson's Bay Company, Eaton's, Woodward's, and Johnstone Walker, as well from local hotels and manufacturers. They also partnered with groups including the Made-in-Alberta Association, the Lions Club, and the Kiwanis Club.

The week consisted of events put on by the event organizers throughout the city. These included exhibitions of Alberta manufacturers' products, students' home economics projects, and interior decorating displays. Events also included lectures on shopping and cooking, dinners and dances for local men's clubs, and table-setting competitions for interested participants. Overall, Home Economics Weeks celebrated the homemaking roles of middle-class women, especially their consumer activities. Organizers claimed that when women shopped locally, purchased in bulk, and avoided bargains, they contributed to prosperity. These habits were of general importance, but the imperative to consume properly increased during times of financial austerity. As the lead organizer of Home Economics Week stated, "women occupy a most important place in the commerce and trade of the Dominion and ... dictate the prosperity of the world."[48]

Home Economics Week functioned as an occasion to promote a pro-capitalist vision of female consumer citizenship, but of special interest here is the role played by domestic science academics housed in the Faculty of Household Science at the University of Alberta. Lecturer Grace Duggan, who was also the president of the Alberta Home Economics Association, sat on the organizing committee.[49] In addition to being a professional home economist, she was positioned by press coverage of the event as a "well-known Edmonton club wom[a]n."[50]

It is difficult to determine which particular events Duggan organized, though it is probable that she facilitated the publication of articles by Household Science instructors in Edmonton's leading newspaper, *Edmonton Journal*, during the week of the event. Duggan authored one of the articles, as did the director of Household Science and associate professor Mabel Patrick. Professor Hazel McIntyre and lecturer Margaret Doyle also contributed pieces. Not only did the articles contain extensive advice on how Edmonton's homemakers could become better shoppers, but they also used the opportunity to promote and secure the place of home economics in the academy, economy, and nation.

Two of the articles written by Patrick and Duggan contained overviews of home economics and proclaimed the importance of the discipline. In each article the author argued that because consumption was paramount to homemakers' work, it was necessary that women learn how to become skilled consumers. In Patrick's estimation, home economics was a crucial component of women's education, teaching them how to manage their homes along "scientific" and "progressive lines." According to her, the average housewife of the 1930s was unfortunately not "trained to meet the problem of home-making." In addition to her ignorance as to "where the waste is and the extra motions are," she is unprepared to make the "complicated" consumer choices that homemaking entailed. Whereas "in colonial times the daughters of the home" learned how to "make candles, clothing and other necessities" from their mother, times had changed to the degree that "the problem of the [modern] housewife is not that of making as much as that of choosing." Specifically, "as the manufacturing processes were taken out of the home[,] the manufacturer began to increase the number and kinds of things made, and experts were employed to make cheaper products and 'just as good' articles." For this reason, it was crucial that "homemakers' training keep pace with that of the expert," and the study of home economics was the manner in which women could become experts. Throughout, the article implicitly suggested that mothers were no longer knowledgeable enough to train their daughters; as such, domestic education had to be taught by experts. The movement of domestic production out of the home and into the factory, Patrick suggested, necessitated new and *expert* methods of homemaking.[51]

Duggan's piece, "Home Biggest Business in This Modern World," echoed Patrick's emphases. Duggan reasoned that because "families as such to a very large extent are consumers rather than producers ... the home-maker [must] spend her money wisely." Indeed, "it is only through the sane use of her resources that she may take care of her family's needs and requirements." As her use of the words *wisely* and *sane* make clear, Duggan assumed that untrained homemakers were poor shoppers. A home economics education, however, could help even the most spendthrift woman acquire consumer expertise. By staying within budget and buying items of "real value," women could meet expenses, pay for unexpected "sickness" and "unemployment," and have enough for perks such as "holidays, education and travel." Wise consumption was positioned of such importance in the management of modern families that it eclipsed the importance of bread-winning: "The health of the family, its education, its pleasures, are determined, not by the amount of the income, but by the wise distribution or spending of that income."[52] For Duggan, all families should be able to make ends meet, regardless of income. If they did not, it was the fault of housewives for budgeting incorrectly.

Stressing the importance of consumer education, Patrick and Duggan revealed the extent to which consumer issues had become a focal point for home economists during the 1930s. In so doing, they laid bare the sense of superiority that accompanied an expert approach to home management and consumption. By suggesting that the average homemaker was not a suitable teacher for her daughter and also that the average homemaker's inability to meet expenses was due to ignorance, these instructors cast women without formal home economics training as backward. Accordingly, they were unscientific, naive, and wasteful. It was only by familiarizing themselves with modern consumer methods – developed by home economics experts – that they and their families could be saved from their own depravity.

While Patrick and Duggan were explicit in their position on proper consumer training, it is likely that their criticism of improper shopping and cooking habits was influenced by their views of the non-white and non-Western European Other. In their articles about the importance of homemaking, they did not single out non-British homemakers' behaviour as deviant, though Duggan's emphasis on shopping wisely indicates her sense that a large number of homemakers did not shop correctly. In another article, this one on cooking, Patrick does imply that non-British homemakers behaved inappropriately. "Adequate Diets Are Very Cheap," declared the article's title. Despite this fact, "few people have an adequate diet and most use luxury foods"; they did so largely for "radical, religious, social and lastly family" reasons, all of which "proved a barrier by setting up life-long habits."

Patrick may have been referring to the diets of Ukrainians, along with those of other continental Europeans, when she wrote about religious and social customs. In the minds of English Canadians, Ukrainian Canadians were particularly troublesome because they refused to assimilate, preferring instead to speak their own language, to belong to either the Ukrainian Catholic Church or the Greek Orthodox Church, and to maintain their own foodways.[53] Although during the 1930s white English Canadians formed the majority of Alberta's population, immigrants from Eastern Europe comprised 16 per cent of the population.[54] Smaller numbers of people of Indigenous, African, and Asian heritage also lived in the province.[55]

Therefore, Patrick may also have been thinking about Indigenous and Asian cuisines, especially since these foodways did not usually include bread or dairy products. Yet, according to Patrick, all diets – even those of the poor – should include "milk, fruit and vegetables, meat and eggs, [and] bread and cereals." Her own view of correct eating, then, influenced her perception of other cultures.[56] It is likely that non-white and non-Western European mothers were perceived as incapable of properly training their daughters. More than this, they might instil deviant cultural norms that their daughters would then reproduce in the setting of their own families. Indeed, Mary Leah de Zwart has argued that home economics training in western Canada during the early twentieth century "promoted White cultural values," despite being labelled as offering neutral homemaking techniques.[57]

For members of the Faculty of Household Science at the University of Alberta, food was an especially contentious consumer issue that required remedial attention. In "Reward of Good Cookery Reaped in Healthy Living," Professor Hazel McIntyre informed Albertans that while some might see cooking as an "art" that simply came naturally to some cooks, cooking was in fact a skill that could be learned through proper application of "intelligence, interest and training." Any "intelligent woman" could learn how to cook; it was simply necessary that she forgo the old-fashioned practice of "'rattling up a cake'" and, instead, "take time to measure" ingredients. Here, home economics mobilized the elevated position of science by claiming that the application of a scientific method (in this case, measuring) was necessary to improve the home. Not only would it improve one's baking, but also it would allow women to follow recipes better in "newspapers, magazines and the latest ... books," all of which were becoming more detailed. McIntyre wrote, "Companies [and] manufacturers are establishing research kitchens which take the guesswork out of ... cooking." Moreover, "equipment has been made which helps to eliminate the possible faulty judgement [of] inexperienced cooks." Such tools included thermometers, ovens, and electrical equipment, with the latter becoming affordable for those on "moderate incomes." Despite the increasing specificity of new recipes, together with the new kitchen products available on the market, some people were still employing out-of-date methods, she felt; they were "beating eggs with a fork" and "do not own flour sifters." This behaviour was positioned as the result of a lack in education: because they had never received home economics training, they had "yet to learn that cooking has become easier with the introduction of efficient tools."[58]

According to McIntyre, then, gone were the days of intuitive baking and cooking by "art" and "guesswork." Practices such as these would not work in the new world of research kitchens and mass-marketed recipes. Both a scientific and a specifically consumer-oriented approach to cooking had become necessary. To succeed in the scientific age, homemakers had to cook by measurement. They also had to purchase the new technologies being developed by manufacturers. These teachings echoed those being developed in the United States during the same period. As Goldstein writes, home economists presumed that their pupils already knew how to cook "by hand"; hence they emphasized precise, market-oriented methods.[59] Such an approach may have simply been intended to acquaint students with the fullest options available. In practice, however, this instruction was often presented in biased terms. Instructors portrayed scientific and consumer-oriented methods as superior to all others. Returning to McIntyre, it is noteworthy that she blamed poor cookery on the ignorance of housewives who were reluctant to learn new methods. She claimed that instead of acquainting themselves with scientific cookery, recalcitrant housewives "served apologies" along with their "inferior" and "ruined products." In McIntyre's view, the time for cookery as an art was over. Scientific approaches and mass-produced tools brought good cookery within the reach of anyone "intelligent" enough to take advantage of them.[60]

For McIntyre, "New Canadian" mothers were especially to blame for improper diets. She claimed, "Many such families are still adhering to food standards deficient in dietary essentials." Indeed, "you will find homes in which the heavy desserts" are still being served, regardless of the advice at the time that desserts be replaced with fresh fruits. It was by training wives and mothers about "proper" nutrition that home economics believed they offered a valuable service. "Children from New Canadian families," she argued, could learn in school about "the available raw materials in this country"; they could also start "practising at home what [they] learned in school." In this way they could help their mothers both Canadianize and modernize, which in McIntyre's mind, were the same thing: "Like any true scientist, when [the cook's] old methods are proved obsolete, she conscientiously tries out the new. She does not confine herself to the recipes of her own country, but makes use of the interesting food combinations of other countries."[61] Through home economics education, then, McIntyre sought to erase the supposedly "deficient" practices of non-British Canadians. For her, the assimilatory effects of home economics education were praiseworthy. As such, pieces written by certain home economics faculty and staff at the University of Alberta and published in the *Edmonton Journal* are consistent with De Zwart's findings about the whiteness of home economics. As she writes, home economics in western Canada tended to "promote White cultural values, specifically British or northern European values," in relation "with groups that were considered inferior by virtue of their race, class, or both."[62]

Other articles in the *Journal* made specific references to the consumer practices of low-income people without alluding to race or ethnicity. In her aforementioned article on diets, Patrick argued that even "people on relief" could purchase healthy food. The trick, she said, was for them to "[buy] in quantity and when it was cheapest." For Patrick, however, because many relief housewives "failed to realize the value of foods or how to choose the essentials," it was unlikely that they would change their ways. Instead of considering why persons with lower incomes rejected "healthy" food, she suggested that poor people had to change their ways. By making home economics research more widely available, she argued, such goals could be accomplished.[63]

According to home economists, in addition to improving their food habits, Edmontonians ought to dress in such a manner that reflected middle-class standards. In her article titled "Success in Good Dressing Lies in Fundamentals," lecturer Margaret Doyle informed readers that "every woman owes it to herself and to the world to make dressing well an individual means of self expression, of personality enhancement." Good dressing, in her view, was both in service to the world and the individual. Through success in fashion, women could "enhance" their personalities and express their own identities.[64] This message was consistent with the early twentieth-century development of what Jane Nicholas has called the "Modern Girl." For Nicholas, this subject is "defined by her mass-market clothing." She consciously constructs her appearance in order to express her individuality.[65] The messaging of dressing as self-expression remains conservative in that it positions women as ornaments for onlookers. In suggesting that women's ability to please others was an important feminine skill, home economists revealed themselves as committed to the reproduction of patriarchal norms.

In as much as women were expected to dress well in service to themselves and others, classed expectations shaped how home economists conceptualized proper appearance. Doyle encouraged women to construct pleasant appearances that would align with and please the bourgeoisie. Women were to avoid "cheap, ill-made, shoddy, extremely fashionable garments." In her view, "one or two really good dresses are in better taste than a larger number of the cheaper sort." More than this, "good hats of conservative line and color" were better choices than "those of the latest fad or fashion." Women were told to "avoid overdressing for any occasion." For example, she wrote that "a bright red dress is not particularly successful as a garment for church services."[66] As her language makes clear, inexpensive clothes were associated with poor taste, whereas expensive and well-made clothing was considered tasteful. Excessive fashion and loud colours were also to be avoided. It was far better for women to dress themselves in an understated manner, Doyle argued, than for them to stand out. For Doyle, this kind of advice was self-evident. It was deeply classed and consistent with dominant narratives about fashion choices as reflective of women's character.

During the nineteenth century middle-class fashion writers had tended to prize "self-effacement" and sincerity. Linking fashion choices with "character," they suggested that women should dress simply and modestly. As Nan Enstad has argued, "to be tasteful one did not become an object of display by using 'too much' ornamentation or color." Furthermore, "fashion without middle-class taste was ... morally suspect." When working women began buying

ready-made clothes that were bright in colour and bold in style in
the late nineteenth century, middle-class onlookers often considered such choices as evidence of "moral deterioration." Notions of
moral deterioration were deeply tied to socio-economic status, as
Enstad showed: "cheap fashion consumption made women themselves cheap, lowering their value and threatening their virtue."[67]
Doyle's emphasis on constructing a subdued appearance reveals
her adherence to middle-class standards. Suggesting that women
should not wear clothing that drew attention, she advised women
to dress with circumspection and decorum. In so doing, they
would retain their modesty. They would also demonstrate their
submission to middle-class standards of taste and commitment to
pleasing the sensibilities of "refined" onlookers.

## Conclusion: Disciplining the Consumer Citizenry

In Canada, consumer issues structured post-secondary home
economics programs prior to the Second World War. From the
1900s onward, issues of budgeting and shopping, along with lessons on how to shop for, choose, and maintain household goods,
infused the curricula. Moreover, subsumed within these curricula
were implicit lessons about the bourgeois nature of modernity. To
be a modern Canadian citizen was to have all the furniture, textiles, and décor that were featured in university home economics
classes. More than this, women had to cultivate a mutually beneficial relationship with the consumer marketplace. Using branded
goods within the classroom and taking field trips to department
stores and manufacturers, students were taught about the range of
goods available for purchase, as well as how to select and use these
products in the home.

Canadian post-secondary home economics instructors taught all
their pupils to consider themselves modern consumers, but their
teachings were nevertheless imbued with ethnic and class-based
characteristics. Canadian home economists, like those in the United
States, tended to portray "the new, modern consumer as a white,
middle-class woman." They did so primarily because they saw
themselves as homemaking experts; they also assumed that their role
was to uplift others into "their own image."[68] In 1930s Edmonton,
post-secondary domestic science faculty and staff encouraged the

public to adopt bourgeois, Euro-Canadian standards of behaviour. Edmonton housewives were advised to do so by avoiding sales, shopping selectively, buying groceries in bulk, preparing Euro-Canadian foods, cooking scientifically, drinking milk, and wearing demure clothes. Women who did not adhere to these practices endangered their own morality, as well as their families' health and pocketbooks.

During the first half of the twentieth century, home economics responded to a *perceived* shift in the nature of domestic labour. Prior to industrialization and urbanization, home economists argued, women's work had been primarily that of production. As more factory goods became available, however, and as more families moved into cities, women's budgeting and shopping roles became increasingly important. Home economists justified their profession by lamenting the extremely complicated new world of mass consumption to such a degree that housewives needed outside help. They positioned themselves as ideally situated to provide this service, and they began researching issues such as budgeting and shopping. They also began teaching students how to acquire expertise in these matters. Their teachings were highly gendered, premised on the notion that women were naturally suited to home-making. They were also pro-capitalist. In developing a science of shopping, home economists did not question the rules of the marketplace or the view that housewives should acquire consumer goods. Instead, home economics promoted consumer expertise in the capitalist marketplace. In this way, home economics helped to create the idea of the modern consumer citizen. This citizen was explicitly white, bourgeois, and feminine.

*Chapter Four*

# Rural Consumer Citizens: Consumption in the Countryside

In fall 2015, CBC News reported that an Alberta farm family was "eating like pioneers for a year." Inspired by her grandfather, who had homesteaded in Manitoba more than a century ago, Albertan farmer Shannon Ruzicka, together with her husband, Danny, and their three young children, had decided to stop buying food. Instead, they were "growing and baking everything that goes into their bellies." Why did they take up this challenge? Because they no longer wanted to "rely on any system for sustainability and happiness."[1]

The decision by Shannon Ruzicka's family to boycott food stores is but one example of the twenty-first century "homesteading" movement, which characterizes store-bought food as toxic. According to homesteaders, store-bought food lacks nutrition and is produced in unfair and unsustainable conditions. Thus, it is better for humans to grow their own food.[2] This homesteading movement is significant, not least for its ethical stance towards labour, nourishment, and sustainability.[3] From the standpoint of consumer history, it is also noteworthy in that it portrays the past as preferable to the present. *Primitive* and *wild* are words that appear often in the movement's lexicon, as does the word *pioneer*. Yet there is a fallacy in portraying earlier systems as pristine.[4] Historian Douglas McCalla notes that pioneers in Upper Canada accessed a whole range of groceries from merchants, including sugar, coffee, tea, candy, spices, and medicines. These merchants purchased their supplies in international markets.[5] Prairie homesteaders, for their part, had access to groceries through national and international catalogues, as well as through itinerant pedlars. As Claire

Meldrum correctly states in the "Comments" section of the CBC article about the Ruzicka family, "yes, [pioneers] grew or raised much of what they ate ... but the idea that they wouldn't have had access to coffee or rennet or baking soda is ridiculous. The catalogue system was at its height and the railways were transporting goods to the far flung corners of North America."[6]

Rather than rejecting outright this romanticization of the past, however, it is more useful to ask why such visions of the past exist. An examination of homesteader literature indicates that a sense of anger fuels rejections of capitalism, as does a fear that the marketplace is "killing us," stated another CBC commentator.[7] For some, a validation of thrift drives the movement, in the sense that it is unnecessary to purchase what can be grown or made at home.[8] There is also an assumption that because today's consumer systems are impersonal, they ought not be trusted. Miles Olson, author of the homesteaders' guidebook *Unlearn, Rewild*, writes that it is time to "build independence and autonomy from the system, stepping into interconnectedness with non-humans and humans alike."[9]

In addition to exploring the roots of the homesteading myth, it is important to examine the conditions of rural life in earlier periods. Doing so helps pinpoint the history of consumer habits and thus offers valuable lessons on how humans acquired and perceived goods in earlier times.[10] Examining rural white Canadian women's consumer engagements between the years 1897 and 1939, this chapter contributes to the historical excavation of the rural consumer past. Along with such scholars as Douglas McCalla and Beatrice Craig, it demonstrates that rural white Canadian settlers participated extensively in the consumer marketplace.[11] Whereas Craig and McCalla focus on the early nineteenth century, however, this chapter examines a time that is typically characterized as one of modernization.[12] For this reason, its findings are perhaps less surprising than studies of earlier periods.[13] At the same time, it is also true that existing studies of twentieth-century consumption tend to focus on urban settings.[14] As such, by exploring rural women's consumer history, this chapter offers an important counterpoint. It shows that rural white Canadian women across the country were keenly interested in consumer research, technology, and advocacy. Between the 1910s and 1930s, in fact, rural white Canadian women saw themselves as consumer citizens. They viewed consumption as a key entrée into public life, and they expected their government to protect them from unfair conditions.

This chapter's findings are based on an intensive review of print materials created by members of the Women's Institute (WI) movement.[15] The WIs, indeed, comprised the largest rural women's organization in Canadian history, with seventy-one thousand members in 1933.[16] The movement officially began in 1897, when women in Stoney Creek (Ontario) launched the first chapter. By 1913 there were local and provincial institutes in all of Canada's provinces. In 1919, institute members from across the country gathered in Winnipeg, where they established a Dominion-wide organization. The movement remained strong into the Second World War and beyond, as Linda Ambrose, Margaret Kechnie, and others demonstrate.[17]

The WIs did not represent the voices of all rural women. It was a predominantly white organization, one whose members agreed with its motto, "For Home and Country."[18] Institute literature characterized its members as cisgendered and rural; indeed, within the institutes the term *farm woman* was synonymous with the terms *farm wife* and *mother*. As such, the institutes were overwhelmingly concerned with matters belonging to what members saw as rural white women's purview, including domestic labour, homemaking, dairying, poultry raising, gardening, and handiwork. Moreover, and in addition to this gendered outlook, women who joined the institutes had certain socio-economic privileges. Simply by demonstrating that they had enough time, energy, and other resources to devote to the institutes, they revealed that they were not simply struggling to survive.

Within this white, cisgendered, and privileged environment some diversities did exist. Kechnie demonstrates, with reference to Ontario, that provincial institute leaders tended to be from urban, bourgeois households.[19] In contrast, and as this study's own research reveals, many women who joined local institutes came from more modest means. Some of them had money to spend, but many were dedicated to frugality. As well, while some of the less affluent lived in towns, a great many more lived on farms. References within the institute literature as to how farm women could get by during difficult economic times demonstrate these latter women's outlooks. For example, in 1923, a member from Beeton (Ontario) wrote, "The hard times of the last two or three years ... brought to the life of many women this question – How can I make some money to help along?"[20] Reflecting these members' concerns, locals across the country studied the problem of income earning. They also shared information on how to create and raise goods for sale.[21]

A study of the WIs thus offers partial understandings of rural people's consumer habits during the early twentieth century. It provides insights into the consumer engagements of rural cisgendered, white women, and within that purview it enables understandings of how both affluent and more budget-oriented women approached consumption. Through reference to the WIs' local, provincial, and national print materials, it specifically demonstrates that a large proportion of rural dwellers before the Second World War made significant investments in consumption. These investments, as we shall see, tended to track along socio-economic lines, with bourgeois women demonstrating more interest in individualized homemaking, and less affluent women demonstrating more interest in peer-to-peer sharing of resources. At the same time, and no matter their priorities, all levels of the WIs worked hard to make farm women's consumer interests more enjoyable, affordable, and rewarding.

## A Rural Canadian Women's Movement

A mixture of government funding, bourgeois leadership, and grass-roots activism characterized the WIs between 1897 and the Second World War. Insiders' lore insists that Adelaide Hoodless, an early domestic science crusader, founded the organization after witnessing the death of her baby boy. Better motherhood training, she argued, would lower the infant mortality rate. Hoodless, however, did not create the WIs single-handedly. Instead, they were part of a broader impetus among educated white women across the British Commonwealth, the United States, and Western Europe to create social organizations that would promote women's interests. Organizations such as the Women's Christian Temperance Union, examined in chapter 1, and the Councils of Women, explored in chapter 2, similarly emerged during this time.

The WI was, however, the first self-identified rural women's organization. According to Ambrose, the early WI members saw the institutes as "parallel to the existing farmers' institutes, where men regularly met to consider the advances in approaches to farming." Instead of studying agriculture, however, the women studied homemaking.[22] During the first two decades of the twentieth century, provincial departments of agriculture funded the groups. In some provinces, such as Alberta, this money was made available in response to lobbying by farm women. In other places urban educators mobilized support. In Saskatchewan, Manitoba, and Nova Scotia college administrators asked their provincial departments of agriculture to fund rural women's education. Particularly, they sought to improve the economy and morale of the countryside by teaching women modern domestic management. The provinces, in turn, were receptive. The British Columbia minister of agriculture told his province's WIs in 1911 that "it had been his aim ever since taking office to help in bettering the conditions of women in the country." He wished to promote "talks to housekeepers" through "public demonstrations and practical work" and to create links with the "WI and colleges in this line of work in other countries and other provinces of Canada."[23]

Certainly in the institutes' earliest years domestic improvement was a primary goal. As Hoodless put it, "a nation cannot rise above the level of its homes, therefore, we women must work and study together to raise our homes to the highest possible level."[24] Yet, and as the organization grew, members demonstrated interest in matters beyond the home. Across the country members held fundraisers for post offices, schools, hospitals, libraries, and halls. They planted flowers around small towns, decorated local buildings, and contributed to school, hospital, and recreation programs. They welcomed newcomers, aided new mothers, raised money for farm women's holidays, and held social events. And they taught each other how to sell such items as eggs, butter, milk, and handicrafts. So single-mindedly did some rural institutes pursue such objectives that the institutes' leadership occasionally felt compelled to intervene. In 1939 an anonymous editorial in Manitoba's *Institute News* stated that over the past two decades "many institutes have functioned to improve the community." As such, it was now time for "the Institute [to] concern itself with the development of the homemaker and the improvement of the individual home."[25]

This conflict between the encouragement of homemaking and the varied interests of local members points to a socio-economic divide that characterized the first three decades of the institutes. Whereas many middle-class leaders viewed homemaking as the best path towards rural improvement, many less affluent members viewed income earning and community building as the best means to these ends. Indeed, in the middle-class perspective, respectable women spent most of their time homemaking. Unstated within this perspective, of course, was that they could afford to do so. As an anonymous writer put it, "a woman does not expect to become a homemaker by the simple expedient of getting married. She realizes that homemaking is a profession which demands preparation, study, genuine interest and a good deal of personality."[26] In contrast, members who prioritized individual and community prosperity tended to operate within a less affluent framework. As such, they saw women's purview as mainly involving thrift and economic improvement. As another member stated in 1931, "when it happens that the income is reduced to a fraction of what it was, then the clothing and feeding of the family ... become exceedingly difficult tasks, demanding very great resourcefulness."[27]

When considering the WIs' consumer engagements, it is important to keep these distinct priorities in mind. Indeed, whereas institute leaders tended to adopt a didactic approach, local members tended to embrace a more collegial framework. In this latter view, it was not the institute's place to cast judgments on members' behaviours. Instead, local women participated in the institutes as peers. As such, they attempted to share resources within an egalitarian context.

## Sharing Information: A Rural Consumer Agency

The WIs engaged in consumption, first of all, through the sharing of consumer knowledge. Given that they focused on rural improvement, there arose plenty of opportunities within the organization for members to share information about matters deemed significant. Through home economics classes, fair exhibits, guest speakers, annual conventions, speeches, special events, industry tours, and printed materials, WI members both taught each other about consumption and distributed personal consumer knowledge. In this way, the institutes functioned as an informal consumer agency.

During the first two decades of the twentieth century, food occupied a major portion of WI programs. Given that food – its

procurement, preparation, and serving – was a major component
of farm women's daily labours, it is not surprising that early members focused on this topic. Food was a responsibility that blended
farm women's producer and consumer roles: through gardening,
dairying, poultry raising, and livestock work many farm women
actually created food. Yet they also acquired foodstuffs through
exchange, barter, and purchase by interacting with neighbours,
local co-operatives, country stores, and international corporations.
They then combined the results of this labour to make three daily
meals, snacks, and treats. Small wonder that when asked in 1932,
"In what branch of Home Economics are you most interested?"
WI members in Prince Edward Island (PEI) overwhelmingly listed
"cooking" and "food values."[28]

At first glance, some of the food activities in which the WI participated had little to do with consumption. It was common, for
example, for WI and Cercles de fermières branches to exhibit their
products at local fairs. Foods produced for small markets (such as
eggs, apples, and butter) were showcased, as were foods produced
for home consumption (such as pies and breads). Nonetheless,
it is also true that members had to shop for some of the ingredients used in fair-worthy recipes. In addition to demonstrating
that members of the PEI Women's Institute sought to share food
research, these recipes indicate that by 1929, Baker's Chocolate
and Crisco had become household products in Charlottetown.
During the late 1920s the WI of PEI printed member-tested recipes
in its monthly newsletter. Usually the recipes contained generic
names for foodstuffs, such as "white sugar" and "corn starch."[29]
Sometimes, though, brand names appeared. A 1929 "Chocolate
Bread Pudding" recipe tested by M.A. MacPhail of Charlottetown
included "2 squares Baker's Chocolate." A recipe for "Date
Dreams," tested by MacDonald College, appeared in the same
issue; its first ingredient was "1/2 cup Crisco."[30]

So concerned were the Saskatchewan groups about fruit prices,
meanwhile, that in 1926 they began to correspond with members
of the Okanagan Valley institutes, who in turn were involved in
growing and selling the region's apples. Three years later "25 prairie women" journeyed to the Okanagan to study production first-
hand. After this visit they conceded that prices of British Columbia
fruit were equitable.[31] During the Depression, the WI again became

concerned about prices. In 1931, topics for the Quebec WI's meetings included "menu for a farm home for a week, where Economy must be considered," and "Family Food Budget."[32] Other topics from the 1930s included "How to Get By on Lower Quality Meat," discussed in Alberta; "low-cost menus," discussed in Nova Scotia; and "Budget and Diet," discussed in Saskatchewan.[33]

Members were also interested in needlework. Sewing courses were offered in every province throughout the 1910–40 period. As well, sewing featured in every exhibition in which the WI participated. Most often members made clothing, but they also made pillowcases, quilts, sheets, tablecloths, curtains, and hats. As with cooking, sewing was a producerist activity in so far as it was a craft. At the same time seamstresses had to procure patterns to follow and cloth with which to work. Sometimes the fabrics that members used consisted of repurposed materials, such as old coats and flour sacks. Members also held pattern exchanges. At other times members did have to purchase items, including needles, thread, textiles, notions, dyes, and patterns. As such, sewing did require some purchasing. Probably the biggest purchase made by individual members was a sewing machine. For this reason locals sometimes invited sewing machine companies, usually Singer, to give demonstrations to members. Of particular value in such demonstrations were the sample gifts and coupons that demonstrators offered.[34]

Knitting, crocheting, and rug making were also popular. Although these activities are generally understood to be productive in nature, they did necessitate the buying of needles, yarn, and related accessories.[35] As a result, the WI invited representatives of the textile industry to give demonstrations to members.[36] Members also shared information with each other about natural and synthetic fibres.[37] As well, courses in these crafts were offered. Such learning opportunities were important because members often sold their needlework. Women's Institutes of Nova Scotia (WINS) developed the most formal system in this regard. In 1929 four different "Handicraft Exchanges," located in Port Maitland, Lawrencetown, Bridgewater, and Amhert, held "Show Days" of members' handmade rugs, quilts, tablecloths, towels, bedspreads, and pillows. Tourists were the primary audience of these events.[38]

During the 1920s, courses on home decorating proliferated, echoing the bourgeoning interest in these topics among home economists. By the 1930s in both New Brunswick and Alberta, home decorating courses were as popular as courses on food and dressmaking.[39] For many members home décor was creative labour that usually involved needlework and sometimes painting, ceramics, and carpentry. Home decorating, however, also involved consumption. In addition to purchasing the textiles, paint, and other materials required for what would now be referred to as do-it-yourself projects, WI members were interested in such consumer goods as dishes, wallpaper, linoleum, lacquer, furniture, and upholstery. Throughout the 1920s and 1930s, informative articles about these products appeared in WI newsletters.[40] Members also entered home-decorating exhibits into local fairs and gave each other talks on the subject.[41]

If interior decoration loomed large in the interwar years, so did new technologies. Both the radio and the telephone received comment within the Quebec WI during the 1930s. Regarding the former, one member suggested that, when used selectively, radios could enhance "family relationships."[42] Regarding the latter, another said that the telephone helped mitigate the "communication problems which exist in rural areas."[43] By far the most commonly discussed technologies within the WIs, however, were "labour saving devices," or electric appliances. By the 1920s institute members were debating the merits of vacuum cleaners, irons, electric ranges, refrigerators, and coffee pots. Thus, although such goods entered Canadian homes at staggered rates throughout the twentieth century, which were dependent upon the availability of electricity, the affordability of the goods, and the preferences of individual purchasers, many rural Canadian women were aware of their existence as early as the 1920s.[44] They also were attuned to their possible benefits.[45] In fact, members often gave speeches about labour savers at monthly meetings. As early as 1910 one Ontario member gave a talk on "dish-washing machines," arguing that while they had "not yet been introduced" into households, these machines were "working successfully in restaurants."[46]

On a similar note, members also taught each other about how to improve their kitchens. Monthly meetings often focused on kitchen design, generating tips on how to make the time spent in the kitchen more enjoyable.[47] As well, in 1928 WINS entered a modern kitchen exhibit into the provincial fair, calling the booth the "Nova Scotia Kitchen." According to WINS, this kitchen was designed to "eliminate needless drudgery." All the "surfaces" were higher than usual to prevent stooping; the furniture was arranged close together to "avoid needless steps"; and the window was positioned over the sink to let in light and offer "a breath of fresh air, and a rest for the eyes."[48]

Staying abreast of consumer trends, rural Canadian women attempted to make their labour more enjoyable. Nevertheless, their interest in kitchen improvement did not translate into a wholesale embrace of the marketplace. Instead, rural Canadian women tended to incorporate new designs according to their perception of the benefits of such improvements. The aftermath of a kitchen-improvement course offered in Manitoba in 1931, in which seven hundred women had enrolled, illustrates this trend. Upon returning home, many attendees put their learning into practice. Some of this work required a modicum of consumer spending, particularly on wood, hardware, and textiles. Yet, for most of the students, the most satisfying component of kitchen improvement was that a big impact could be made with a relatively small expenditure. Eight rearranged their "large" kitchen "equipment," 260 rearranged their "small" equipment, 30 raised the height of their tables, 75 "adopted the habit of sitting at work," 90 re-covered their "work tables," 200 repainted their kitchens, 100 fixed their curtains, and 40 made their "garbage disposal" more efficient. One student even made a "tea cart, a bread board, pot holder rack and a small plant table out of a discarded washstand," which she had purchased for eighty cents. In contrast, only one woman paid to have her "whole kitchen" remodelled.[49]

Thrift was a constant theme in the WI newsletters. According to the Manitoba organization's annual report of 1921, members spent just over one hundred dollars on material that allowed them to make clothing that would have otherwise cost six hundred dollars at retail prices.[50] Four years later the Home Economics Committee of WINS declared "thrift" the "watchword" of the year.[51] During meetings institute members traded thrift ideas, such as making goods out of flour sacks, shown in a 1930 Nova Scotia demonstration.[52] Thrift tips also appeared throughout institute newsletters. In 1931, for example, a PEI woman contributed an article about using every single component of various kinds of fruits.[53] In 1938 the

Quebec convener of home economics noted that the topics being investigated by the province's locals that year included the "uses of old silk, making kitchen curtains from voile dresses, home-made Xmas gifts and decorations [and] refooting cashmere stockings."[54]

So important was the issue of strategic budgeting to the WIs, in fact, that when visiting speaker Miss Julia O. Newton of Minnesota stated during her opening address at the Manitoba WI's 1930 convention that "the greatest woman in history is the wife of a man with an average income," she "won her way into the hearts of her audience."[55] Much of the budgeting advice that circulated within the WI during this time was similar to that promoted in home economics classes.[56] Whereas many home economists tended to adopt a didactic approach, however, many local members viewed budgeting as key to everyday survival. As the author of a 1922 Manitoba article explained, "in these days of hard times it is necessary to economize wherever possible."[57]

### Rights and Duties: A Rural Consumer Citizenry

Sharing consumer knowledge was one method by which the WIs functioned as consumer organizations. Making consumers' concerns public was another. Throughout the 1897 to 1939 period the institutes articulated a close link between consumption, on the one hand, and citizenship, on the other. Indeed, for many members in the WI, consumption was not simply an individualized activity, done in private and with little public consequences. They saw consumption as a political issue, one that tied their activities to their communities, provinces, and country.

An early indication of institute members' sense of themselves as consumer citizens emerged in 1915. In that year the Quebec WI called for the provincial government to begin inspecting leather goods.[58] Through this demand the WI suggested that the Quebec government was responsible for ensuring consumer rights. By the 1920s, other institutes were making similar declarations. In 1922 the Manitoba WI began calling for "Canadian government inspection" of "imported eggs."[59] In 1923 the WINS began lobbying for compulsory wrapping of baked bread. According to this organization's petition, which was sent to the Department of Public Health, unwrapped bread risked "contamination from flies, dust and unwashed hands."[60] Calling on both provincial and federal governments for greater intervention into the consumer marketplace, these actions demonstrated the institutes' assumption that governments should protect consumers from fraudulent businesses. In this way they suggested that WI members considered themselves to be consumer citizens, ones whose rights to high-quality goods should be protected by the state.

During the interwar years the quality of wool available for sale and the potential for its adulteration were also a concern. Wool quality was indeed important, given that members made knitted goods both for personal use and for sale. In 1921 the Manitoba WI began to lobby for "a law compelling manufacturers to stamp as such all goods that are 'not pure wool.'" In 1938, when such a law had still not been enacted, the British Columbia WI joined forces with the Alberta Sheep Breeders' Association and the Western Canada Livestock Union to "ask the Federal Government of Canada to enact legislation ... requiring all goods or fabrics made of wool ... to bear a label stating the quantity or percentage of virgin wool, and of all other materials (including re-worked wool)."[61] In these ways they demonstrated their determination to make the state responsible for consumer protection.

By 1939, consumer issues had become sufficiently important that WI members began to see the need for formal organization. In that year the Saskatchewan Homemakers Clubs spearheaded a push to create a "Canadian Consumers' Bureau."[62] Experiences with fraudulent merchandisers, whose advertising was filled with "extravagance" and "part-truths," had led members to demand independent consumer action.[63] Noting that "the average homemaker must protect the health of her family on a small budget," the Homemakers Clubs argued that a consumers' bureau that researched "correct information on all brands and makes of all classes of goods" would be a boon to housewives.[64]

In calling for organization, the Saskatchewan Homemakers Clubs demonstrated similarities with activists south of the border. As Lawrence Glickman argues, American consumer activism swelled in the 1930s.[65] During these penny-pinching years a range of American activists argued that since consumers faced both profiteering and complexity, it was time for consumers to organize. As part of this movement, major "consumer education organizations" formed at both the local and the national level. The latter included the Consumers' National Federation, founded in 1937 and "representing more than thirty organizations."[66] It is unknown whether the Saskatchewan Homemakers Clubs had direct contact with American groups. Yet, given that American organizations produced a vast number of publications including *Consumers' Digest*, it is probable that the clubs were at least familiar with them.[67]

Various actions undertaken by the WIs between the 1910s and 1930s reveal that many rural Canadian women thought it completely justifiable to ask the state to protect their consumer interests. In their view they were citizens who were spending money. As such they were entitled to consumer protection. Yet, just as the WIs argued that consumers were entitled to certain rights, so they suggested that consumers had certain responsibilities. Indeed, according to the WIs, shoppers' actions had public ramifications that affected their local, provincial, and national communities. For these reasons it was important to shop responsibly.

One way by which the institutes urged responsible shopping was through intelligent buying. At times the WIs echoed the home economics literature on this subject, indicating the close links that existed between the two movements. During the early 1930s a poem called "The Shopper's Creed," originally adopted by the American General Federation of Women's Clubs, appeared in both the Quebec and the Alberta WI press. It summarized the buyer's duties:

> I believe that the woman, through control of a large share of the family budget, exerts a vital influence upon today's economic order.
>
> Therefore, I hold it my duty to help make this influence constructive; to govern my buying so that waste will be reduced and the greatest good to all realized from my expenditures.
>
> I believe that, as measures of true economy, I should:
>
> Make known my merchandise needs and preferences in advance whenever the opportunity is presented;
>
> Remember that cheapness is not always a bargain, and consider suitability and durability as well as price;
>
> Avoid merchandise known to be produced under unfair competitive conditions, such as sweat shop or prison made goods;

Be reasonable in my demands for service, such as credit, alterations and deliveries;

Refrain from returning merchandise unless the goods or the store is at fault.

That is my Creed. I believe in it; I shall support it.[68]

By republishing this poem, institute members indicated their awareness of the consumer trends taking place south of the border. Simultaneously, they demonstrated support for the assumption, common within home economics at the time, that women could create prosperity by adhering to principles of rational, ethical shopping.

Whereas intelligent buying received a modicum of interest, another form of responsible consumption received sustained support. After the First World War the WIs joined forces with other organizations, including the National Council of Women (NCW) and the WCTU, to promote Canadian products.[69] While the provincial institutes frequently encouraged their locals to study Canadian industries, local institutes launched their own "Buy Canadian" campaigns. In Edmonton in 1929 the institute encouraged merchants to display Canadian-made goods in their store windows.[70]

Interestingly, however, while those working at the national level often called for members to buy Canadian, those working in provincial and local contexts often thought of economic citizenship in regional terms. In some instances, in fact, members were outright hostile to certain Canadian companies. In 1922 the Graysville (Manitoba) Institute resolved "that the country store is of more benefit to the community than the mail order house."[71] During this period two of the largest mail-order houses serving rural Manitoba were Eaton's and Simpson's, both assertively Canadian.[72] Hence, by declaring preference for the country store, members of the Graysville institute prioritized supporting their local community over large companies. Four years later the convenor of home industries for WINS made a similar suggestion. If women would simply purchase Nova Scotian products, she said, then "trade will surely advance in our neighbourhood and Eaton's parcels coming to the local Post Office will not be so large nor so frequent."[73]

By calling for neighbours to shop locally, members unwittingly affirmed the argument of citizenship theorist Nira Yuval-Davis, discussed in this book's introduction, that people's conceptions of citizenship are often "multi-layered," linked to communities both within and beyond the nation.[74] In the case of the WIs, local affiliations especially were compelling. Of all the provincial institutes, Nova Scotia's had the most sustained "Buy at Home" campaign.[75] In 1926 the Province of Nova Scotia helped fund a "Demonstration Train" to travel the province, carrying some of the exhibits featured at the provincial fair. WINS contributed an exhibit called "The Nova Scotia Pantry," which was "stocked with all the foods which are produced or packed in Nova Scotia," including "a wide variety of fruits, vegetables, fish and meat" in addition to "beans, cereals, spices and condiments, coffee, tea, cocoa, ... lard, butter ... ginger ale, cake, biscuits [and] bread confectionary." As WINS stated, the pantry's diversity was "a real eye-opener."[76]

Over the years, WINS engaged in other campaigns, including convincing merchants to feature Nova Scotian products in their windows and educating homemakers about government-issued labels that identified these products (fig. 4.1).[77] Perhaps the most unique consumer-citizenship event in which WINS participated, however, was the "Consumer's Pledge." In 1933, in partnership with the League of Loyal Nova Scotians, WINS encouraged Nova Scotians to sign a card indicating consumer loyalty: "In order to stimulate trade in Nova Scotia and to furnish more employment, I promise to buy the native products of Nova Scotia when these will meet my requirements, quality and price being satisfactory." WINS sent blank pledges to each local institute, which in turn collected signatures and mailed the pledges to the Nova Scotia minister of agriculture.[78]

Other provincial and local institutes also endorsed the "Buy at Home" movement.[79] In 1930 the British Columbia WIs joined with the "manufacturers and producers, distributors, retailers and press of the province" to launch an annual "Buy in British Columbia Week." Throughout this campaign the BC WIs had "expert speakers" and "prizes for the best window-displays of B.C. products." They "urg[ed] all members and women shoppers to buy at home first." In Minburn (Alberta) members "composed four songs for a 'Buy at Home' campaign."[80] In Quebec, members entered into

This label is being issued by the Department of Natural Resources to all manufacturers in Nova Scotia. The purpose is to single out and identify Nova Scotia products and advertise them in the markets of the world. It will also assist our Nova Scotia people in their efforts to buy home products and thus help to support our industries. Women's Institute members who have been interested in our Home Industries work will welcome this assistance.

WATCH FOR THE LABEL!

4.1 "Watch for the Label!" *Home and Country* (Nova Scotia), October 1928, 1, courtesy of the Women's Institutes of Nova Scotia.

the national exhibition a "Flax from the Field to the Loom and from the Loom to the Wearer" exhibit, which featured flax grown in the province.[81] For the 1931 Charlottetown exhibition the PEI institutes entered a booth featuring breakfast, dinner, and supper meals made from PEI goods. On the walls members hung blankets and brooms made by PEI businesses; they also put up "painted posters showing the advisability of buying island goods." Shelves featuring the products of over twenty-six island manufacturers were also displayed.[82]

More than any other activity in which the WIs engaged, however, the Home Economics Weeks of the early 1930s best exemplified how the members understood consumer citizenship. In Alberta and Quebec, and particularly in the centres of Edmonton, Calgary, Abbotsford (Quebec), and Sherbrooke, local WIs collaborated with merchants, chambers of commerce, city councils, manufacturers, Councils of Women, provincial and local Home Economics Associations, and other groups for one week in April to promote local shopping, intelligent buying, nutrition, fashions, and home décor. Particularly notable about these events was the assumption that the primary identity of the homemaker was that of consumer citizen. It was through their consumption habits that women contributed to their communities. As a journalist writing for a Sherbrooke newspaper wrote, "the idea [behind Home Economics Week] is that massed purchasing, right across the Dominion, will take stocks from dealers' shelves, send new orders into factories, create new jobs, [and] put the wheels of industry back into motion again."[83]

Events featured during the Home Economics Weeks reflected the partnerships that the WIs and other women's organizations sought to create with business and the state. In Edmonton in 1933 Mayor D.K. Knott opened the week with an address at the Tivoli showroom, following a luncheon for the Kiwanis Club. Members of WIs, together with the Shrine Ladies' Auxiliary, served the meal. Entertainment consisted of "orchestral music," "tap dancing," and "an address by the general secretary for the British and Foreign Bible Society for Canada and Newfoundland."[84] After the mayor's speech Mrs. J. MacGregor Smith, the convenor of the home economics committee for the Federated Women's Institutes of Canada (FWIC) and the chair of the Home Economics Week committee, presented Knott with a "basket of Alberta products" (fig. 4.2).[85] The choice to give a basket of Alberta goods to the mayor makes clear that shopping was pivotal to proper homemaking.

As part of the event the Tivoli was stocked with forty exhibition booths, including entries from Canadian Bakeries, the Edmonton City Dairy, the Blue Willow Product Company, Northwestern Utilities, Jonstone Walker Limited (a department store), Ogilvie Flour Mills Limited, Birks Limited (jewellers), Vets Sheet Metal Works, the Great Western Garment Company, and Safeway Stores Limited.[86] To show their appreciation to the companies for their participation in the event, the institutes endorsed the products being exhibited. For example, an advertisement that appeared in an Edmonton paper during the week stated: "The Women's Institute are USING and HIGHLY RECOMMEND All These Blue Willow Quality Products" – including the company's cocoa, tea, and coffee.[87]

Department stores, too, participated. In 1933 the Johnstone Walker of Edmonton store displayed a notice for "Home Economics Work of the Public, High, Technical, and University Study Students"

4.2 Mrs. J. MacGregor Smith presenting a basket of Alberta-made goods to Edmonton mayor D.K. Knott, April 1933. Photograph ND-3-6666; ND-3-6673. Used with the permission of Glenbow Archives, Calgary, Alberta.

throughout Home Economics Week.[88] Woodward's department store, also in Edmonton, partnered with the FWIC to offer daily lectures in its groceteria on "the value and preparation of foods."[89] Eaton's and the Hudson's Bay Company were, however, the biggest sponsors. In Calgary these stores hosted week-long exhibitions of students' home economics work. Restaurants in Eaton's and the HBC also offered demonstrations in cooking and table setting and put on fashion shows.[90] In conjunction with the WI, Eaton's featured "A Display of Interior Decorating" that showcased a "combination living-and-dining room" and a "colonial bedroom." Both were "assembled and entirely decorated by Home Economics experts."[91] The HBC held a dressmaking competition; after purchasing fabrics at special prices from the store's fabric department, contestants had three weeks to submit their creations to win "prizes."[92] Finally, Eaton's and the HBC hosted daily lectures by local home economics instructors. Subjects included shopping and the importance of home economics in schools, as well as "The Art of Interior Decoration," "Furniture in the Home," and "Table Setting for Home Entertainment.[93] All of these events were popular. In Calgary in 1933, average attendance numbered "one hundred women and girls" per lecture.[94]

During the early 1930s, then, the Alberta WIs had especially embraced the notion of consumer citizenship. Indeed, according to MacGregor Smith, shopping "occupied ... a key role in the commerce and trade of the Dominion" and as such enabled women to "dictate the prosperity of the world."[95] This was a responsibility that many WI members took seriously. In fact, one of MacGregor Smith's reasons for organizing the Home Economics Week in Edmonton was that women should be "leading the way along the road to better times."[96]

### Debating Consumption: Frugality versus Entitlement

A final way in which the WIs engaged in consumption was by discussing the pitfalls and possibilities of consumer spending. At meetings and in the organization's press, institute members discussed consumption's many dimensions. Within these conversations, matters of expenditure and self-fulfilment received sustained attention. How much time and money should one devote towards consumption? Did women deserve consumer goods? At the heart of the institutes' concerns was a tension between frugality and entitlement. Whereas some members argued that thrift was the ultimate goal, others suggested that it was time for rural women to embrace the opportunities that the marketplace offered.

A close reading of institute literature reveals that some members genuinely enjoyed making household goods. The act of creating objects combined three cherished activities: being thrifty, being creative, and being productive. Whether knitting an afghan for a sofa, sewing a curtain for a child's room, or transforming a flour sack into an apron, WI members poured labour and love into their endeavours. An article by Eva M. Bishop of the WINS well describes this producerist ethic. She wrote: "I believe every woman should have some craft at which she is skilful ... It satisfies the creative impulse, soothes the nerves, provides a delightful pastime and gives us beauty at little cost."[97]

Evidence that members valued home crafting appears frequently in WI literature. FWIC president Nancy Adams recalled that when she was nine years old and living in interwar Saskatchewan, she attended a meeting with her mother where they learned hat making. She "made one ... from red flannelette" and was "so proud ... that next Sunday [she] wore it to church."[98] A 1932 report in the Quebec newsletter indicated that members gave each other demonstrations on "Reed Basketry," "Stool Making," "Rug making, "How to re-seat a chair," "Glove making," "Salad making," and "Making and Colouring Icings." Not only were these activities creative, tactile, and purposeful, but they were taught by members to other members without the aid of an expert. This indicates that members took pleasure in sharing their crafts.[99]

For the WIs, and unlike within home economics curricula, ideas about home production were not restricted to the individual homemaker. Local institutes often shared both creative knowledge and creative labour and in the process built a sense a community. One notable effort occurred during the First World War, in Parkhill, Ontario. Caught up in the spirit of conservation, members opened a community canning centre. After securing an old armoury to house the centre, they arranged the donation of an industrial-sized boiler and a canning machine. They had originally planned to can food solely for donation to the war effort, but by 1918 they were canning enough produce to charge the Canadian Expeditionary Forces for their goods. In 1922 the centre was still in operation, with members using it both to can their own household goods and to prepare foods for market. According to members, the industrial-scale facility was a boon, for it "compresses into one day the drudgery of weeks."[100]

Closely related to some members' creation of community through resource sharing was a strong emphasis on thrift. Not only does the canning experiment illustrate this trend, but so do two Manitoba events. In 1931 the Makaroff institute hosted a "Country Store" evening; it was free for all to attend. Several products donated from Canadian manufacturing firms, as well as gifts donated by institute members, were displayed on a stage in the town's hall. Each person was given a numbered ticket; numbers were then drawn, and "holders of corresponding numbers received parcels from the store."[101] This event was similar to the popular "Poverty Balls," or local dances that took place across the province. These were hosted by local institutes; attendees of the events wore "patches."[102] Both the Country Store and the Poverty Ball brought people together during tough economic times. Acknowledging the possible scarcity that people were experiencing, they fostered a sense of solidarity. In 1933 this same sense of thrift and community pride galvanized the Manitoba WI to encourage members to exchange homemade goods with others in their community as a way to save money.[103]

For some members, then, thrift offered a way for them to share knowledge, build community, and combine resources. At the same time, others valued thrift primarily for moral reasons. In ways similar to those of some WCTU and NCW members, discussed in chapters 1 and 2, some institute members voiced disapproval of what they saw as excess. Following the opening plenary of the 1919 convention of the Western Ontario WIs, Miss A.H. Clayton of Listowel asked, "Are we as Institute workers setting the proper kind of example in the matter of thrift and economy?" In her view, "we have been so prone to consider we were doing the right thing only when we are extravagant and making a show."[104] According to Clayton, respectable women were modest; they were also mindful of the examples they were setting.

Despite some members' misgivings, such concerns were in the minority. As early as 1915, members were questioning whether financial restraint was always in a woman's best interest. That year, in Haldimand (Ontario), members debated this very topic. Their June meeting was about "the Difference between Frugality, Economy and Parsimony." The details of this meeting are unknown, but its title suggests that some members saw reason to temper their impulse towards saving. Indeed, one year later, this same institute held a meeting on the topic of "Mothers: What She Owes to Herself and What She Owes to the Community."[105] As this title illustrates, some members saw self-care as at least as important as community work.

By the interwar years a strong contingent of institute members had been arguing that in certain instances consumer spending should be embraced. Labour saving, especially, was applauded. In 1923 Mrs. C.W. Farran from Farran's Point (Ontario) spoke on "Co-operative and Individual Labour Saving" at an annual WI convention. She urged members to "form a club," "paying equal shares," and to "buy a vacuum cleaner, to be used by each of them in turn." She also suggested that they purchase an "electric floor waxer and polisher." Members could build "community kitchen[s]" and "sewing room[s]" furnished with top-of-the-line equipment and available for all to use. Even if someone was unable to join a labour-saving group, they could purchase items for home use. Dinner wagons, fireless cookers, and mop wringers all saved time and energy. These devices allowed women to avoid stooping, lifting, and scalding themselves and prevented "overstrained muscles and nerves." As she said, "it is no economy to do with as little as possible, in order to save and have a good bank account. Some day there may be a doctor bill amounting to more than the combined cost of all the articles mentioned." Women's time and health were "worth it."[106]

Suggesting that families spend money on women's needs, Farran's speech validated women's desires for respite. Nonetheless, it also waded into controversial territory. As historian Veronica Strong-Boag demonstrates, Canadian farm families typically held fast to the belief that all money should be saved for future generations or reinvested into capital equipment.[107] Since labour-saving devices did not generate the same visible capital as did crops and livestock, some farm families viewed them as unimportant. As home economics lecturer Ethel Chapman said in her 1921 address to the Ontario WI, "to the farmer with heavy payments to meet, any complete mechanical equipment for the house may seem to mean a rather questionable expenditure."[108] Yet labour-saving devices were necessary, she argued: many women leave farms because they "cannot stand farm work." If a family were to invest in water, electricity, and appliances, women would be more likely to stay.[109]

The issue of financial control within farm families was indeed contentious. In 1916 the Sheffield (Ontario) institute resolved that a "Separate Purse is an Advantage to the Home," after a debate on the subject.[110] Some members may have been in favour of a pooled income, but WI literature indicates, too, that some farm women wanted to earn their own money. According to a Toronto lecturer in 1923, "one farm daughter made a bargain with her father ... by which in return for the [chicken] feed and shelter she was to keep the household in eggs, turn the sale proceeds from the young cockerels into the family exchequer, and retain the rest of the hen money for herself. Out of this she clothed herself, started an embryo library, and her first bank account."[111] This girl's determination to buy clothes and books, as well as start a savings account, indicates that she thought her own appearance, education, and future to be worthwhile investments.

Over the years institutes repeatedly asked whether the interests of girls and women were worth the financial costs. In 1921, at Plum Coules (Manitoba), members had a debate titled "Whose Fault Is It?" It addressed "the question of why home-makers put up with out-of-date methods of doing housework when so many modern conveniences can be purchased."[112] Recognizing that farm women were exhausted, the Manitoba WI arranged a "Farm Women's Vacation Week" in 1930. Working with the Manitoba Agricultural College in Winnipeg, the institute invited farm women to spend the week of 14–21 June at the college, where for the small fee of "$7.50" they could spend seven days "do[ing] what you wish and when you wish." Excursions to department stores, cinemas, and lectures would be offered, but women could also take a "pleasant walk," read an "interesting book or magazine," or have "a quiet nap."[113] As such, they could finally enjoy some down time after working so hard for so long.

All over the country farm women yearned for respite. One PEI member wanted time to herself so much that in 1937 she developed a "Time Budget." Dividing her chores into "daily work," "occasional work," "special work," and "extra time," which was put aside for "emergencies," she planned her daily schedule. Working rigorously, she was eventually able to have one free hour in the morning and three hours in the afternoon. At first she spent this new time resting. After she felt she had caught up on her health, she decided to "be of good to others in [her] community." Of particular enjoyment was "act[ing] as a leader" for the local girls' "food club." Significantly, this member felt that "good equipment," particularly in the kitchen, was key to her success.[114] For this writer, as perhaps for others, both time to rest and time to contribute to one's community were worthwhile endeavours.

Given members' yearning for respite, it is not surprising that within the institute press the commodities that members most frequently desired were labour-saving devices. They were not, however, the only ones. In 1930 the monthly institute newsletter of PEI included a piece written by Cecilia Williams MacKinnon, which argued that "new clothes" could be a boon. They lifted one's spirits, and they invited admiration from others. To illustrate this point she relayed a "true story": "A tired, dejected-looking little woman once entered a doctor's office ... The doctor talked to her in a casual manner ... then said abruptly[,] 'You don't want medicine, you want new clothes, in your nervous run down condition you have got it into your head you're not going to live long and so you've not bought yourself a single new dud for months, your clothes are all as ancient as the ark. My dear lady, when a woman loses interest in her personal appearance she has about lost her grip on life.'" The doctor's solution was to "get a stylish bright dress, smart shoes, a sweet little hat, and ear-rings." After the woman objected, saying that people would gossip, the doctor replied, "Say! They'll say that Mrs. Black looks ten years younger and as well-dressed and fine-looking a woman as walks in shoe leather." The woman followed her doctor's advice, and was soon experiencing "a speedy and permanent cure."[115]

As this story reveals, MacKinnon thought not only that farm women deserved new clothes but also that dressing well was important to their health. Mothers "work away day in and day out ... forgetful of self and appearance ... until they make their children feel almost ashamed of them." She told mothers to "get all the labor saving devices you can afford in your homes, conserve your energy, take a nap at noon every day, dress up every afternoon, and don't think you are too old to enjoy a trip to town occasionally." Doing so was not selfish but was important for both one's own health and the well-being of one's family.[116]

In this view, it was a question not of whether women deserved consumer goods but of whether women were smart enough to avail themselves of the items the market had to offer. Such a position defended women's consumer entitlements. In MacKinnon's opinion, and in those of writers like her, farm women deserved to feel pretty. They also deserved to have some time off. Consumer goods, in their minds, offered one method by which to achieve these goals. For these reasons it was acceptable for farm women to put aside their concerns of frugality and to embrace the possibilities of the marketplace.

## Conclusion: Producerist Consumers

Despite living in the countryside, many Canadian women between 1900 and 1939 engaged in consumer activities. Through WIs they shared consumer knowledge, lobbied for better consumer conditions, practised consumer citizenship, and suggested that certain consumer goods could help emancipate farm women from drudgery and blight. Some farm women felt guilty about consumer excess, and many preferred to practise thrift. Some WI members indeed displayed a producerist ethic, taking immense pride and satisfaction in home production. Some rejected the individualist values associated with personal consumption, preferring instead to hold such events as "poverty balls" and "country store" evenings that offered broad material support to all community members. Throughout this period, however, tension existed between those who valued thrift and those who believed betterment could be accomplished through consumption. For some members it was acceptable to purchase labour-saving devices, lovely dresses, and attractive furnishings in order save time and brighten one's day. For these women personal happiness was directly tied to down time, fashion, beauty, and new home décor.

By examining Canadian WIs during the first four decades of their existence, this chapter brings into clear focus the ambiguities related to consumption in the early twentieth century. Although many farm women valued thrift, home production, and handicraft, many also valued the efficiency, beauty, and cheer that new consumer goods provided. For individual women, spending decisions became delicate acts of balancing both the family's needs and savings targets and whatever benefits new commodities might provide. At the same time the consumer status of WI members remained unquestioned. The WIs recognized the involvement of their members in consumer issues. They often functioned as consumer organizations, in which members shared consumer advice and engaged in formal consumer advocacy.

Many early twentieth-century rural women in Canada found their endless rounds of chores to be both fulfilling *and* exhausting. Some yearned for labour-saving devices, holidays, new clothing, and new furniture and appliances. For these women, new consumer products may have been fraught with vestiges of excess and greed; yet, they also held promises of freedom. Indeed, for many rural white Canadian women before the Second World War, being a consumer meant much more than the fulfilment of another domestic responsibility. It meant engaging in political and economic affairs as an active, responsible citizen. It meant potentially influencing the prosperity of one's community and one's nation. As such, consumption held out the possibility of liberation.

*Chapter Five*

# For Whom Do We Dress?
# Feminism and Fashion

"NoBraNoProblem," declares the social media hashtag of a recent protest movement calling for liberation from constrictive underclothes. This movement gained strength in 2015, after a high school student in Montana, Kaitlyn Juvik, reported on Facebook that a teacher had told her to go home and put on a bra because she was making "a lot of male teachers ... uncomfortable." She was "embarrassed" and "angry," calling on contacts to fight double standards in dress codes. Juvik's story has since been covered by international media; she herself has organized protests against dress codes and has encouraged others to do the same. Her anger is about more than the right to go braless; it is "about ending body shaming" and "about women everywhere being able to be comfortable in their own bodies."[1]

Juvik's experience is specific to Montana, but it is also indicative of a recent international backlash against sexist dress codes. In Canada, Kayla Touchette of Landmark (Manitoba) recently filed a complaint with her provincial human rights commission because a teacher had "told her to cover up" her shoulders and "put on a sweater," though "boys in the school wear basketball jerseys without problem."[2] Certainly social media has emboldened young women to take action against body shaming, in that the platform enables them to connect with people around the world. Yet the movement is also more widespread. After her boss sent Nicola Thorp home in January 2017 from her job at the firm PricewaterhouseCoopers in the United Kingdom because she had contravened the company's dress code by wearing flat shoes, she started a petition calling on the British parliament to ban high-heels requirements. Her petition gathered 152,000 signatures, but the government rejected such legislation.[3] Canada has witnessed a similar up-tick in complaints during recent years. As a result, Earls Restaurants has revised its dress code, stating that women can wear high heels and skirts or "varying heel heights" and "pants."[4]

Enquiring into how white wives and mothers in English and French Canada perceived fashion during the early twentieth century, this chapter demonstrates that although controversies over women's fashions are currently erupting, the struggle to liberate female bodies from onlookers' preferences has a long history. Through a detailed analysis of the white club-women's press in both English and French Canada this chapter reveals that for well over a hundred years many Canadian cisgender female activists have been challenging sartorial norms. At the same time it also illustrates that the preoccupations of past advocates were both similar to and different from those of today. As do contemporary critics, many in the past called on women to throw out fashion's restrictions. Some also declared that double standards in dress arose largely from men's powers over women. Nonetheless, historical activists were also much more concerned about respectability. In both English and French Canada several women's advocates suggested that conformity to moral precepts – and not comfort and creativity – should guide fashion norms. Influenced in some cases by Protestantism and in others by Catholicism, these writers argued that women could only be respectable once they embraced modesty. Thus these activists were also in favour of reform, but their recommendations were very different.

This chapter explores all sides of the fashion debate in the white Canadian women's press before 1940, historicizing the contemporary international push against sexist dress customs. Simultaneously it offers new insights into the history of Canadian fashion. To date, this topic has received moderate attention, with researchers probing subjects ranging from the influence of the fur trade upon Coast Salish dress to white men's sartorial habits in New France to the work of twentieth-century fashion writers.[5] The period between Confederation and the Second World War has been well covered, featuring studies of the rise of ready-to-wear, the portrayal of women in advertising, and the influence of war upon fashion.[6] For the purpose of this chapter, four recent research areas especially stand out: the history of dress reform, the perspectives of female consumers on dress, the connections that moral reformers made between fashion and sin, and the heightening of visual culture.[7] The following pages draw extensively upon this literature, making particular reference to research conducted by Laurie K. Bertram, Jane Nicholas, and Katrina Srigley.[8]

Blending recent scholarly findings with an analysis of print materials dating from the early twentieth century, I show that white Canadian women have a long history of fashion criticism. This chapter thus offers a slightly different interpretation of feminist fashion critique than that put forward by Barbara Kelcey. According to Kelcey, white anglophone female activists in late nineteenth-century Ontario were lukewarm towards American feminists' criticisms of tight corsets, long skirts, and other constricting aspects of Victorian dress. Many English Canadian feminists recognized the restrictions of fashionable female attire, Kelcey argues, but their own attachments to style prevented them from taking up the dress-reform cause.[9] Unlike Kelcey, I focus on the early twentieth century, but my findings do indicate that the history of Canadian dress reform is more nuanced. Many early Canadian feminists were in fact quite vocal in their fashion criticisms. For example, in 1914 Toronto dressmaker and suffragist Flora MacDonald Denison argued that women should abandon all restrictive modes of clothing and embrace comfortable, practical styles.[10] Many advocates, as well, argued against ornate designs, urging women to adopt more simplicity. Moreover, as fashions changed between the 1900s and 1930s, so did women's criticisms. During the 1910s, when high heels became fashionable, authors criticized this trend. And, during the 1920s, when the "flapper" style emerged – featuring knee-length hemlines, bare arms, and loose tunics – women in Quebec launched a major campaign against modern dress. Such actions, this chapter argues, reveal that although some Canadian women may well have been indifferent to dress reform, many others were intensely interested in the topic. They also sought to shape Canadian women's habits in ways that matched their own proclivities.

My findings are based upon references to clothing and fashion contained within white women's periodicals published before 1940. These periodicals were created by the largest women's organizations in Canada, namely the WCTU, the NCW, the Fédération nationale Saint-Jean-Baptiste, the Cercles de fermières du Québec, and the Canadian Women's Institutes (WIs). All these groups had different orientations, but – and as the preceding chapters have argued – they were also similar in that they each embraced an ideology that can best be described as Euro-Canadian maternalism. That is, their leaders tended to argue that the supposedly natural roles of English and French Canadian women as wives and mothers made them moral authorities. As well, all these clubs tended to adopt middle-class views. This is not to say that they avoided grass-roots activism, for many of them were actively involved in their communities. Rather, it suggests that the spokeswomen of these groups tended to be affluent. As such the opinions generated by their presses did not represent all women in Canada; rather they represented the views of a privileged movement leadership.

### The Joys of Fashion

In their recent studies of women and clothing in late nineteenth- and early twentieth-century Canada, historians Laurie Bertram and Katrina Srigley each have found that for many women during this period, fashion carried certain attractions. According to Bertram, several young Icelandic Canadian women in Manitoba kept up with Anglo-Canadian fashion trends. They did so partially to deflect potential ethnic discrimination, but also because they enjoyed doing so. As Bertram writes, the "eagerness with which urban Icelanders embraced Anglo-Victorian clothing ... speaks to their attraction to it."[11] Similarly, according to Srigley, many working-class women who lived in Toronto during the 1930s enjoyed window shopping. They could not afford new clothes, but they found satisfaction in seeing new apparel.[12] Such pastimes indicate that for these women, fashion was a pleasurable hobby, one that combined an admiration for artistic design with a pleasure in remaining *au courant*. As such, these women revealed a keenness for modernity. To be considered "modern" during this time, as Nicholas writes, was a desire to keep "up with the pace of change."[13]

The club-women's press offers further indications of the pleasures that many women took in apparel. It reveals that for many white Canadian wives and mothers of this period, fashion was a source of novelty, sensuality, and creativity. According to the NCW's journal, *Woman's Century*, fashion had many aesthetic qualities that could be enjoyed. In 1921 that journal began a column called "Fashion Wise & Otherwise." Authored by Kitty Hardcastle, it discussed the latest fashions, usually in a breathless, admiring tone. One iteration, for instance, fawned over wedding trousseaux, going into detail about "lace" and "crepe silks."[14] Another praised new styles in spring clothing, which were described as "poetry"; these included the "soft velvety surface of duvetyn and velours" in the new "wraps and capecoats," and the "light colors" of new blouses in "crepe de chine or canton crepe."[15] Through such prose, *Woman's Century* celebrated clothing's sensuality and intimated that readers might do the same.

In introducing the "Fashion Wise & Otherwise" column, *Woman's Century* may have been trying to stay relevant. During the 1920s, mass-market American magazines including *Ladies' Home Journal* were flooding Canadian news-stands.[16] These periodicals, together with such domestic offerings as the *Canadian Home Journal* and *Everywoman's World*, were entertaining, offering features on homemaking, celebrity news, and fashion, among other subjects.[17] As such, they were more popular than the reform-minded *Woman's Century*. Nevertheless, it is also true that some Canadian club-women appreciated fashion. During the late nineteenth century, many Anglo-Canadian club-women turned up their noses at dress reform, which advocated banning corsets and long trains, because they preferred to look stylish.[18] Into the twentieth century several Anglo-Canadian club-women remained suspicious of dress reform. In 1912 the *White Ribbon Bulletin* of the WCTU noted with relief that it was possible to be both politically active and smartly dressed. According to a correspondent who had attended the Women's Liberal Federation in England, the women who attended wore "dainty lingerie blouses" and "pretty frocks" underneath their "well tailored" outerwear.[19]

In addition to praising fashion, the club-women's press also expressed appreciation for dressmaking. Throughout this period members of the WIs and the Cercles de fermières demonstrated interest in sewing, indicating a widespread assumption that needlework was integral to wives' and mothers' identities. Such interest was reflected in the regular sewing courses offered by both the institutes and the *cercles*, available at most of their many locations.[20] The courses allowed participants to learn practical skills, but they also enabled artistry. As Julie-Anne Bureau wrote of a *cercles* course offered in 1932, "l'invention et l'imagination jouent un rôle non moins indispensable que celui des ciseaux ou de l'aiguille."[21] Appreciation by the institutes and the *cercles* of homemade clothing was also reflected in their written materials. Dorothy M. Walsh of the Quebec WI wrote to her periodical in 1937 to say that "while clothing may now be bought for very little, this cheap clothing is practically always cheap in material and workmanship." It was hence better to make one's own dresses. This practice allowed updates and enabled wearers to keep garments "attractive and artistic."[22]

Of the women's clubs examined in this chapter, the WIs and the Cercles de fermières placed the most emphasis upon needlework. Yet other clubs were interested, too. In 1921 – the same year that the Kitty Hardcastle column was introduced – *Woman's Century* began carrying advertisements for McCall's sewing patterns. Unlike the magazine's other advertisements, which tended to run on the outer columns of individual pages, these advertisements were full page and carried detailed illustrations of models wearing clothing made from the patterns on offer. By browsing these advertisements, readers could learn about new styles, including that for winter 1921 the "straight-line silhouette predominates."[23] They could also order patterns. Certainly one should not extrapolate too much from these advertisements; their appearance reflected the precarious financial situation of *Woman's Century* as much as it reflected other concerns. Still, the appearance of McCall's patterns in *Woman's Century* does hint at some club-women's assumptions that sewing patterns were relevant. Indeed, despite the availability of ready-to-wear, many Euro-Canadian women of this era made their own clothes. They did so not only because it was affordable but because they enjoyed it. As Srigley notes with reference to women who sewed clothing for themselves and others in Toronto, many people took satisfaction in being both thrifty and creative.[24]

By expressing pleasure in clothing, the club-women's press demonstrated that many Canadian women found fashion exciting. So important was fashion, in fact, that a few suggested that clothes could create happiness. In 1911 one Ontario WCTU member asked rhetorically, "Where is the woman who will not work to better advantage when she knows that she is looking nice?" According to this writer, a "pretty ... frock" could take the edge off one's "monotonous routine."[25] Thus, in contrast to another WCTU member's 1912 pronouncement in the *Toronto Daily Star* that "young women" should "form clubs eschewing 'undesirable dress,'" this writer suggested that attractive clothes could ease housework's burdens.[26] In her view, the knowledge that one looked nice while homemaking was more important than other considerations. In 1930 a member of the PEI WI offered similar thoughts. Simply because a housewife might value thrift and devotion, wrote Cecilia Williams MacKinnon, does not mean that she has to ignore her "appearance."[27] In her opinion, a "stylish bright dress, smart shoes, a sweet little hat, and ear-rings" made all the difference between being "tired" and "dejected" and being happy. Indeed, in MacKinnon's view, women's self-worth was tied to their ability to feel modish and "young" – or not "antiquated," as she put it. Wearing "out-of-date" clothes made one feel old and was equivalent to losing one's "grip on life."[28]

Fashion, then, was an antidote to isolation. Housewives might be lonely, but this did not mean that they had to neglect their interests. Indeed, a pleasing appearance could be key to a woman's confidence. Certainly women might have wished to appear attractive to impress those with whom they interacted. Yet they also wished to please their own selves. As MacKinnon argued, fashion enabled wives and mothers to hold on to their youthful spirit. This argument reflected her investment in fashion as a tool of self-respect. It also, and more subtly, indicates that for at least some women in PEI the ability to appear young and modern was key to feminine identity.

## Fashion as Communication

Within the white club-women's press before 1940 there was a recognition that many women enjoyed fashion. They did not say as much, but the writers who discussed the aforementioned components of fashion did so from the perspective that wearers were fashion's primary audiences. In other magazine articles, however, different assumptions were made. For many contributors, in fact, fashion was primarily a form of communication. In their view the selection of fashion pieces had as much to do with sending messages out into the world as they did with wearers' own sartorial preferences.[29] For these reasons it was important to consider one's choices carefully.

A minority of contributors who adopted the fashion-as-communication perspective suggested that the wearers' peers were their audiences. In 1920 the Victoria (British Columbia) correspondent for *Woman's Century* reported that the Local Council of Women in that city had started a campaign to bring in dress codes for high school students, particularly girls. "Standardization," noted the report, would reduce "much of the rivalry caused by the wearing of silk stockings and fancy waists."[30] In this view, fashion was a method by which wearers communicated their status to their peers. Stylish clothing on the schoolyard caused girls to compete for each other's esteem.

More often, however, writers with this perspective assumed that fashion's audiences were men, specifically heterosexual men, whom women were trying to attract. According to a report in *Woman's Century* on the 1919 National Conference of American Women Doctors, a Dr. Edith Swift of Boston had stated that there were "two extremes in clothes – those worn by women who used them as a means of luring the opposite sex, and the useful and hygienic clothing adopted by the professional or business woman."[31] The anonymous author clearly preferred the latter type. Indeed, by contrasting these two extremes, both Swift and the author suggested that whereas clothes worn for public life were meant to communicate efficiency, those worn for "luring the opposite sex" were meant to communicate impurity. Clothing here was an instrument of professionalization, one that could be used to demonstrate briskness and deflect unwanted sexual attention. At the same time, this binary between professionalism and sexualization depended on the existence of the sexualized woman, one who used clothing to signify her attractiveness to the male gaze. In other words, the asexualized, professional ideal depended on making moral judgments about women who wore clothing that was deemed promiscuous – judgments that objectified and sexualized the bodies of fashion wearers.

Female objectification was in fact central to most discussions that assumed that heterosexual men were women's clothing audiences. Rather than presenting women who wore alluring clothes as subjects who made rational decisions, authors who assumed that heterosexual men were women's audiences presumed that fashionable women were objects of public consumption. As such, they were available for both the male gaze and public debate. One anonymous article that appeared in *Canadian White Ribbon Tidings* in 1919 illustrated this approach well. According to this article, a Dr. Margaret Patterson of Toronto had recently given a speech to young women entitled "Healthy Girls." Patterson stated that if young women wanted "to get the respect of their male companions," they had to "give proof by sensible, decent and healthful attire that [they] respect [their] own bodies."[32] She hence suggested that certain types of women wore provocative clothing and that such clothing sent signals to men that the wearers' bodies were not valuable. As a result, men would not "respect" such women. What remains unstated is the inference that male disrespect could translate into sexual aggression. If, however, the women were wearing clothing deemed not "decent," they were at fault for whatever actions men might take. Such women had thus given up their personal agency.

If Patterson's indecently dressed women were objects of the male gaze, so were they object lessons in virtue. By referring to "sensible, decent, and healthful attire," Patterson indirectly held up supposedly indecent and unhealthily dressed women as examples of depravity. When it came to morality, this pattern repeated itself often within the women's press. Not only did authors represent women who wore supposedly risqué fashions as sex objects, but they also suggested they were personifications of immorality. As such, their personhood was doubly denied.

In keeping with its Catholic commitment, *La Bonne Parole* emerged as the most judgemental of all the presses. In article after article this magazine denounced "l'impudeur du costume féminin."[33] According to several articles the fashions of the post-war years were especially immodest. Authors railed against low necklines, high hemlines, short sleeves, transparent silk blouses, visible lingerie underneath shirts, and sleevelessness. Said Mademoiselle Phaneuf, the representative of the Association des employées de

manufacture, women who wished to preserve Christian (*chréti-
ennes*) morals should not wear "jupes trop courtes, de corsages
trop décolletés et de tissus trop transparents."[34] As did Patterson
before her, Phaneuf set up a dichotomy between respectable – in
her case, Christian – women and those who dressed indecently.
Whereas Christian women were rational beings who made good
decisions, indecently dressed women were object lessons, people
who existed to help Christian women realize the pitfalls of taking
modern fashion to its extremes.

Whether criticisms of immoral fashions were written in French
or in English, all ultimately assumed that heterosexual men were
fashion's true audiences. In either language, showing too much
skin, wearing bright colours, and revealing the silhouette of one's
body through tight clothing were attributes of immorality. As the
*White Ribbon Bulletin* put it, "the freakish fashions, which shame-
lessly display the physical ... charms of young girls, are a disgrace."
Especially to be avoided were "transparent waists, skirts reaching
but a few inches below the knee, so tight that the figure is boldly
displayed at every step," and "stockings of the thinnest and bright-
est silk."[35] As this quotation reveals, commentators assumed that
when girls and women showed too much skin, wore tight clothing,
or wore conspicuous colours, they drew undue attention to themselves. They were hence inviting the sexual gaze. For this logic to
work, of course, commentators had to make the assumption that
girls' and women's bodies were inherently sexual. Certainly, wearing tight clothing, bright colours, and showing skin would not be
problematic if girls and women were considered agentive beings
deserving of universal respect. Instead, moral reform discourse
presented women's bodies as objects of the sexualized gaze. It was
therefore of pressing importance to keep them as hidden as possible.

## "Slavery" and Liberation

A further theme within reform women's fashion writings was the
notion that fashion was a form of "slavery." In English Canada
writers railed against a "slavish attitude towards the dressmak-
ers' authority," while in Quebec writers urged "d'abolition de l'es-
clavage de la mode."[36] Their frequent employment of the slavery
metaphor, though certainly melodramatic, indicated a widespread

desire among writers to lessen fashion's influence. Nonetheless, even if they agreed that fashion held too much sway over women, they differed as to what exactly they viewed as fashion's restraints.

According to some, it was the time women spent on fashion that was the problem. Hattie Orchard of Ontario expressed the opinion in 1911 that women spent too "much time and physical and mental energy ... studying and discussing the various fashion magazines, the catalogues and the clothes of all the women we meet." In her view, it was better to be more "temperate"; doing so would enable women to think about "higher, better things," particularly those involving the "cultivation of the mind."[37] In 1919 the noted reformer Anne Anderson Perry of Winnipeg made an even stronger argument: "Now that women have the vote, [they should abandon] the slavery of fashion," which she referred to as "the shackles of sex." When women "spend so much of their time and thoughts on the length of skirts," they cannot "enlarge their minds."[38]

If some writers yearned to escape the time investment that fashion demanded, others sought freedom from styles that restricted their mobility. During the First World War and into the early 1920s the NCW campaigned against high-heeled and pointed shoes, arguing that such footwear caused "hammer toes, bunions, corns, weak muscles, fallen arches, ... backaches, and ... nervous irritability."[39] So serious was the problem, said a 1917 *Woman's Century* article, that almost "90 per cent of Canadian people have deformed, sick, weak and painful feet" due to wearing fashionable shoes.[40] Other lamented styles included "tight lacing," "dragging skirt[s]," overly puffed sleeves, "hobble skirt[s]," tight armholes, and tight collars.[41] When women wore such fashions, argued noted dressmaker Flora MacDonald Denison, they "deformed and crippled" themselves.[42]

Fashion's cost, too, was lamented. *Woman's Century*, *La Bonne Parole*, and *La Bonne Fermière* all printed pieces arguing against the ongoing expenses required by staying in fashion.[43] One article in *Woman's Century* articulated this problem well. "Fashion decrees that a woman's cloak, say, should take the form of a ... jacket" in one year, and "the form of a cloak" in another; moreover, one year it will have "two rows of buttons," the next, "one." Due to constantly shifting fashions a woman will toss "aside a garment" still in excellent condition." Consequently, "dire waste" is produced, and, due to spousal arguments over money, "marital misery" results.[44] Although this writer did not see a way out of fashion's conundrum – she preferred to stay in fashion and suffer the consequences – other writers urged cost-reducing solutions. One member of the Cercles de fermières urged women to practise restraint when it came to shopping.[45] Another woman, this one a member of the NCW, recommended starting an "Old Clothes League," in which members would dedicate themselves to wearing old dresses in order "to combat the cloth merchant and tailor."[46]

The simple fact that many women were responsive to fashion at all was the issue that bothered some writers. Contributors who took this tack bemoaned women's lack of free will. Argued one writer, it was time to say to the "makers of fashions" that "we are not apes, we are women."[47] For Eleanor G. McFadden of the Manitoba Agricultural College, it was the idea that women wore unflattering clothes just to appear stylish that proved troublesome. Rather than dressing in ways that enhanced wearers' "individuality," fashion's followers wore ill-fitting garments.[48] Why did they do so? According to another writer, it was women's "vanity."[49] A further writer reminded readers that fashion was the result of specific decisions made by people in the fashion industry; therefore, given that fashion was not fate, one did not have to submit to its demands.[50]

The idea that women should stop following fashion with "sheep-like docility" was related to another notion much decried in the women's reform press, that women's fashion addictions caused them to dress immorally.[51] If women would stop obsessing about style, they would start dressing with more decorum. In keeping with its Catholic commitments, La Bonne Parole was outspoken in this demand. After criticizing women's beachwear for showing too much skin – apparently, the writer had seen women's cleavage, arms, and shins at the beach – one article asked rhetorically, "N'est-il pas temps d'ouvrir les yeux et de nous insurger contre une tyrannie qui escompte trop notre tolérance?" Especially to be avoided were the new lines of blouses made of sheer materials; these fashions were "scandaleux et suggestif."[52]

Despite La Bonne Parole's status as the strongest critic of fashion in all of Canada, a few English-language writers also condemned so-called extravagance. Stated one, "It is well known that outré fashions originate for the most part at the dictate of the demi-monde and others of like kind," a group that the author viewed with derision. These kinds of people "use certain allurements of dress to capture the lower senses" and to hence induce people to buy their wares. Unfortunately, due to their desires to appear fashionable, many "decent" girls and women were purchasing "dresses that are nothing short of indecent." It was time for women to stand up to the "dressmaker [who tries] to force a 'Vamp' dress" upon them; it was time for women to be "appropriate and modest."[53]

When contributors called on women to overthrow the chains of fashion so that they could dress more modestly, they demonstrated a different position than those who said that women should have greater bodily mobility. When women said that they wanted more comfort, they were suggesting that they wanted to do things other than keep up appearances. In contrast, when women said they needed to liberate other women from fashion's constraints to bring a sense of decorum back into the world, they were arguing that women should always consider themselves on display. For these writers, only when women conformed to norms of respectability could they be free. Implicit in these arguments was the view that women's bodies were under intense scrutiny. Hence it was better to master the code of respectability than to risk having people make moral judgments.

### Standing Up to Fashion

According to the women's reform press before 1940, fashion had a number of difficulties. For some, it was too risqué; for others it was too confining. Still others thought it was costly, time consuming, shallow, flashy, and capricious. Given all these problems, it is not surprising that, in addition to criticizing fashion, many writers put forth solutions to what they perceived as fashion's difficulties.

In 1920 a Methodist reformer in Calgary named Emily Kirby, who went by the pseudonym Constance Lynd, put forth one of the most original solutions. In her view, men should simply stop ogling women. "From the dawn of creation," she argued, "man has decked himself out to please himself. He then reached out and began to dictate the dress for woman." Indeed, "man to-day dictates our fashions, and then persecutes us for adopting them." Notable for its bluntness, Kirby's argument laid bare the problem of the male gaze. One of the only writers to challenge male influence, she pointed to the sexism that restricted women's freedom. She wrote that instead of telling women how to dress, "man should control his sex functions." As such she argued that women's liberty was curtailed by men's presumed dominance over women's bodies, not only in private but also in public.[54]

Despite Kirby's pinpointing of the male gaze, most other contributors suggested different responses. In 1919 *La Bonne Parole* reported that the daily newspaper of the Vatican was calling upon women around the world to fight against indecency in dress. It was time, argued the Vatican, for women to channel their superior moral instincts and to condemn anyone who promoted "les modes indécentes."[55] Not a year after this pronouncement, Catholic women in Quebec created what was referred to in English as the "league against indecent fashions."[56] *Woman's Century* described the initiative: "Already 10,000 women have taken the pledge not to 'exceed the limits of good taste in a desire to be fashionable,' and also to establish correct standards for women's dress in Canada." As this report indicates, many women had taken the Vatican's words to heart.[57]

Into the interwar years Quebec women's protests continued. *Bonne Fermière* reported in 1921 that the Cercles de fermières had joined other organizations in writing letters to retailers, asking them to stop promoting immodesty. The *cercles* had two specific demands: retailers should stop selling clothing with low necklines, transparent materials, and tightness around the hips; and they should stop distributing catalogues with illustrations of women wearing lingerie. By ending these practices, retailers could regain the confidence of respectable female shoppers.[58] Again, in 1927 and 1928, the French-language women's press reported upon organized attempts to combat immodest fashions. In the former year, noted *La Bonne Parole*, the Saint-Lambert section of the Fédération nationale Saint-Jean-Baptiste had started a formal league against indecent dress, an initiative much lauded by local priests. And, in the latter year, *La Bonne Parole* carried a note from a Dominican priest who was proud to report that Catholic women in Quebec were still active in the league against immodest fashions.[59]

In 1935 Quebec women tried a further tactic. That spring *La Bonne Parole* announced a new swimsuit created by the Fédération nationale Saint-Jean-Baptiste, designed by member Florine Phaneuf. Endorsed by the Ligue catholique féminine and the Catholic diocese of Montreal, the suit was available in stores under the name "costume L.C.F." The garment was, according to Mme Georges Morel, proof that beach attire could be at once "comfortable, élégant, et décent."[60] Available in a range of colours and made with Quebec textiles, the suit featured a tight bodice with an open neck and bare arms, a belted waist, and a pleated skirt that stopped at mid-thigh (fig. 5.1).[61] Rather than simply railing against indecent fashions, the women behind this suit took more direct action. Phaneuf's efforts, together with the FNSJB's work to get the dress in stores, demonstrates the depth of many club-women's convictions that women needed to demonstrate decorum.

These actions against indecent dress were the most organized responses to fashion's perceived problems. Beginning in 1917 the NCW did campaign against high heels and pointed shoes, as discussed, but their efforts did not reach the same levels of activity as did the Catholic effort in Quebec.[62] Nevertheless, it is also true that through the late nineteenth and the early twentieth century, the English Canadian women's press was replete with calls for reform. In a number of articles both during and immediately after the First World War, anglophone authors railed against what one called the "High Selfishness of the Dresser."[63] One such article appeared in 1916, when contributor M. Alberta Deards expressed outrage that although "sacrifice of life, health, limb, and eyesight" was being made overseas, "the crowds of fashionably and expensively dressed women do not diminish in our streets." In her view, "in these days of blood and tears we women ought to forego our artistic tastes and be content with plain, inexpensive dress, even if it bears the stamp of last year upon it." Not only would avoiding fashion demonstrate respect for soldiers, but it would free up women's resources for more virtuous causes. If women stopped worrying about their wardrobes, argued Deards, they could knit more socks for soldiers; they could also spend more money on "Red Cross work, on flour, milk, etc., for the starving Belgians, on field comforts for the boys in the trenches."[64] As this argument made clear, its author associated an interest in fashion with the

5.1 Bathing suit designed by Florine Phaneuf. *La Bonne Parole*, May 1935, 16.

Christian sins of the body, particularly greed, pride, and sloth. Far better for women to put their efforts towards more spiritual causes.

By calling out fashionably dressed women as selfish, Deards's article – together with others written in similar veins – exposed the assumption of some contributors that women's bodies were barometers of social morality. Indeed, many commentators tended to reserve their harshest critiques of luxury for women, even as they recognized that both men and women pursued material pleasures. In the 1918 piece "Luxury and Womanhood," for example, author E. Blakely noted that during the war Canadians "lounge[d] in magnificently upholstered motor cars," even while "our men" overseas "[lay] writhing in unutterable agony for hours at an advance dressing station" for want of motor ambulances. Presumably, both men and women enjoyed automobiles and other comforts, but it was the fashionably dressed woman particularly who received condemnation. Despite Canada's duty to support the Allies' cause, "milady throws 'needs' to the winds and indulges in luxuries," including costly blouses, "sheer waists," "extravagant lingerie," "gayly [sic] coloured, fashionable sweater-coat[s], "Milan hat[s]," and other "foolish finery," argued Blakely. She then made a similar argument to that of Deards. Instead of spending money on fashion, women should send their money overseas, where it could be used to "feed a Belgian kiddie." They should also buy Victory Bonds, and they should further buy only Canadian goods. Through economic nationalism they would support their country's manufacturers and hence indirectly aid the war effort.[65]

Just as Deards wanted women to engage in selfless charity work and spending, so did Blakely want women to donate to virtuous causes. Each of them grew aggrieved when they saw fashionable women; to them, such women's clothes indicated that the wearers were selfish people who, despite having disposable time and income, directed their resources towards their own bodies. Not only were such women greedy, but they were also morally suspect. Implicit in this line of argument was the assumption that women had particular social roles, ones that were both supportive and chaste. When women did not conform to these expectations, they upset existing codes of femininity.

When other women's reform writers adopted the view that fashion was selfish, they tended to write along the lines typified by

Deards and Blakely. A few, however, did offer slightly different justifications. In 1915 *Canadian White Ribbon Tidings* published a fictional story in which an adolescent girl becomes disappointed that one of her friends will not attend her birthday party. When the girl enquires as to why, her friend tells her that she does not have a new dress to wear and that she would therefore feel inadequate. Upon hearing that news, the birthday girl mandates that only old dresses should be worn. Her friend is appeased, and the birthday party proceeds.[66] Through this story the WCTU suggested that thrifty styles were a kindness to those who could not afford new clothing. In 1920 a report by *Woman's Century* on the Woman's Citizens' League in Hamilton (Ontario) offered a similar message. Members of this league decided to adopt modes of dress that would be "a rebuke to the woman who excited envy in others by her selfish spending."[67]

So concerned were some writers about the assumed sensitivities of lower-income people, in fact, that they advocated restraint in dress to avoid unfortunate outcomes. These included the notion that poor women, after seeing a beautiful "georgette blouse," would starve and even prostitute themselves to be able to purchase one.[68] Articles also included the idea that humility would dampen class conflict. According to *Woman's Century*, it was necessary for affluent women to combat "luxurious habits," particularly "display in dress," in order to stifle "class animosity and discontent." In this view, poorer women's awareness of "luxuries" caused them to aspire above their class station. Such an outcome would be "amongst the worst evils of our day."[69]

## Mastering the Gaze

Despite the general consensus within the women's press that fashion was a problem best avoided, there was one final response to fashion that merits attention. This was the view that instead of avoiding fashion, one should confront its problems head on. In other words, some writers suggested that women should master the art of attire. In this way they could subvert potential critique and simultaneously enhance their status. As WI member Mrs. Walter Hooker of Hillview (Ontario) said in 1910, "do not make the mistake of thinking that it does not matter how you look." Instead, homemakers should wear "nice clothes" at all times so that their attire could help their families appear "attractive, refined, and uplifting."[70]

The connection of clothing to status has a long history. According to Jan Noel, government officials in seventeenth- and eighteenth-century New France wore expensive, showy clothes to demonstrate their elite status.[71] Into the 1930s people in northern North America tied clothing to social rank. In interviews with women who lived in Toronto during the Depression, Srigley found that, time and again, interviewees mentioned clothing as a "marker of status."[72] According to some, it was important to wear one's finest attire when heading "downtown"; doing so would ensure they were treated "legitimately and respectably."[73] Women wishing to secure sales and clerical work paid especial attention to attire, as did women who wished to gain entry into sororities. For these women, dressing stylishly but modestly was key. Entry into dance halls, too, required certain forms of finery, as did engaging in protests on the street. For all of these occasions, Srigley argues, women took care to dress in ways considered "respectable" by the groups with whom they were interacting.[74]

An examination of the white club-women's press of the 1890s through the 1930s offers further indications of how many northern North Americans have tied clothing to social rank. According to many writers, in fact, clothing helped to demonstrate superiority. This superiority, in turn, was connected to class, in the sense that high-status clothing was defined as that not worn by poor women. It was also connected to nationalism. For some white wives and mothers, it was important to cultivate an elegant appearance. In this way women's bodies could symbolize the stated ideals of the English and French Canadian nations.

For writers in this vein, evidence of sophistication was a first consideration. When women neglected their looks, they demonstrated naivety. For example, according to Kitty Hardcastle, most contemporary women were "ugly" and needed training in the "art of dress." In her view, it was time for all women to learn the "principles of beauty" so they could become "beautiful."[75] On one level, of course, this passage purports to democratize beauty: Hardcastle promises to teach all readers her tricks. Yet, on another, it represents an equation of beauty with skill. Only by learning how to be beautiful, she argued, could women elevate their appearances.

Which skills in particular were needed? For many the key was simplicity. "Simplicity is always in good taste," said Hattie Orchard of the Ontario WIs in 1911.[76] Material of good quality, such as fine wools and linens, should be used, as Myrtle Hayward of the Manitoba WIs stated in 1922.[77] Moderation, too, was important. According to an anonymous 1920 article, true sophistication was achieved when women chose simple but well-tailored cuts that flattered and covered their bodies. Such cuts had to be made of high-quality materials, and furthermore they had to be in soft, muted tones. When women mastered the art of dressing according to these principles, they could demonstrate their sophistication. Moreover, their appearances would inspire both admiration and repose.[78]

Defining sartorial perfection in these ways, authors gave readers advice on how to appear attractive. At the same time they also revealed the profound sense of class superiority upon which their tastes were based. As Bourdieu reminds us, standards of taste are always constructed through class conflict. Notions of "self-imposed austerity, restraint, [and] reserve" are particularly prized by those in socially "dominant" positions, he says, for they reflect the "ease" and "asceticism" that their privilege allows.[79] Indeed, Canadian club-women's embrace of elegance demonstrated a clear bourgeois aesthetic. As American historian Nan Enstad points out, during the late nineteenth century bourgeois fashion experts argued that elaborate trimmings, bright colours, and eye-catching patterns were garish. Defining gentility in opposition to boldness, they developed a language of taste that prioritized muted colours, simple lines, and modest cuts. These characteristics, in turn, reflected the bourgeois feminine ideal, specifically the notion that virtuous women were simultaneously chaste and beautiful.[80]

If class privilege underlay many women's definitions of taste, so too did an assertion of nationalism. According to one 1920 article in Woman's Century, which was titled "Grace and Beauty: True Patriotism," it was only when a woman dressed with elegance that she revealed her nobility. After going through four years of war, its author wrote, it was time for women to step up and "exalt the people of our country." The author was especially bothered by the shortened sleeves and raised hemlines of the post-war era. By "chang[ing] extravagance into moderation" and "abolish[ing] ...

a lack of modesty," she said, women could "lead the way in ... matters spiritual as well as moral." Implied in this argument was the sense that war was a moral cleanser. Canadians had "prove[n] themselves" through war "to be of the same fine fibre as their fore-bears," the author claimed. Thus, it was time to abandon the out-landish styles of the post-war years and return to simplicity.[81]

At no time did this article employ the word *race* in its equation of modesty with nationalism. Nevertheless, by referring to the "fine fibre" of Canadians' forebears, she was employing the same kind of language that was common in racial rhetoric at the time. "In turn-of-the-century Anglo-Saxon thought," notes Mariana Valverde, "the paradigm of the human 'race' was the Anglo-Saxon Protestant ruling bloc, with other groups ... being regarded as human only by analogy." More than this, English thinkers tended to see reason and morality as specifically Anglo-Saxon traits, ones that kept the British "race" civilized and prevented it from descending into barbarity.[82] In that the "Grace and Beauty" author associated modest dress with nobility, and immodest dress with depravity, she revealed her own adherence to racist precepts. By dressing with decorum, she implied, women would return the Canadian nation to its ancestral – and hence Anglo-Saxon – glory.

It was not only English Canadian writers, however, who con-nected a moralistic and racist form of nationalism with modesty in dress. From the 1910s into the 1930s both the English and the French women's presses advised women to cover up. At issue were such features as low necklines, high slits, tight skirts, sleeve-less garments, bright colours, eye-catching materials, and any-thing transparent. All of these styles, they argued, made women ugly and promiscuous. As such, they threatened French Canadian womanhood.[83] The Cercles de fermières argued in 1921: "En sup-primant dans les toilettes tout ce qui sent le débraille et le vul-gaire, le remplaçant par la simplicité et la grâce qui constituent la véritable élégance et en perfectionnant ainsi le goût de nos femmes françaises."[84]

In suggesting that French women should aspire towards mod-esty, the *cercles* were connecting the identities of French Canadian women to their abilities to appear both chaste and sophisticated. This special mixture, they suggested, was the epitome of French womanhood. In making this claim, the *cercles* demonstrated their similarities to their English Canadian counterparts, revealing that class-based notions of taste were key to the *cercles'* definitions of beauty.

## Conclusion

In her 2005 book *Fresh Lipstick*, American writer Linda Scott takes issue with what she calls a desire among feminists to "reform the dress of others." In her view, white feminists in particular have been giving "higher moral value" to "simple, colorless, [and] asexual" dress since at least the eighteenth century. The "neo-Marxists" of the 1960s and 1970s were no different than "scholastic suffragists from the turn of the century" or even the "Puritans of the colonial period." All these groups privileged a "natural" look over a seemingly artificial one; each rejected the taint of fashion in favour of simplicity. Scott argues that it is time to reject the moralist strain running through feminist thought on fashion; it is also time to recognize that the "meaning of dress and grooming habits varies according to each woman's place in race, class, and history."[85]

Through a detailed examination of the writings of English and French Canadian women's advocates before 1940, this chapter helps clarify the issues that continue to structure feminist debates. Most obviously, it shows that despite the recent tendency to dismiss all previous feminists as puritanical do-gooders, not all twentieth-century women's advocates adopted moralist perspectives. Some authors, as we have seen, argued for a balance between comfort and fashion, stating that it was in fact possible to achieve both. Some writers took issue with the costs involved in staying in fashion, noting that if one wanted to maintain the respect of one's peers, one had to invest considerable sums of money into yearly fashion trends. For a few the moralists themselves were the problem. Surely by wearing shorter hemlines, as one writer put it, women could enlarge notions of social propriety, thus gaining more mobility and more respect in the process. And, for others, it was the objectification of women – not fashion – that was the real issue. Only when the power relations that made it possible for men to ogle women at will were dismantled, one advocate suggested, would the issue of what women wear cease to be a topic for discussion.

In addition to revealing the diversity of perspectives on fashion in the Canadian women's press, this chapter highlights the strength of the notion during this period that men had the right to ogle women. This point had two components: first, that men were widely perceived to be instigators of sexual activity; and second, that women's bodies were sexual icons and therefore also standard-bearers of morality. Regarding the first, it is clear that some writers worried about young women's appearances because they feared that when young women dressed in ways coded promiscuously, men could become emboldened to sexually attack them.

In terms of the second implication of the presumed sexuality of women's bodies – that it was women's bodies that symbolized the morals of society generally – this issue played out somewhat differently. For several Canadian writers it was necessary that women dressed modestly. Unlike those authors who called on women to do so to safeguard themselves from sexual assault, however, these writers said that women should dress modestly to protect the values of the English and French Canadian races. Along the same lines, some also said that in addition to dressing modestly, women should dress with refinement and elegance. In making such claims, these writers were clearly imposing race- and class-based standards upon all women who came within their purview. In their judgment, modest dress, together with subtle colours and high-quality fabrics, was the best path towards moral uplift. These writers, then, made explicit connections between modest, sophisticated appearances and the worth of the bodies upon which such appearances were constructed. Implicit in the arguments was the view that all who dressed in ways that contravened these values were themselves somehow degraded.

When considering such arguments, it is useful to return to contemporary rejections of purity within feminist debates on fashion. Certainly we can reject Scott's caricatures of all past feminists as strident moralists. At the same time, her arguments against morality carry weight. Even more so than today, English and French Canadian writers before 1940 viewed women's fashions in moralist terms. For many, to dress modestly and with sophistication was the pinnacle of female achievement. Elegant dress was a way to demonstrate high status within one's nation; it was part of the journey towards full citizenship. Unfortunately such constructions of womanhood denied the dignity and worth of all who dressed in ways that reflected either difficult economic circumstances or different value systems, or both. More than this, they upheld the view that women's bodies, by virtue of the sexualized status, were the moral standard-bearers of their nations. In this way they reinforced the belief that women's bodies were meant to be interpreted in sexualized terms. It fell to women, as sex objects and as mothers of the race, to promote their own worth by virtue of their carefully chosen attire. Such presumptions were obviously and in many ways profoundly unliberating.

*Chapter Six*

# Challenging Capitalism? The Limits of Collective Buying

In 1995, feminist historian Sheila Rowbotham argued that the contemporary marketplace was characterized by "individual consumers in individual homes buying individual products." This was not inevitable, however. "Markets," she wrote, "are social structures which have been shaped and reshaped historically." In the early twentieth century the rise of the individualist marketplace was not a "foregone conclusion." Instead, "there were alternative associative visions of how American society might develop, there were co-operative projects and movements which sought social control over consumption."[1]

This chapter suggests that during the first half of the twentieth century a variety of groups sought to make the Canadian marketplace more responsive to the needs of consumers. Women featured prominently in these efforts. Indeed, and as a growing number of scholars now demonstrate, co-operative movements led by female consumers flourished not only in North America but also in Australia, the United Kingdom, the Netherlands, France, Switzerland, Germany, Italy, and Spain before the Second World War.[2] Each movement was unique, but the campaigns can be broadly categorized as either price oriented or socially oriented. The central goal of price activists was to bring down prices in a manner responsive to the budgets of housewives. Social activists sought to shape the consumer marketplace in ways they perceived to be more just.[3]

To date, few scholars have paid attention to Canadian women's roles within consumer co-operation. In his work on English Canadian co-operatives Ian MacPherson notes that the movement embraced the "doctrine of domesticity."[4] Across the country, men managed most co-operative societies and comprised most of the membership base. They largely assumed that women were more suited to domestic labour and social organizing and thus were not suited to leadership.[5] Research by Rusty Neal on Nova Scotia co-operatives corroborates MacPherson's findings. From the 1910s through the 1930s, Nova Scotian co-operators assumed that women's chief roles in the movement were not as leaders but as supporters.[6]

Examining the role that women played in consumer co-operative movements in early twentieth-century Canada, this chapter shows that a variety of Canadian female consumers sought to transform consumption. They did not always accept the capitalistic premise that shopping had to be a solo activity, carried out by individual buyers in a profit-oriented marketplace. They promoted alternatives. In some cases they sought to lower prices and hence to divert profits from the market back to the consumers. In others, they sought to participate in a larger community collective, one that valued co-operation not only in the consumer but also in the producer and distributor realms.

Proponents of co-operative consumption in Canada had laudable aims. In practice, however, it was difficult to sustain their initiatives. Prior to the Second World War the mainstream co-operative movement foundered on gender. As this chapter demonstrates, male co-operators recognized that successful consumer co-operation depended on housewives, but they found it difficult to understand their consumer priorities. Men also had difficulty in sharing authority. In this way they resembled their counterparts in the United States. Studies on the Seattle labour movement and the Chicago consumer movement show that consumer co-operatives in these cities were unable to reconcile issues of gender. In as much as male leaders demanded the loyalty of female shoppers, items available through the co-operatives did not meet women's demands for quality, affordability, and convenience.[7] Rather than taking the working conditions of housewives seriously, however, male co-operators insisted that they should patronize co-operative stores, despite resultant increases to their domestic labour. It is therefore unsurprising that many women did not heed this call. Similar issues hindered the mainstream Canadian co-operative movement.

The Canadian women's co-operative movement, for its part, suffered from difficulties relating to class. As this chapter will show, some middle-class female co-operative initiatives contained implicit bias against lower-income women. For example, lower-income women – with their supposed penchant for convenience foods and cheap fashion items – were blamed for causing inflation. Through female-managed co-operative food stores, middle-class women attempted to make lower-income women purchase *only* foods in bulk. Such initiatives, as will be shown, were ineffective in convincing these women to become loyal co-operative shoppers.

Gender and class were not the only issues impeding the middle-class co-operative movement, however. Non-profit co-operatives were difficult to sustain over time. Offering items at low prices depended largely on volunteers – a model that was unsustainable in the long term. Other problems included being approved for permits, securing sale space, finding wholesale bargains, and forming commodity chain networks. Ultimately, gender, class, and logistical issues hindered Canadian consumer co-operation prior to the Second World War.

Analysing women and consumer co-operation within (a) the mainstream Canadian co-operative movement and (b) the middle-class women's movement, this chapter demonstrates that women's consumer co-operation in Canada stretches back to the 1910s.[8] In Canada as elsewhere, not everyone agreed that atomized and alienating modes of shopping were the only or best approach. Instead, many struggled to create new forms of consumer citizenship that prioritized affordability and community support. Even though such initiatives failed, they remain notable for their attempts to ameliorate the individualist nature of the capitalist marketplace.

## Gender and Co-operation

Most Canadian co-operative societies in existence before the Second World War were managed by men. Countrywide the membership structure of most co-operatives was premised on the family unit, not the individual. As such, members had one vote, and only one membership could be held within a family. Male heads of households overwhelmingly held these memberships. Furthermore, male-dominated producer and marketing co-operatives were much more powerful than consumer co-operatives. This disparity was the result of male members having a greater interest in production and marketing, as well as the presumption that consumption was less profitable – and hence less important – than production and distribution.[9]

Despite the dominance of men, women did have a role. In his overview of the *Canadian Co-operator*, Canada's largest co-operative periodical before the Second World War, MacPherson finds that the co-operatives' press occasionally featured such exceptional female co-operators as "Nellie McClung, Francis Marion Beynon, Agnes Macphail, and Irene Parlby." Sometimes these references noted the "potential" of women and co-operation. For the most part, however, they aimed at teaching women "how to become better homemakers."[10] Rusty Neal, who also studied the *Co-operator's* coverage of women, affirms MacPherson's findings. According to Neal, the periodical suggested that women's greatest value to the co-operative movement lay in "buying, distributing, and processing consumer goods from the marketplace for use in the family/household."[11] *Co-operator* advertisements echoed this messaging. According to advertisements placed by the Co-operative Wholesale Society throughout the interwar years, "the role of women as consumers" was as implicit as it was in "other retailers' advertisements ... in the national daily newspapers."[12]

In addition to studying the role of women in the *Co-operator*, MacPherson and Neal have explored further how George Keen, Canada's leading co-operative advocate in the first half of the twentieth century, envisioned women. According to MacPherson, Keen "accepted fully the doctrine of domesticity." Given that women were in charge of domestic affairs, he thought that their main contribution to the co-operative movement would be through "their loyal patronage."[13] In keeping with this view, Keen spearheaded two "national drives," one in 1910 and one in 1933, to "establish women's co-operative guilds."[14] He did so with a view to facilitating individual guilds that would then affiliate themselves with local co-operative societies. Together they could form a national women's auxiliary that would perform the educational work necessary to building the co-operative movement.[15]

By suggesting that Canadian women form co-operative guilds, Keen was following the British model. During this period the

British Women's Co-operative Guild boasted approximately fifty-eight thousand members who were dispersed throughout smaller guilds in England, Ireland, and Scotland. Together these guilds engaged in important movement-building work, including education and social organizing. Crucially they were also independent from the male co-operative societies.[16] According to Margaret Llewelyn Davies, the general secretary of the English guilds, women's autonomy was key to "obtain[ing] the experience and self-reliance which is necessary for really effective work."[17] Keen, however, disagreed. As he wrote in a letter to Davies, the "large areas and small population" in Canada "contribute to a purely parochial attitude of mind." As a result, he claimed that, unlike British women, Canadian women were uninterested in progressive reform.[18] For this reason, Keen ignored Davies's suggestion to make women's guilds independent and instead went ahead with an auxiliary model.

Despite Keen's paternalism, some women did form auxiliaries. In Saskatchewan in 1918, a Mrs. Yates, "wife of a Wheat Pool employee," formed a Regina-based guild. It was affiliated with the co-operative store on Dewdney Avenue, and its purpose was to "help inform the women who supported the store and to interest others in joining." The guild remained active until the co-operative store closed. In 1935 a new store opened on Albert Street, and the guild was revived. In Moose Jaw a co-operative guild formed around a "purchasing group [that] bought coal and bulk commodities." Women in interwar Yorkton and Lafleche also participated in guilds. The group in Yorkton was a "rural" guild, while the Lafleche group was interested in banking and investing. The guild in Saskatoon was tied to a store, and when the store closed, so did the guild. Nonetheless, its members revived the guild in 1948.[19]

Saskatchewan was also home to one of most prominent female co-operators of the time, Violet McNaughton. McNaughton was a seasoned political organizer who had been prominent in the agrarian movement since the 1910s. She was especially active in the Saskatchewan Grain Growers Association and was once president of the Women Grain Growers.[20] In her view, co-operation in all three realms of economic activity – production, distribution, and consumption – was the only way to eradicate selfishness from the marketplace.[21] In keeping with this vision, she promoted consumer co-operatives. As she stated in 1927, "co-operative marketing of our produce ... touches ... only one side of our economic life." For this reason, "co-operative buying must come if benefits of co-operation are to be realized."[22]

Despite McNaughton's support of consumer co-operation, she engaged in few initiatives. During the winter of 1913–14 she and her colleagues from the women's auxiliary of the Hillview Grain Growers' Association started an Eaton's buying club. Tired from their "much needless journeying to and from the [rail] station" to pick up individual parcels, the Hillview group had decided to form a club by which individual orders could be submitted in one letter to the T. Eaton Company department store in Winnipeg. Eaton's, in return, would package all the orders together into "one large shipment." A member of the women's auxiliary then collected the shipment at the rail station and notified the others that their parcels had arrived.[23] Other efforts included organizing "a beef ring to distribute fresh meat" and managing a "buying and distribution" initiative for "farm supplies."[24] These ventures, however, did not last long. McNaughton devoted more energy to producer co-operatives, reflecting the fact that, on the prairies, producer co-operatives were more successful than consumer ones. Indeed, under the 1939 Saskatchewan Co-operative Associations Act, there were 595 co-operatives in the province; of these, 332 were dedicated to marketing "bulk commodities or petroleum products," and 136 existed for maintaining community halls. By contrast, only 47 co-operatives were "organized to operate stores."[25] Given the relative scarcity of co-operative buying organizations, it is unsurprising that McNaughton had concluded by 1927 that "consumers' co-operation [remained] unsuccessful ... both in the United States and in Canada." Nonetheless she remained a supporter of consumer co-operatives in principal. Whereas "producers' co-operation is confined within a certain occupational group [such as wheat farmers], the consuming group includes every man, woman and child in existence," she said. For this reason, consumers' co-operation, even more so than producers' co-operation, could "furnish the basis ... for what is often spoken of as 'The Co-operative Commonwealth.'"[26]

Women's guilds also appeared in Nova Scotia. In 1919 a women's guild was established by members of the British Canadian

Co-operative, a store located in Sydney Mines on Cape Breton Island. In keeping with Keen's vision of male oversight, this guild became an "affiliate" of the Co-operative Union of Canada. According to Neal, the "all male Education Committee" of the British Canadian store managed the women's guild.[27] Until 1951, the year the guild disbanded, the auxiliary engaged in educational, social, and other forms of community labour. The British Canadian Co-operative had been an important institution in eastern Nova Scotia. For example, in the 1940s it employed more than 160 individuals and had "3,000 member families," in a town with a population of just over 8,000.[28] Due to the size of the British National Co-operative, it is likely that the women's guild was also influential.[29]

According to Neal, the guild was most active during the interwar years. In the 1920s it "organized massive local parades of up to three thousand children" and "sponsored picnics for the entire town and surrounding region." During this time the guild also established a "stamp scheme" that allowed children to visit the co-operative and obtain goods. When the coal miners went on strike, the guild ran soup kitchens and "showed up in the protest demonstrations." Other activities included holding public lectures, teaching children about co-operatives, and organizing various social events.[30]

As the history of co-operative guilds in Saskatchewan and Nova Scotia shows, many of Canada's co-operative guilds operated in connection with co-operative stores. This link reveals the dominant belief held by co-operators about feminized consumption. By the late 1920s the connection between female consumers and co-operation had become so commonplace that the phrase *woman with the basket* had become a standard trope. This message is illustrated by an undated photograph taken in Sydney Mines that shows an adolescent girl holding a basket with the slogan "Canadian Success of Co-ops Depends on the Woman with the Basket" (fig. 6.1).[31]

Continuing into the 1930s and beyond, Canadian co-operators suggested that the shopper, not the leader, was the chief role of women in the movement. An example in Antigonish (Nova Scotia) during the Great Depression provides a case study. Between 1930 and 1940 approximately seventy co-operatives were created in that town, half of which were consumer co-operatives.[32] Spearheaded by the Department of Extension at St Francis Xavier University, the

6.1 Participant in Co-operative Day Parade, Sydney Mines, Nova Scotia; name unknown, c. 1920s. Library and Archives Canada, PA 188169.

Antigonish movement aimed to cultivate a sustainable economy in eastern Nova Scotia. This region had suffered numerous setbacks early in the twentieth century. Steel and coal production had declined, fisheries had become less profitable, and farming had become less viable. As a result, the region was in a state of "generalized distress."[33] Co-operation, according to faculty members Moses Coady and Jimmy Tompkins, would allow Nova Scotians to take control of their circumstances. As a popular slogan put it, Nova Scotians would become "Masters of Their Own Destiny."[34]

While the majority of people involved in the Antigonish movement were men, some of the promoters were women. During the 1930s female staff members at St Francis Xavier were central to the efforts of the Extension Department. For example, the department's administrative assistant, Kay Thompson Desjardin, travelled with Coady to provide secretarial services. Departmental instructors and librarians Sister Marie Michael MacKinnon and Sister Mary Anselm served as home economics instructors; MacKinnon was also the department's librarian. Towards the latter half of the decade St Francis Xavier economics graduate Ida Delaney joined the department and took over MacKinnon's responsibilities. Together these women organized conferences, arranged study clubs, and wrote course curricula. Many of them also travelled, performing the consciousness-raising work of the movement.[35]

According to the literature produced by Extension Department staff, women were necessary to co-operative success. Nevertheless, the department portrayed women's roles narrowly. In her study of the treatment of gender in the *Extension Bulletin*, a newsletter written by the staff and distributed between 1933 and 1939, Neal found that women were represented as "mothers, wives and home economists." Men, by contrast, were shown to be involved in the "formal economy." Overall, the *Bulletin* portrayed co-operation as a male "preserve."[36]

Given these representations, it is unsurprising that during the Second World War, the Extension Department created a pamphlet called *What Can the Women Do?* It was meant to encourage "All Members of Women's Study Clubs" to become interested in "co-operative stores, credit unions, canning factories, better farm homes, improvement of rural conditions, [and] handicraft work."[37] Since 1934 the Extension Department had been running women's study clubs, which were meant to teach Nova Scotian women about co-operation. The clubs were popular, with 350 "active" clubs recorded by 1938.[38] Nevertheless, Nova Scotian women remained marginal. Men dominated the co-operative boards throughout the province, and because only one membership per household was allowed, they also constituted the majority of the membership base.

Even as Extension Department staff members portrayed women as homemakers, they also viewed them as consumers. During the early years of the Second World War, department worker Ida Gallant Delaney wrote a booklet called *Shopping-Basket Economics*. Intended as a text for short courses, it was also distributed to the women's study clubs. The booklet promoted the principles of "intelligent buying" that were being taught in home economics classes. Yet, whereas the home economics movement taught students to shop for the sake of the nation, Delaney's text encouraged readers to shop for the sake of co-operation. According to Delaney, co-operative "women know that without them the co-operative store will not succeed, nor will the co-operative wholesale succeed." Indeed, "it is on their purchases that the co-operative ventures of the future will be built."[39]

The text opens with an anecdote about "Mrs. Consumer" who has forgotten her shopping list. She arrives at a store in a frenzy, trips over a cereal display, and, because she feels overwhelmed, buys items in a haphazard fashion. This tizzy, the reader is told, was brought on by Mrs. Consumer's lack of preparedness and by the volume of advertisements in the store: "The soap flakes were surrounded by a bewildering array of signs. Mrs. Consumer changed her mind twice and then finally shut her eyes and speared a box of soap flakes with her hatpin [because] that was easier than deciding which kind to buy" (fig. 6.2).[40] Delaney and home economists hence agreed that the proliferation of advertising and products caused by mass distribution had made buying more complicated: "There are thousands of more things to buy, new products, old products in new forms ... many brands ... many sizes."[41] Her booklet was similar to home economics lessons in so far as Delaney recommended that money could be saved by buying in bulk and by increasing home production. If Mrs. Consumer would make her own bread, beans, porridge, and baby food, instead of buying pre-packaged and canned items, she could save approximately a hundred dollars per year. In Delaney's estimation, the time that Mrs. Consumer saved by purchasing convenience foods was not worth the higher financial costs. In the same paragraph where she advised women to save money on food, Delaney suggested that Mrs. Consumer could use these savings to purchase an electric washing machine.[42] Accordingly, Delaney thought it was better to spend time cooking than doing laundry. For many housekeepers, however, it was more practical to purchase convenience items than it was to save money. This was especially the case for those who had to provide their families with three meals a day.

By arguing that housewives should purchase washers, Delaney showed the same support of household modernization that was common in many rural improvement programs. She presumed that rural Nova Scotian women desired modern appliances especially. In another *Shopping-Basket Economics* passage Delaney describes Mrs. Consumer's visit to a "small tourist home." The visit was a revelation for Mrs. Consumer because "the number of labor saving gadgets simply amazed her." She was impressed by the electric cake mixer, potato peeler, toaster, and electric washer. As a result, Mrs. Consumer resolved to study the capitalist marketplace in order to teach herself and others how to be better consumers. Delaney wrote, "Consumption is a little raggedy, undernourished dog running after the streamlined train of production," and "something must be done to put the breath of life in the dog."[43] As this passage indicates, Delaney assumed that modern living conditions would improve the lives of rural Nova Scotians. She assumed that they desired modern appliances and that it was her responsibility as an adult educator to provide rural women with the training required to emancipate themselves from pre-industrial conditions. In this view, modernity was akin to happiness. Despite the fact that modern lifestyles required new forms of domestic labour in terms of learning about, shopping for, and spending money on electric goods, Delaney assumed that *consumptive* labour was preferable to so-called pre-modern cooking.

If *Shopping-Basket Economics* resembled the many treatises on consumption coming out of home economics during this period, it also supported a similar consumer ethos. According to both home economics theory and *Shopping-Basket Economics*, consumerism – or a conscious shopping practice informed by politics, economics,

Mrs. Consumer changed her mind twice and then finally shut her eyes and speared a box of soap flakes with her hatpin.

6.2 Overwhelmed consumer in need of guidance. Ida Gallant Delaney, *Shopping-Basket Economics* (Antigonish, NS: St Francis Xavier University, c. 1942), 5.

and morality – was a new phenomenon. Delaney's portrayal of Mrs. Consumer aptly highlights this focus. In the story Mrs. Consumer is portrayed as unable to make good decisions. She states that "'the sellers make a great fuss about selling; the art of salesmanship is pretty well developed ... but I, I just buy with no skill at all in the art of buymanship.'" Accordingly Mrs. Consumer concludes that "'it should be up to consumers to figure out how we can put order in the economics of our shopping baskets. We are the people who have to catch up.'"[44] By depicting consumption as a new phenomenon in which women had to gain expertise, Delaney laid out a new identity for women. She implied that under pre-modern conditions women had slaved away at thankless domestic tasks, whereas, with the arrival of modernity, women could assume new, glorious roles. It was through the professionalization of consumption that individual housewives could help direct the economic future.

Yet, while in many ways the approach of Delaney to shopping resembled that of the home economists, the location in which shopping should occur varied. Whereas home economists imagined homemakers as individual shoppers making choices among various stores, Delaney portrayed Nova Scotian consumers as members of a larger co-operative society. As such, it was their responsibility to shop in ways that benefited co-operation. According to Delaney, shopping at non-co-operative stores helped to "keep up a system" that "has denied [the reader's] family a decent and a happy livelihood." Shopping at the co-operative, by contrast, contributed "a plank in the structure of industry controlled by the consumer."[45] Unlike home economists, co-operative consumers had to investigate the production and quality of each item, but Delaney encouraged housewives to trust the co-operative board. For example, many co-operative stores in Nova Scotia sold goods branded with a "CO-OP" label. For Delaney, this label meant that "the wholesale has made a study of different lines of goods, and has arranged for manufacturers to prepare certain products specially for the co-operatives." Accordingly, by purchasing goods with this label, shoppers were assured that other co-operators had vetted the items.[46]

That women should base their shopping decisions according to the "CO-OP" label of approval was contentious. As Delaney herself acknowledged, while the male boards were responsible for ordering store items, they were also clueless as to women's shopping preferences. Delaney wrote, "There were, for example, the [unfashionable] housedresses that Mrs. Consumer's co-operative could not sell although they were sturdy enough to wear forever." The fictitious co-operative store frequented by Mrs. Consumer also stocked "expensive hemstitched sheets which the majority of the members could not afford," with the result that "they had to buy sheeting elsewhere." Women's fashions and sheet prices, Delaney explained, "are very simple things to the housekeeper" but are not so simple to "an all-man Board of Directors."[47]

In her call for housewives' support, Delaney recognized that other shopping options were available. She was also familiar with the reasons that women chose to shop elsewhere, one being lower prices. By acknowledging that many women shopped elsewhere, Delaney made a careful argument for prioritizing co-operation over budget. She explained that co-operatives in Nova Scotia charged "market prices" in order to cover costs. For Delaney, however, shopping was not merely about the consumer but about the producer. She urged readers to consider the consequences of "loss leaders" for co-operative stores. When shoppers visited private stores to purchase loss leaders (items marked below cost so as to attract customers), they hurt the co-operatives. Delaney opined that it was better for individuals to pay higher prices for items at a co-operative store, which would in effect be repaid to them at the end of the month through members' profits. It was through this practice that co-operative stores could gain strength and, over time, compete with private retailers.[48]

Shopping conditions also affected co-operative business. Proponents of co-operatives were of the position that it was not the responsibility of the store to meet the "standard of cleanliness" and "courtesy" available elsewhere. Rather, according to Delaney, it was the fault of shoppers who, instead of complaining to their boards, shopped elsewhere. As such, she admonished female shoppers to fulfil their responsibilities as co-operative supporters and to raise their complaints with store directors. Delaney surmised that if boards were aware that shoppers found their stores unsatisfactory, the situation would be rectified.[49]

Given the amount of work involved in co-operative shopping, it is unsurprising that co-operative stores were a hard sell in rural

Nova Scotia. Conflicts between all-male management boards and female shoppers, combined with poor service, dirty stores, uncompetitive pricing, and inadequate stock, meant that many women preferred to shop elsewhere. As demonstrated in *Shopping-Basket Economics*, many Nova Scotian housewives preferred low prices, clean stores, and courteous service to supporting the co-operative store. Being a good co-operative consumer entailed much more than merely shopping at a certain location. It meant less convenient shopping and more bulk shopping, reliance on co-operative grocery brands, involvement in co-operative store management, and work towards long-term store improvements. For these reasons many women preferred to continue to shop at for-profit retailers. Indeed, while any kind of shopping could be a frustrating endeavour, shopping at a co-operative store that demanded total loyalty could be even more arduous. For women in interwar and wartime Nova Scotia, as for women elsewhere in Canada, shopping remained a predominantly private activity, one that was shaped by their individual needs and proclivities.

## Middle-Class Women and Co-operation

Whereas co-operation offered limited emancipation from the marketplace, it was possible that the women's movement – focused on female leadership and theoretically responsive to women's needs – offered better opportunities for those seeking freedom from capitalism. This section considers such a possibility by exploring the middle-class English Canadian women's movement and asking whether it offered better alternatives.

The Women's Institutes (WIs), the National Council of Women of Canada (NCW), and a number of smaller groups demonstrated sustained interest in co-operation between 1900 and 1940. Unlike the male-dominated co-operative movement, the middle-class women's movement approached the topic from a consumer perspective. These women were often homemakers who shopped daily. Their chief interest in co-operation hence stemmed not from a producer or distributor viewpoint, but from the disadvantages that individual consumers faced. They argued that it was better for women to pool their resources to defeat the profit principle than for individual women to keep going it alone.

One of the earliest references to co-operation in the English Canadian women's press occurred in 1912. That year the British Columbia WIs applauded a suggestion made by the BC minister of
agriculture for housewives to begin "securing ... supplies and commodities for home use by whole-sale." Doing so, he stated, "will
result in a material saving to each individual member."[50] Throughout the war years organized rural women demonstrated interest.
One year into the war, the women's auxiliary of the United Farmers of Alberta looked into "co-operative buying of fruit from the
producers in B.C."[51] Again in 1915, the Women Grain Growers'
Association of Normanton (Manitoba) discussed "co-operative
buying amongst the women," with members assuming that it was
"likely to go ahead."[52]

Co-operation was not limited to rural settings. During this early
period women in urban areas were also interested in the topic.
The Housewives' League movement, active in Ontario, Quebec,
and Nova Scotia between 1913 and 1917, was one of the largest
collective-buying initiatives to emerge in Canada before the Second World War. The league was inspired by the New York–based
National Housewives' League (NHL), which had made international headlines due to a 1912 butter boycott in which 165,000
housewives had participated. Holding boycotts and conducting
collective-buying experiments, the NHL formed local branches
throughout the northwestern United States. Their main goal was to
lower food prices, but they also sought to improve food quality.[53]

One of Canada's first Housewives' Leagues formed in Toronto
in response to living costs. In the fall of 1913, tension had mounted
over increasing food prices. According to the *Toronto Daily Star*,
milk had risen to "10 cents ... a quart," and "lamb chop bones," due
to their high cost, were "being carefully scraped."[54] The price of
eggs was egregious; prices had increased from less than 10 cents a
dozen in the summer to "30 cents a dozen" in December.[55] As a re
sult, Toronto members of the Canadian Household Economic Association (CHEA) formed a Canadian chapter of the Housewives'
League. Several association members sat on the league's executive,
including "Mrs. Deans, Mrs. Rainey, Miss Venn, Mrs. MacIver,
Mrs. Fotheringham, [and] Mrs. MacVicar."[56] By the end of January 1914 the league had a hundred members.[57] Four months later,
five hundred women had joined.[58] The league was guided by three

steadfast "rules": "To reduce the high cost of food, to obtain sanitary conditions wherever food is sold, and [to work towards] honest [food] weight."[59] These rules related to the overarching goals of the league: to lower food prices, improve vendors' facilities, and reduce food profiteering. The organizers assumed that these goals would ultimately help the housewife buy more nutritious fare.

The Toronto Housewives' League embarked on several initiatives to accomplish its goals. First, it sought to change how housewives shopped. At an early meeting the executive informed members that it "expected" them to "buy fresh produce where the middleman has as far as possible been eliminated." Members were advised also to "watch market prices and boycott stores with unnecessarily high prices; to refuse to purchase cold storage products held to advance prices or to the detriment of condition; to plan orders so that only one delivery a day need be made; and to pay cash or settle credit promptly."[60] It was hoped that the collective pursuit of these goals would lower prices and ensure quality. By calling for such practices, the executive demonstrated its belief in the strength of numbers; only through collective action could better conditions be created. At the same time, the executive also positioned housewives as responsible for high prices. Along with Julian Heath, president of the American National Housewives' League, members agreed that "the housewife who supplies the demand [is] to blame" for poor quality and high costs.[61] Guest speaker George Putnam, the superintendent of the Ontario WIs, repeated this sentiment. He told members that "women do not understand the comparative values of foods and comparative prices." For Putnam, it was imperative to "educate our women in the wisest methods of buying," in as much as "many housekeepers ... are wasteful through ignorance." His statements were received with applause.[62]

The league's position that housewives required education in order to bring down prices echoed that of both the home economics movement and the co-operative movement. Middle-class club-women, home economics instructors, and co-operative educators alike assumed that if they could change how women shopped, the marketplace could be reformed. Yet these approaches were condescending and unrealistic for lower-income women, many of whom had little choice but to purchase goods within their budget. Furthermore, by focusing on the behaviour of shoppers, club-women scapegoated individual women rather than challenging major corporations.

To help spread the message of intelligent housekeeping, the league invited guest speakers to its meetings. Members heard lectures on consumer issues by such prominent speakers as Lockie Wilson, Julian Heath, and Christine Frederick. Wilson's lecture, delivered in January 1914, was particularly well received. According to Wilson, distribution channels between producers and consumers required immediate improvement. He described western Canadian wheat distribution as inefficient because it was shipped to England before it was returned to Canada. Toronto milk production was also chaotic: "On Huron street one morning I saw as many as 12 wagons delivering milk, crossing and re-crossing one another." He reasoned that if distribution could be improved, consumers would benefit.[63] Frederick's lecture, given simultaneously to the Canadian Business Women's Club and the Housewives' League, was titled "The Business of Housekeeping."[64] Frederick, an American author known for her publications on scientific homemaking, was a proponent of both advertising and intelligent shopping.[65] The content of her Toronto speech is unknown, but she may have promoted the modernization of Canadian homemaking.

The Housewives' League also engaged in lobbying and outreach. Members presented their views to the commissioners of the federal Cost of Living Inquiry in February of 1914 in Toronto. Angry that local farm produce was being left to rot outside of Toronto due to a lack of distribution, the league suggested that the parcel-post system be modified so that farmers could ship directly to consumers.[66] A couple of months later, the league's president and her colleague Miss Lucy Doyle travelled to the new suburb of Oakwood to give a talk on "the high cost of living" to the British Imperial Association. They argued that big food "combines" were responsible for high prices. It was then up to women to form "the biggest trust in the world's history" to "make the manufacturer pay attention."[67] The league's appearance at the association is important; it suggests that the league was seeking an alliance with British-identified groups. According to Doyle, the league was "best qualified to speak" to the British Imperial Association.

While the Housewives' League had many initiatives, sales were its most significant one. Beginning in January 1914 the league began purchasing merchandise directly from local farmers. Members then hosted large sales where they sold the merchandise directly to consumers. Acting on a volunteer basis, they held these sales to cut out the middleman and offer lower prices. In addition, league members hoped to eliminate dishonesty from food dealings. By buying directly from producers, they inspected and priced their food accordingly.[68] Sales were also a way for members to improve the quality of food available to Torontonians. Whereas packaged foods were often "adulterated" with cheap preservatives, whole foods purchased directly from local growers were assumed to be "pure."[69]

The first sale put on by the Toronto Housewives' League occurred at the end of January 1914. Given its success, the league had to secure a larger venue for the next one. The most successful sale in its history was held on 3 February 1914 at the St Andrew's market on Richmond Street. It was open to all "women in town, whether members or not."[70] Patrons could purchase 300 dozen eggs priced at 40 cents per "two dozen," and 200 pounds of butter priced at "27 cents a pound." Chicken was sold for 20 cents a pound, duck for 18 cents a pound, and grapefruit for 5 cents. Customers could also buy large portions of apples. The sale was so anticipated that two hundred women lined up at the entrance (fig. 6.3). According to the *Toronto Daily Star*, the crush resulted in the entrance doors being broken. Consequently two police officers – already assigned to the market – began admitting the shoppers "two by two." Women continued to arrive throughout the day, many of whom disembarked from the "Queen street cars, with fruit baskets, club bags, string bags, and paper bags suspended from their arms."[71]

Following the success of its February sale, the Housewives' League took stock. It was obvious that there was a huge demand for affordable, good-quality food. At the same time they realized that it was difficult for a volunteer organization to meet this demand. In addition to contacting local suppliers and arranging for the delivery of goods, league members had to inspect and price the merchandise, arrange sale locations, sell food to customers, handle all financial aspects, manage emergencies, and clean up after each event.[72] Selling local good-quality food at cost required large amounts of volunteer labour. For this reason league members decided that future sales would only be for members. Following

CRUSH TO BUY HOUSEWIVES' PRODUCE BARGAINS.
It was a sad day for the "High Cost of Living" yesterday when the Housewives' League sold produce at cost.
The crush was great while the bargains lasted.

6.3 Shoppers and their children waiting in line to enter the Housewives'
League Sale, 3 February 1914. The caption reads: "Crush to Buy Housewives'
Produce Bargains. It was a sad day for the 'High Cost of Living' yesterday
when the Housewives' League sold produce at cost. The crush was great
while the bargains lasted." ("Crush to Buy Housewives' Produce Bargains,"
*Toronto Daily Star*, 4 February 1914)

this decision they created three tiers of membership. Women who
wanted to attend sales but not participate in the league could purchase white-button memberships for "ten cents." Blue buttons
could be purchased for fifty cents by "active members." "Sustain-
ing members," meanwhile, could pay one dollar for membership
Presumably, by establishing this membership hierarchy, the league
hoped to offset some of its operating costs. It also attempted to
give the best buying advantages to those who were most active in
the association.

By April 1914, Toronto newspapers had stopped reporting on
league sales. Either the Housewives' League had ceased to report
its sales to the press, or, more likely, the sales were no longer open
to the public. League members continued to purchase food for their
own use. Towards the end of May, local farmer John Pringle attended a league meeting to discuss the difficulty of delivering vegetables to each member. While he was committed to bringing his
produce directly to consumers, he required "a sufficient number

of customers ... in a convenient radius" to do so.[73] As he indicated, direct trade between farmers and consumers was difficult. Either the farmer required time and resources to make deliveries, or the consumer had to do the same to pick up merchandise. Either way, the experiment by the Housewives' League was starting to make it evident to both producer and consumer that distribution required more resources than the league had available.

At this point, the Housewives' League shifted its focus from League-organized sales to establishing permanent farmers' markets or "curb markets" throughout the city. The St Lawrence market was in operation, but league members argued that it was too far from residential neighbourhoods to allow for convenient daily shopping. Worse, "meat was left exposed on low shelves and in places where poultry plucking went on." Vendors at the market, meanwhile, used scales that "were alleged to vary." The market further lacked accountability mechanisms. For example, there was "no registration of sellers so that the woman who is cheated, or thinks she is," had no place to turn for "redress."[74] Given this state of affairs, the league began campaigning for four kerbside markets in each quadrant (west end, east, north, and south) of the city. It asked the city's board of control for approval, stating that the league's markets would cost the city "little except their approval." Moreover, the markets "would cost the farmers nothing in the way of rentals." The board, however, declined to discuss the proposal and promised to respond to the league at a later date.[75]

In July 1914, as a result of its advocacy, a Mr. P. Graham offered the Housewives' League a piece of land in the Oakwood neighbourhood on which they could hold farmers' markets. Given that Oakwood was a new suburb, developers likely thought that a market would attract buyers.[76] There is no evidence to indicate that the league accepted Graham's offer. In fact, considering the records of that summer, members probably refused it. Their meeting on the 19 May appeared to be their last meeting of the season. It was common for Toronto club-women to put their activities on hold over the summer.[77] When the league resumed in late August, it submitted only food-price reports to the *Toronto Daily Star*.[78] During the association's meeting at the end of September the CHEA announced that the Housewives' League would now "confine its activities strictly to the matter of the food supply, watching the price markets and communicating with the Government." According to the president of the CHEA, due to the outbreak of war in August between the British Empire and Germany, women's time was to be spent solely on the war effort. She further stated that "most of the members were at present busily working with knitting needles and machines in aid of the Patriotic League." As such, "the year's work ... would have an altered horoscope."[79]

Given that the Housewives' League continued submitting price reports to the *Star* during this time, it is likely that members remained committed to food issues. Thus the virtual disbandment of the league in September 1914 was probably related to the sheer scope of volunteer activities required for its efforts, rather than to the war effort. Over the previous six months the league had changed its executive, as well as continuously searched for representatives to co-ordinate food sales and deliveries in specific districts.[80] By September, members likely accepted that the work involved to cut out the middleman exceeded the capacities of volunteers. Their criticisms of the food industry, while valiant, were simply too much to tackle given their limited resources.

Despite facing increasing obstacles, Toronto's club-women continued to pursue co-operative initiatives for the rest of the decade. In December 1916 the CHEA used the parlour at the Young Women's Christian Association to discuss the "high price of eggs," noting that each of Toronto's three farmers' markets sold eggs at a different price. Members blamed distributors for markups and afterwards launched a citywide egg boycott. As a part of this action they resolved to "establish direct communication between producer and consumer" and to purchase eggs at cost. Their inspiration to do so came from the American Housewives' League, whose goal was to lower the prices of household staples,[81] In a 1916 letter to the editor, published in the *Toronto Daily Star*, a contributor by the pen name "Another Housekeeper" argued that profiteering was the cause of wartime inflation. She called on readers to "get a number of friends or neighbours to order together, and buy in large quantities" to fight this "greedy monster." She suggested that they do so particularly for soap, "canned goods," flour, and sugar.[82] Given the content of her letter, it is likely that she was part of the club-women's movement.

Women elsewhere also organized during this time. The Housewives' League in St Catharines held its first meeting in late

January 1914, during which fifty members joined. They "bought beef and pork in quarters on the market and had it cut up for them by a man who used to work as a butcher." This allowed members to get the "finest steak and beef roasts for eighteen cents a pound against twenty-five cents in the stores, and as low as ten to fourteen cents for coarser cuts." They also purchased wholesale potatoes, which netted them a savings of ten cents a bushel. By the end of January the league had planned to buy butter in bulk, which they would divide among themselves. In so doing, they could buy butter at "five or six cents" less than the price of packaged butter in stores.[83]

Women in Ottawa also began to organize. In January 1914 a group of affluent women formed their own branch of the Housewives' League in response to the rise in food prices during the fall of 1913. By March the league had five hundred members.[84] Well aware of the commonly pointed-to culprits of rising food costs, members took it upon themselves to address the factors that were within their own sphere of action. They pledged to "pay all accounts promptly" and keep their orders to "one delivery a day." In so doing, they sought to minimize overhead. The Ottawa league was more conservative than were its counterparts in Toronto, in that it did not explicitly blame farmers and merchants for markups. Instead, it attempted to work with these groups. For example, the Ottawa league declared that it would not hold sales "to compete with retailers" provided retailers acted responsibly. Members would, however, hold sales in the event that prices rose, and "a boycott [was] found necessary." They also viewed farmers as potential allies. This is reflected in one of the league's goals, which was to "bring together producer and consumer, that prices may be satisfactory to both."[85]

Despite the fact that the Ottawa league employed a delicate approach, members vowed to defend the interests of shoppers and to raise awareness of poor shopping conditions. Members pledged to "demand clean shops"; "co-operate with the retailer in trying to secure commodities which are in quantity and quality what is paid for"; "insist on full weights and measures"; and "report to the society all cases of dirty shops, particularly in which food is exposed to contamination." Primarily, the Ottawa league sought to curtail profiteering, which they took as a personal affront. According to a league organizer, there are "certain people" in the food business "who ... smile as they pocket the housewives' money."[86]

By March of 1915 an organization called the Ottawa Household League had opened a co-operative store that was designed to help the town's housewives procure healthy food. It is unknown whether the Ottawa Household League was affiliated with, or comprised the same membership base, as the Ottawa Housewives' League. However, given that each organization was affiliated with the Local Council of Women, it is likely that they were the same group. In addition to buying in bulk to eliminate the costs added by middlemen, the Household League wanted to teach women how to shop. To do so, the president of the league, Mrs. Wilson, explained that its store "refus[ed] to stock wasteful and extravagant foods." In this way it would limit options, thereby helping to reduce the cost of living, while promoting wholesome living. Wilson told the following anecdote to convey her intentions: "One woman came in with a charitable order for one dollar" and wanted to buy "cold meats," "pickles," and "biscuits." Wilson informed her that "the shop had none of these things." As a result, the shopper had to "take out her order in many pounds of flour, rolled oats, rice, beans and similar valuable foods." Wilson said that she gave the shopper "recipes of simple, inexpensive dishes," copies of which the shop always kept on hand.[87]

As Wilson's anecdote implies, the Ottawa Household League considered cold meats, pickles, and biscuits to be "wasteful and extravagant." Its position was that charity recipients should purchase unprocessed foods and make their food from scratch. By doing so, they would eat more nutritiously and save money. Wilson failed to consider the reasons that those "receiving help from the city" – meaning municipal charity – would choose processed food and suggested that poor people had bad shopping and eating habits and needed to be disciplined. Through her anecdote she assumed a binary between the Ottawa Household League and the city's poor. Wilson positioned league members as experts on food, and relief recipients as foolish creatures who needed to be taught about nutrition and thrift. By denigrating those with different foodways, the league justified its existence. Poor women were also blamed for rising food prices. Specifically, because these women did not cook and shop appropriately, middlemen were able to profit from markups. However, the Ottawa Household League reasoned that if poor women would consume properly, the overall cost of nutritious food would decrease.

Less information about the Montreal Housewives' League is available than about the Ontario leagues. Available evidence does suggest, however, that the Montreal league pursued similar goals. Its first meeting was held in February 1914, at which the vice-president, Mrs. Thos. Fesenden, stated that the organization stood for "fair prices, clean shops, purer products ... and to bring producer and consumer nearer together."[88] Despite this ethos the Montreal league did not commit to collective buying. Instead, it remained a watchdog organization dedicated to helping housewives reduce living costs, as well as to publicly promoting housewives' interests.[89]

Women in Quebec City, too, started collective-buying initiatives. In May 1917 anglophone women formed an English-speaking branch of the Housewives' League. A French branch, according to the *Quebec Telegraph*, already existed. For its part, the English branch vowed to monitor prices, to give custom only to retailers with fair prices, and to raise awareness about poor conditions in stores. At no time during its first meeting did members suggest that the English league would buy and sell its own merchandise.[90] Fortunately for shoppers the existing Ligue des ménagères did participate in collective buying. In October 1917 the francophone league contacted Ontario butter producers to solicit "tenders for between 30 and 40 tonnes of butter for its members."[91] The next month the league's "Conseil supreme" purchased a wagon-load of flour, which it then divided and distributed to members at cost. The league also purchased 4,500 sacks of potatoes, which were sold to members for one dollar and eighty cents each.[92]

Six months later francophone women in Montreal formed a similar group, called "Le Syndicat economique des ménagères." Group membership was restricted to Catholic "Canadiennes-Françaises." The executive committee was made up entirely of women, and Father Piette, a Catholic priest, acted as the group's spiritual adviser. With the goal of purchasing products in bulk and passing the savings onto members, the association contacted various suppliers. By April 1918, members had been in touch with local producers of butter, milk, cheese, cream, eggs, potatoes, flour, bread, and sugar.

Financing for the group came exclusively from memberships. According to *La Bonne Parole*, each member contributed one dollar per month.[93]

On the east coast, women in Halifax had established a household league in the spring of 1914. Created by the city's Local Council of Women, its purpose was to "reduce the cost of living."[94] By early 1915 the group was purchasing "country produce at wholesale rates" and distributing it to members. Members paid "about $25 per week for various commodities."[95] Further information about this group is not contained in the available records, but hopefully future research will provide more evidence.

Women in western Canada also established collective consumer organizations, though they generally did not call themselves Housewives' Leagues. In Calgary in 1913 the Local Council of Women launched a committee on house economics, a group that subsequently became known as the Calgary Consumers' League. According to the president, Georgina Newhall, its agenda was to "reduce the cost of living" and to develop "a new order of things wherever trade conditions touch the household."[96] Although the Calgary Consumers' League was affiliated with National Consumers' League of the United States – whose main purpose was to advocate for better industrial conditions – this affiliation meant more in name than it did in agenda. For Newhall, "the name 'Consumers' League of Calgary' [was] a misnomer." As she stated, its "proper cognomen should be the 'Housewives' League.'" This statement indicates that Newhall was aware of other Housewives' Leagues operating in Canada and that she aligned her organization with those groups.

In June 1913 the Calgary Consumers' League took over the operation of the city's public market. This year-round facility had been operating since 1911, but only four stalls were being rented when the league assumed responsibility. The building was perpetually empty, with shoppers actively avoiding its dirty interior. Under the league's stewardship, however, conditions improved dramatically. The market was cleaned, and twenty stalls were rented. By September 1913 the league had earned three thousand dollars, an amount that had taken the city two years to garner.

The league accomplished this revenue by purchasing in bulk and soliciting producers to sell at the market. Their first purchase was a "carload" of fruit and vegetables from British Columbia, which they then sold. Following this success, they wrote more than five hundred letters to Alberta producers and their organizations to invite them to set up shop in Calgary. The mailing resulted in fourteen new regular vendors at the market. Through their letter writing league members learned that there was more than enough supply to feed the city of Calgary. However, they also learned about wasteful food practices. Newhall described receiving "stories [that] were written of potatoes, carrots and turnips dumped into coulees as filling, because of the hopelessness of finding a market for them." This news was "maddening," she wrote, as "the consumer in Calgary was paying fancy prices" for vegetables often imported from the United States. The league's successful lobbying for changes to the city's meat laws also contributed to the success of the market. During its earlier years the city had restricted the size and quantity of the cuts of meat that could be sold in the city. By lobbying the city for looser restrictions, the league opened up the meat trade.[97]

Through the public market the Calgary Consumers' League helped to lower the cost of food for its customers. Under its leadership the market was a clean and attractive shopping space that allowed local producers to sell directly to consumers. As such, the market served as a food co-operative. Consistent with the sentiments of the emerging co-operative movement on the prairies, Newhall stated, "Wherever the regulation of prices is in the hands of the merchant alone, these are bound to be high, because he is working for his individual benefit." She wrote that, by contrast, a "market built by the people for the people, with its expenses and profits open to investigation, enables the consumer to properly estimate the cost of production and distribution, and allow a reasonable margin of profit."[98]

Throughout the First World War, bulk buying remained popular in western Canada. In July 1915 the Vancouver-based BC Consumers' League announced that it had reached an agreement with Okanagan cherry growers. The league would purchase a train car of cherries and then sell the cherries directly from "a railway siding at the city market." By doing so, it aimed to lower the overall price by eliminating transport and packing costs, while ensuring that cherry growers received a fair price. Bulk cherry purchasing was

a new venture that had "never before been tried in the province."
Following this the league hoped to purchase apricots and peaches
in bulk.[99] Women in Saskatchewan, Alberta, and Manitoba also
remained interested in co-operative buying. In September of the
same year, the women's section of the Grain Growers' Association
in Saskatchewan organized a large fruit purchase.[100] Simultaneously the women's auxiliary of the United Farmers of Alberta also
enquired into the "co-operative buying of fruit from the producers
in B.C."[101] In Manitoba members of the Women Grain Growers'
Associations in Normanton and Crestwynd planned to create consumer co-operatives.[102]

## Women's Co-operation Interwar

Following the war and into the 1920s, middle-class women continued to buy co-operatively. In 1920 the Local Council of Women
in Montreal partnered with "five far-seeing men of the city," one
of whom was a director of a "night school," to create the Collective Buyers' Association. By April of that year the association had
saved up to seventy per cent on goods. At this point it had only
purchased groceries but planned to purchase other items including "drugs, clothing, [and] hardware" in the future.[103]

By 1920 the Toronto Housewives' League had changed its name
to the Consumers' League, perhaps because it wished to be affiliated with the Calgary organization of this same title, which had
been reporting in *Woman's Century*.[104] The name change might also
have reflected the growing prominence of the National Consumers League in the United States.[105] Unfortunately for the Toronto
league's enthusiastic members, however, interest in their organization was declining. According to its May 1920 report, "an extremely
small percentage of the executive of 125, to whom notices are sent
each time, showed ... a determination to stay with the effort." As a
result the league postponed its plan to have a "Municipal Stall in
the public markets." Nonetheless, it did resolve to ask the "Board
of Commerce" to ensure "that the supply of sugar used in candy
factories ... be regulated during the fruit season." It presumably
made this request so that members could obtain reasonably priced
sugar for canning.[106] It also resolved to lobby the federal government to intervene and lower the excessive potato prices, prices it

believed to be artificially high because wholesalers withheld potatoes from market in cold storage.[107]

In western Canada women's groups continued to buy Okanagan
fruit. By 1929, WIs in each of the four western provinces, together
with the region's provincial Councils of Women, had created a
"system of relaying news notes" about this product. In using this
system, organized women across the prairies ordered large ship-
ments at reasonable prices. By sharing resources, female buyers
thus directly paid female suppliers for their goods. Buyers and
sellers reported fair prices, and for-profit wholesalers and retailers
were removed from the supply chain. The success of this venture
led the Okanagan Valley WI to host "25 prairie women" during the
second week in July 1929 to discuss further business possibilities.[108]

The Calgary Consumers' League also continued its work. Its
stall at the farmer's market was operational in 1921 and sold
butter, eggs, and apricots at cost. As they were in frequent communication with Okanagan fruit suppliers, members considered
instituting a fruit-box order system. They also debated whether
to open a local canning factory so that the housewives of Calgary
could go "away for the summer" and "leave this part of their
household duties ... in competent hands." Despite this ambition,
the Calgary Consumers' League had difficulty managing its work.
According to a 1921 report, the large amount of produce delivered
to the league was such that "the ladies in charge of the stall were
unable to handle" it all. Not having volunteers, they had to distribute the extra fruit to other market vendors, who would receive
"ten percent for selling it."[109]

Even with this flurry of activity during the 1920s, the middle-class
English Canadian women's movement had all but abandoned collective consumption by the 1930s. Indeed, none of the major Canadian women's periodicals mentioned co-operative buying ventures
at all during this decade. In the late 1930s, a small show of interest
did occur in Quebec. The November 1937 issue of *La Bonne Parole*
reported that a group in Montreal, the "Femmes d'affaires," had
met to discuss consumer co-operation.[110] Over the next two years,
study circles of the Fédération nationale Saint-Jean-Baptiste in various locations also studied the topic.[111] One of the largest meetings on the subject took place in Montreal in January 1939. There,
Mme Alfred Thibaudeau presented a treatise on the advantages of

collective buying. By facilitating a feeling of goodwill among members, it would also enrich the lives of individuals, families, and communities. Moreover, it was pope approved: "Le coopératisme est une oeuvre approuveée par le Pape." Yet the greatest advantage of co-operation was that it enabled men and women to participate equally in economic decision-making. Stated Thibaudeau, "C'est encore la seule organisation où légalité des sexes est reconnue." Unfortunately she did not elaborate on this position.[112]

In considering the reasons for the silence apparent in the anglophone club-women's movement regarding co-operation during the 1930s, it is useful to examine the writings of Calgary consumer activist Georgina Newhall. In 1916 she had argued for the establishment of "a Dominion-wide union of Consumers" who would work to lower prices.[113] Yet her resolve diminished over time, and she became discouraged by what she perceived to be a lack of will among Canadian female consumers. In 1917 Newhall wrote to Woman's Century to celebrate news of wartime "milk investigations, egg boycotts, turkey boycotts, [and] potato boycotts." At the same time, she was also critical that the initiatives had been carried out on an ad hoc basis. In her opinion, "organization from coast to coast" was the only responsible method of organizing. Newhall reasoned that, without nationwide coordination, co-operation would be hampered "by little groups of somewhat hysterical women, who exhaust themselves in the very effort to protect."[114]

Newhall was indeed often hostile. In her view, "Canadian born women" were "fickle buyers" who make unpredictable decisions and who were duped by the whims of fashion.[115] More than this, they were too "lazy" to organize. She became critical of both the Housewives' Leagues and the Consumers' Leagues, stating that while they had sometimes implemented "satisfactory results," over the long term they had not "accrued" any "lasting benefit."[116] By 1919 she had abandoned the idea of a national consumer organization.[117] For Newhall, Canadian women were too enthralled by "the glittering temptations of the department store" to have any real interest in the issues that mattered. Accordingly, they would never have the wherewithal to organize effectively.[118]

Newhall's writings indicate that she was a supercilious, disagreeable person. That she abandoned the establishment of a large-scale consumer co-operation, however, does highlight the difficulties encountered by middle-class consumers who were trying to organize. Given the local and short-lived nature of consumer activism, it was difficult for leagues to sustain momentum over the long term. Not only was co-operative buying arduous for those co-ordinating sales, but also some consumers were unwilling to give up the convenience, selection, and quality afforded by mass retailers. Given these factors, it is unsurprising that the middle-class English Canadian consumer movement before the Second World War was piecemeal and sporadic. Club-women simply did not have the resources to sustain what many of them recognized as their own consumer interests.

## Conclusion

Prior to the Second World War thousands of Canadian women participated in an international movement against individualized consumer capitalism. Some of these women joined the mainstream co-operative movement in order to participate in alternative consumption practices that were consistent with their principles of sociability and justice. Other, often middle-class women, used their connections in the club-women's movement to buy and sell groceries co-operatively.

Many initiatives were initially successful. Women's consumer co-operative guilds in interwar Saskatchewan and Nova Scotia raised awareness about the importance of consumer co-operation to all co-operators. As well, during the 1910s, the Toronto Housewives' Leagues hosted sold-out sales of farm products at wholesale prices. Moreover, the sheer interest demonstrated by club-women in co-operative alternatives to mass retailing, particularly within the realm of food, suggests that they were cognizant of the limitations of individualized consumption. It also shows that they were interested in pursuing alternatives to the for-profit model.

In the long term, however, such initiatives foundered. In the mainstream co-operative movement there was a lack of understanding between male leadership and female shoppers. Female leaders were also unresponsive to the needs of customers. Ida Delaney, for example, had difficulty understanding why housewives preferred convenience, quality, and affordability over supporting their local co-op. Instead of taking the realities of women's lives seriously, these leaders dismissed women's shopping preferences as whimsical and ignorant. In this way the co-operative movement's depictions of female consumers had, by the early period of the Second World War, come to resemble those put forward by home economists. The failure to properly address housewives' shopping expectations hampered both the mainstream co-operative movement and the league initiatives. In Ottawa, for instance, Mrs. Wilson, the manager of the Housewives' League's co-operative store, expressed frustration over what she viewed as the wilful ignorance of poor shoppers. She opined that their desire for convenience foods represented the problems of modern consumerism.

While difficulties in bridging class and gender differences hampered co-operative initiatives, co-operators also struggled to manage their ventures over the long term. As the experiment of the Toronto Housewives' League reveals, volunteers were unwilling to devote large amounts of time to wholesaling projects for an indefinite period. Selling food at cost was labour intensive and required more volunteer work than expected. The notable exception of the Calgary farmers' market notwithstanding, by 1921 the upswing in consumer co-operation that had characterized the club-women's movement during the 1910s had dissipated. Although later generations of club-women, including those of the 1930s, expressed interest in co-operation, their initiatives would not match those of their predecessors in Toronto and Ottawa during the earlier period.

Despite the fact that women-led consumer co-operation did not become a lasting movement prior to the Second World War, that women with diverse political orientations and affiliations with various social movements remained interested does indicate an ongoing commitment to challenging the for profit marketplace. Nonetheless, while this chapter provides an overview of Canadian women's consumer co-operation before the Second World War, it is true that more research is needed. Future research should consider how leftist women, as well as women of racialized and ethnic backgrounds, approached collective shopping matters. A focus on political orientation, race, and ethnicity will allow for a more nuanced understanding of the history and obstacles faced by those seeking alternatives to consumer capitalism.

*Conclusion*

# Empowerment and Exclusion: Consumption in Canadian History

In 1932 the federal minister of trade and commerce, H.H. Stevens, announced that "Canadian women hold in their hands today, what is perhaps the most powerful factor in Canadian life – the terrific power of the buyer." Thus, they had to act responsibly. "When they, as a national unit, realize the power they have, and wield it for the studied good of the country, the effect cannot escape being a great step forward and upward in economic conditions."[1] In Stevens's view, women were important consumer citizens whose spending decisions influenced the nation. His statement reflected a broader 1930s interest in consumer spending as a route out of the Great Depression.[2] Yet it also pointed to another theme: women's consumer power. According not only to Stevens but also to many white Canadian women's groups, housewives were crucial political and economic actors. As such, they should be taken seriously. In the same year Mrs. J. MacGregor Smith, the national convenor of home economics for the Federated Women's Institutes of Canada, put it this way: "Women occupy a most important place in the commerce and trade of the Dominion and ... dictate the prosperity of the world."[3]

This book has considered the relationship between citizenship and consumption. It demonstrates that during the early twentieth century the federal government (and many white Canadian women) tended to view white Canadian women as consumer citizens. This book has also shown that citizenship was not the only frame through which white Canadian women viewed consumer issues. Due to their positions as homemakers within the gendered division of labour, thousands of these women were involved in a host of simultaneous consumer projects. They often turned to consumption to ensure the survival and well-being of themselves and their families. Yet they also saw consumption as an opportunity to engage in artistic experimentation and status creation. Furthermore, they engaged in consumer activism. Organizing on behalf of consumers in their own and broader communities, they fought for reduced prices, monitored retailers' accountability, and distributed product information.

This concluding chapter reviews the consumer engagements of white Canadian wives and mothers during the early twentieth century. Its analyses underscore the usefulness of turning to women's history in order to understand consumption's significances. Indeed, whereas some commentators tend to view consumption as a contemporary issue, lamenting particularly what they see as an invasion of the public sphere by commercial and consumer interests, a study of early twentieth-century white Canadian women proves that for well over a hundred years Canadians have been making connections between their civic and consumer roles.[4] A study of the consumer history of white Canadian women also builds awareness of the particular meanings that certain Canadians have attached to consumer issues. Specifically, since Canadian wives and mothers were highly invested in the consumer realm, a study of their writings and actions gives extended insights into how they understood such matters as shopping, commodity ownership, and consumer activism.

To begin, it is clear that many of the women in this study connected consumption to personal and collective liberation. According to the Women's Institutes (WIs), wives and mothers worked long and hard. As a result it was acceptable to turn to consumption. For some, labour-saving devices such as vacuum cleaners and floor polishers offered respite. Fashion, too, was a form of liberation. Both the Women's Christian Temperance Union (WCTU) and the WI argued that putting on new clothing helped mothers feel better, particularly since they worked long hours at home. A few members of these groups also appreciated the sumptuous pleasures afforded by such pursuits.

Consumption was linked to liberation in another way as well. The WCTU argued that men should stop drinking so that their wives and children could buy more consumer goods. By the 1930s the WCTU had specified what wives and children needed: better housing, more home furnishings, new pianos and Victrolas, new clothes, new shoes, more dresses for mothers, and what members called small luxuries and comforts, such as jewellery, magazines, and home decorations. As such sentiments indicate, part of the WCTU's push for temperance was motivated by the attempts of some mothers to wrest more money from the family purse. In this way temperance was linked not only to a widening of consumer spending but also to the desires of individual mothers for greater financial power. Responsible for nurturing their families, wives and mothers were more than familiar with the goods necessary for domestic fulfilment and social respect. By calling for prohibition, temperance advocates sought greater clout for Christian mothers. Along the way they helped usher in a more sober and family-oriented consumer culture.

Yet, if some women found opportunities for empowerment and potential liberation in consumption, other women perceived a series of drawbacks in consumer activity. Some women in this study evinced widespread distrust of retailers and manufacturers. In the early twentieth century the WI held several discussions about false advertising. During the inflation years of the late 1910s and early 1920s, members also held meetings about unfair prices. Many rural women of this period indeed guarded their pocketbooks, putting their interests ahead of the businesses that sold products to them.

Another issue that consistently plagued many women was what they perceived as women's addiction to fashion. According to a variety of women in the WCTU, the WI, the National Council of Women (NCW), and the Fédération nationale Saint-Jean-Baptiste (FNSJB), the fashion industry demanded too much of women, causing them to spend an inordinate amount of time following fashion's dictates and money buying clothes. Fashion, moreover, caused many women to confine themselves within uncomfortable corsets and footwear, and thus hobble their bodies and, according to some, their minds. Hence for many women, participating in consumer culture came at a cost. Not only did capitalist consumer culture endanger women's pocketbooks, but it also required women to give up too much time, energy, and freedom.

Whereas some of the women in this investigation were sceptical of consumer capitalism, others criticized consumption because they saw it as wasteful. This critique had several components.

A few Manitoba women suggested during the 1930s that since not everyone could afford nice things, it was better for one's entire community to wear clothes that reflected thrift. In this way people could feel in solidarity with each other. Some suggested, as well, that thrift was pleasurable. During the war years, when the federal government was calling on all Canadians to conserve food, fuel, and metal, some women took special interest in exercising their thrifty acumen. For them, such actions as growing their own produce, following war recipes, and re-using household materials were enjoyable activities, which they found pleasure in discussing as well as pursuing. For these women, conservation brought a feeling of camaraderie; it gave them an opportunity to use the time-worn skills of budgeting and thrift for new, celebrated purposes.

Others saw thrift as a moral imperative. Running through the press of the WCTU, NCW, and FNSJB was a strong distaste for what many perceived as consumer excess. During the war years especially, authors criticized the decadence into which their compatriots had apparently descended, and decried the contrast between what they saw as indulgent Canadians and suffering Europeans. New clothes, automobiles, and jewellery came under critique, as did attendance at dance halls, restaurants, and theatres. Such critiques, in turn, reveal the strength of the moralist invective against luxury in Canada. They also demonstrate that despite some Canadians' apparent enjoyment of commercial entertainment and new commodities, not all Canadians applauded these activities.

Closely related to writers' appeals for thrift was a widespread call for modesty. Particularly when discussing fashion, writers suggested that modesty should be the deciding factor when one chooses commodities. During the war some women suggested that modesty in fashion sent the right message to sufferers overseas, indicating that Canadians respected Europeans' war traumas. Modesty in fashion continued to be a major theme after the war. According to authors in both the English- and the French-language women's press, modest clothing was a key tool in the prevention of sexual assault. Conservative authors had further opinions. Modesty protected not only the virtue of the wearer but also the virtue of the entire community. When women wore revealing fashions, they provoked lust in onlookers and thus brought shame to themselves and others. Far better for women to dress modestly. In this way they could protect both themselves and everyone around them.

This book has further demonstrated the importance of producerist values within Canadians' consumer pasts. Today, the term *prosumer* has gained currency; it denotes "a consumer who becomes involved with designing or customizing products for their own needs."[5] Most often, those who employ the term refer specifically to technology users who design new products out of existing materials; website creators are excellent examples. Nonetheless, the practice of prosumption stretches back to at least the middle of the nineteenth century and is especially relevant towards work performed in the home. Homemakers, in fact, have been prosumers par excellence. They have purchased products in the consumer marketplace and have transformed them into usable goods. Cooking, sewing, and knitting are typical prosumer activities and were common during the early twentieth century, when ready-made meals, clothing, and linens were less commonly available than they are today. As the example of the WI reveals, a great number of rural women took pleasure in prosumerism, enjoying the recipes they followed that enabled them to create sumptuary delights, and the crafting instructions they followed that enabled them to make attractive clothing and home furnishings. For the WI and its members, in fact, prosumption was fulfilling. It enabled them to be both creative and nurturing. Indeed, for many women at this time, consumption was an active – rather than passive – event, one that enabled some joy, even as it also created much stress.

Wives and mothers of the early twentieth century, then, applied both moral and cultural values to their consumer experiences. At the same time they saw consumption in political terms. Women in the WI and the NCW organized to protect and enhance consumers' lives. As well, during the interwar years, the WI began lobbying for greater product standards, including those of wool quality, as chapter 4 demonstrates. Consumer enhancement activism also occurred in other ways. Throughout the period under study the WI acted as a consumer agency, sharing product knowledge across its membership. On the prairies, moreover, institute women raised money and donated time and energy to create community centres where rural women could relax when not running errands.

Yet if white wives and mothers organized as consumers to improve their experiences, so did they work to protect their pocketbooks. During the inflationary years of the First World War, white women across the country sought to bring down food prices. Widely suspicious of markups, middle- and lower-income women formed what became known as Household Leagues; these were especially prominent in Halifax, Quebec City, Montreal, Ottawa, Toronto, and St Catharines. In these cities members worked with growers to purchase produce, meat, and dairy directly. In some cases they formed buying clubs; in others, they purchased food and then resold it – with no markups – at special membership-only sales. Such activities had mixed results. As the case of the Toronto efforts indicates, these actions were difficult to sustain. Over the long term, volunteers grew tired of donating time and labour to the cause. Hence, when prices began to stabilize in the interwar period, the Household Leagues disbanded.

The formation of Household Leagues, however, was not the only attempt to transform the consumer marketplace. Throughout this period wives and mothers, intent on bypassing capitalist consumer venues, formed co-operative ventures. Some women did so by joining the formal co-operative movement, creating so-called women's guilds that focused on consumer co-operation. Such groups were generally short lived. Indeed, and as the study of the Antigonish movement illustrates in chapter 6, the male-dominated co-operative movement had difficulty in convincing female shoppers to patronize co-operative stores, for these stores did not offer the same convenience, selection, and affordability as did their capitalist competitors. At the same time, when women joined together to create consumer co-operative ventures, some success did occur. This was especially the case with the Calgary farmers' market, organized during the 1920s by the Calgary Consumers' League. The venue transformed the purchasing patterns of many urban wives and mothers, enabling them to buy food directly from producers.

Prior to the Second World War many women who were involved in the WCTU, the NCW, the WI, the FNSJB, the home economics movement, and the co-operative movement thus sought to transform the consumer marketplace, making it more responsive to wives' and mothers' needs for convenience, affordability, and quality. Such work can be considered a form of politicized consumption, in the sense that it challenged existing structures. Yet wives and mothers also engaged in other forms of politicized consumption. In ways similar to today's "political consumers," who argue that one's purchasing decisions have political ramifications, women in these movements asserted that consumers' choices had clear political impacts.[6] In this way they demonstrated a similarity to many consumer activists in the United States during this period. According to Glickman, the late nineteenth and early twentieth centuries were rife with consumer activism, with many advocates arguing that shoppers' decisions could effect broader changes. Through the use of selective boycotts and "buycotts" – the latter term meaning purposeful patronage of particular products and companies – activists suggested that they could improve working conditions, challenge corporate policies, contribute to local prosperity, and pressure governments into reforms.[7]

Women in this study also engaged in political consumerism. The WCTU promoted boycotts of all businesses that made and sold alcohol; they also urged buycotts of businesses that actively supported temperance. These included, as chapter 1 demonstrates, Eaton's and Simpson's department stores, Red Rose Tea, and Purity Flour. The WI, too, practised political consumerism. During the 1920s and 1930s, institute members in Nova Scotia and Alberta launched "buy local" campaigns; according to members in both provinces, buying locally enriched local businesses. As such, it also boosted local employment, injected more money into local circulation, and hence contributed to overall local prosperity. More nationalistically minded thinkers also engaged in "buy local" initiatives. For them, supporting Canadian-owned businesses – rather than locally owned – was key. During the early 1920s the WCTU, the WI, and the NCW all promoted patriotic purchasing. By buying from Canadian-owned businesses and purchasing Canadian-made products, they said, shoppers could contribute to Canadian economic development and thus national progress.

By considering the forms of political consumerism in which the women in this study engaged, it is possible to determine the political values that many of them held. Clearly, when the WCTU supported temperance businesses, they indicated their abhorrence of alcohol. More subtly, though, they also evinced support for capitalism. As chapter 1 reveals, the WCTU endorsed capitalist

economic development, viewing it as integral to Canadian improvement. WCTU consumer activists can hence be considered
fiscally conservative. In this way they were much different from
their contemporaries on the left. As Sangster, Parr, and Guard have
separately argued, female consumer activists in the Co-operative
Commonwealth Federation and Communist Party during this period called for the government to actively intervene in food prices
to keep certain foodstuffs affordable and hence institute greater
equality among consumers.[8] The WCTU wanted greater access to
goods, too, but they sought to do it not through price policy but
through changing the personal dynamics of family budgets.

Closely related to many women's engagement in political consumerism was a widespread conflation of consumption with citizenship. Citizenship, as many point out, is often thought of as
inimical to consumption.[9] As Kate Soper puts it, many critiques of
consumption hinge on the assumption that consumers are selfish
while citizens are public spirited. She writes, "[Consumers] have
most often been presented as obedient to forms of self-interest that
either limit or altogether preclude the capacity for the reflexivity,
social accountability and cultural community associated with citizenship." Citizens, in turn, are often portrayed as consumers' op-
posites: they "look above the parapet of private needs and desires
[and] have an eye to the public good."[10] Yet, Canadian women
before the Second World War made several links between citizenship and consumption. Patriotic conservation campaigns during
the First World War hinged on the assumption that by making appropriate consumer choices, housewives could demonstrate their
civic engagement. Similarly, when women promoted buying locally and nationally made goods, they revealed their assumption
that civic engagement could be achieved through responsible purchasing. For its part, the home economics movement was especially supportive of the consumer-citizen ideal. By training girls
and women to shop in ways that supported personal, local, and
national improvement, the home economics movement sought to
elevate homemakers' social status.

So important was consumption to certain women's civic identities that some suggested that consumers should be considered
equal partners with business and government. According to the
WCTU, such temperance-supporting companies as Red Rose Tea,

Purity Flour, and Eaton's were important allies. Rather than simply being upstanding businesses, they were partners in the temperance crusade. Many conservationist women during the First World War, meanwhile, welcomed the federal government's newly found interest in female shoppers; they even travelled to Ottawa in 1918 to attend the federal Women's War Conference, which celebrated housewives' consumer sacrifices. Nowhere were the ideas of consumer-business and consumer-government partnerships more on display, however, than in Edmonton in April 1932 during Home Economics Week. Organized by home economics instructors at the University of Alberta, together with the WIs and a few other local groups including the Edmonton Creche Society, this event raised the status of female homemakers by demonstrating their importance as consumers. Through public lectures, product exhibitions, media campaigns, and special events Edmonton's Home Economics Week showed female shoppers to be integral to the political economy.

Taking up the consumer-citizen mantle, many wives and mothers studied in this book sought to demonstrate that their domestic labour had importance outside the home. Seizing upon their economic agency as consumers, they connected their spending decisions to broader political and economic matters, including the fate of their country and the prosperity of their local communities. Whereas classical political-economic thought held that consumers made private decisions and thus existed outside of the marketplace, and whereas the gendered division of labour meant that most wives and mothers existed outside of the labour market, many white Canadian wives and mothers nevertheless claimed political and economic roles for themselves through consumption. As Lizabeth Cohen has written in reference to Depression-era Americans, "for social groups not otherwise well represented [in the political arena], identification as consumers offered a new opportunity to make claims on those wielding public and private power."[11] For many of Canada's wives and mothers, such claims were specifically about gaining respect. In this time when men dominated the political, business, professional, and employment arenas, women had little opportunities for public influence. Through consumption, however, they asserted their own importance.

Even as such wives and mothers struggled for respect as consumers, however, it is also true that many tended to entrench particular gender roles. In their claims for citizenship status via consumption, wives and mothers emphasized that shopping was a woman's duty, particularly. As prominent NCW member Jessie McIver put it in 1917, "ninety per cent of the buyers of the nation are women."[12] For the women in this study, indeed, shopping was a woman's duty precisely because it was a component of domestic labour. From the temperance campaigners studied in chapter 1, to the patriotic purchasers in chapter 2, the home economics experts in chapter 3, the rural women's advocates in chapter 4, the fashion commentators in chapter 5, and the co-operative movement activists in chapter 6, all the subjects in this study agreed that consumption and femininity were intricately connected. Not only was consumption a suitable venue by which wives and mothers could proclaim their civic agency, but it was their natural duty due to their gender. Indeed, for the subjects of this book, the issue was never whether it should be women specifically who went out shopping. Rather, their dominant concerns were related to how they could achieve their goals through consumption.

In that the subjects of this study adhered to conventional definitions of femininity, they can be considered to have been cisgendered. In other words, they drew upon their biological status as females to construct their own social identities as heterosexual women. More than this, it is clear that the subjects of this study drew upon their feminine biological status to construct images of themselves as nurturing. In other words, they portrayed themselves to be maternal. As feminist researchers make clear, maternalism is a form of political expression that assumes that a woman's natural role is to be a mother.[13] During the late nineteenth century and into the 1950s, maternalism was especially common among white settler women. According to Joan Sangster, "some women, largely from middle-class backgrounds ... argued that women's distinct role as homemakers and mothers and their commitment to family and moral issues ... would provide an important antidote to male political perspectives."[14] Indeed, no matter their views on other matters, many of the subjects of this study would have agreed with Mrs. Drummond, president of the Montreal Council of Women during the 1880s, when she said in 1884 that "home will ever be our chosen kingdom, but ... we shall order our homes with greater wisdom ... [by] taking a woman's part in helping the great world."[15]

Since they embraced their maternal roles, the women of this book cannot be considered transgressive, at least from a feminist perspective. Rather than seeking to change the gendered division of labour, which relegated women to supportive roles, these wives and mothers instead adopted the voice of the feminized subject and tried to instigate change from that vantage point. In other words, they had no interest in changing the patriarchal order; rather, as cisgendered women they simply sought to gain footholds within the existing system. In this way they were similar to many of their contemporaries. As scholars Mariana Valverde and Carol Bacchi have pointed out, many white, female-identified activists in late nineteenth- and early twentieth-century Canada drew upon maternalist rhetoric to portray white women as morally superior to white men and to hence justify their attempts to gain greater access to political, educational, professional, and employment opportunities.[16]

If many women in this study resembled their contemporaries in deploying maternalist views, so did some offer similar assertions of racial and ethnic superiority. As works by Cecily Devereux, Mariana Valverde, and Jennifer Henderson make clear, many advocates of female suffrage, both in Canada and in other white settler nations, built an ideology of "imperial feminism."[17] This construct was an assertion of British women's moral superiority over all men, as well as their moral and biological superiority over all non-British women. These forms of superiority were based on the status of white British women as "mothers of the race," a term frequently used by suffrage-era feminists to describe them.[18] Asserting that their righteousness stemmed from their biological status as white child-bearers, as well as from their moral status as British Christians, many woman-identified activists of this period justified their claims for enlarged entitlements on the basis of race, gender, and religion. In so doing, they elevated their own status within settler nations. At the same time, however, they also buttressed the prevailing conditions of white supremacy, conservative gender norms, and discrimination against non-Christians.

This book did not explore imperial feminism per se, but it did examine statements made by women in the NCW, the WI, the home economics movement, the WCTU, the FNSJB, and the co-operative movement in relation to race, ethnicity, and consumption. I found that the arenas of home economics and fashion particularly were rife with assumptions regarding white women's superiority. Home economics experts especially saw consumption in racialized and ethnic terms. Chapter 3 demonstrates that some home economics theorists held up Western European standards of taste, cleanliness, restraint, and nutrition as the pinnacle of consumer achievement; they also portrayed women of other cultures as coarse, backwards, and unhealthy. Fashion, too, was an avenue by which some demonstrated superiority. Chapter 5 shows that certain writers thought that dressing with elegance was important for national purity. When they dressed with "grace and beauty," as one anglophone writer put it, women could "lead the way in ... matters spiritual as well as moral," instilling "true patriotism."[19] This author's assertion of white superiority was subtle in that she did not actually employ the term *race*. Nonetheless, by connecting purity to patriotism, she referenced a racial hierarchy that constructed white women's bodies as the most virtuous and therefore as the most valuable.[20] The French-language press offered similar sentiments. According to one priest quoted by the FNSJB, when women dressed immodestly, they triggered male lust. They hence turned back the clock of racial progress, bringing Christianity down to the level of the "savage."[21]

If we consider these discussions in relation to theorist Pierre Bourdieu's investigations of taste, as considered in this book's introduction, we can see that some women in Canada's past constructed moral hierarchies by contrasting their own consumer habits with those of others. The articulation of these hierarchies was related to class in the sense that one needed to spend certain amounts of money to appear sophisticated, but it was also related to race. As both the English- and the French-language presses made clear, only white women were apparently in possession of proper consumer tastes. Such actions reveal that not only the gender affiliations of white women but also their racialized and class identities affected the ways in which they approached consumption. Indeed, even as white women's feminized roles within the gendered division of labour encouraged these women to make high investments in their consumer roles, their overall positions of class and racial privilege encouraged many to use consumer display as a venue by which to judge who – and who did not – meet the criteria for membership in the modern Canadian polity.

During the early twentieth century, then, the consumer sphere was multifaceted. For thousands of white Canadian women, it was connected to survival, liberation, morality, personal expression, upward mobility, and political impact. At the same time, however, and as this conclusion makes clear, the consumer interests of white Canadian women were ultimately connected to their quests for power. By turning to the consumer realm, they sought to empower themselves. They sought to improve not only their personal situations but also their collective political strength. Simultaneously they also turned to the consumer realm to disempower others. By criticizing other people's consumer habits, often on the basis of class, ethnic, and racial prejudice, white women in early twentieth-century Canada tended to define their own superiority against the supposed inferiority of others. In this way they proved the saliency of Bourdieu's 1979 observation that "taste classifies, and it classifies the classifier."[22] They also showed that just as Canadians have frequently turned to consumption as a tool of empowerment, so have they wielded it as a tool of exclusion.

# Notes

CAM       Centre d'archives de Montréal
Glenbow   Glenbow Museum and Archives

## Introduction

1  Mary Quayle Innis, diary, 25 January 1922, B91-0029/058, Harold A. Innis Family Fonds, box 57, file 2, University of Toronto Archives (hereafter cited as Quayle Diaries).
2  Donica Belisle and Kiera Mitchell, "Mary Quayle Innis: Faculty Wives' Contributions and the Making of Academic Celebrity," *Canadian Historical Review* 99, no. 3 (Fall 2018): 456–86.
3  Quayle Diaries, 23 February 1923, 19 July 1923, 3 December 1932, 4 June 1940, 10 May 1955, 17 March 1954, 5 February 1957, 21 February 1968.
4  Canadian consumer historiography is constantly expanding. The best works offer intersectional analyses, such as Laurie K. Bertram, "New Icelandic Ethnoscapes. Material, Visual, and Oral Terrains of Cultural Expression in Icelandic-Canadian History, 1875–Present" (PhD diss., Department of History, University of Toronto, 2010); Jane Nicholas, *The Modern Girl: Feminine Modernities, the Body, and Commodities in the 1920s* (Toronto: University of Toronto Press, 2015); Franca Iacovetta, "Recipes for Democracy? Gender, Family, and Making Female Citizens in Cold War Canada," *Canadian Woman Studies* 12, no. 20 (2000): 12–27; and Alison Norman, "'Fit for the Table of the Most Fastidious Epicure': Culinary Colonialism in the Contact Zone," in *Edible Histories, Cultural Politics: Towards a Canadian Food History*, ed. Franca Iacovetta, Valerie J. Korinek, and Marlene Epp (Toronto: University of Toronto Press, 2012), 31–51. Other important works are cited in the bibliography.

5  This literature is vast. See, for example, Veronica Strong-Boag, *The New Day Recalled: Lives of Girls and Women in English Canada, 1919–1939* (Toronto: Copp Clark Pitman, 1988); Joy Parr, *Domestic Goods: The Material, the Moral, and the Economic in the Postwar Years* (Toronto: University of Toronto Press, 1999); Lorraine O'Donnell, "Le voyage virtuel: Les consommatrices, le monde de l'étranger et Eaton à Montréal, 1880–1980," *Revue d'histoire de l'Amérique français* 58, no. 4 (Spring 2005): 535–68; Donica Belisle, *Retail Nation: Department Stores and the Making of Modern Canada* (Vancouver: UBC Press, 2011), 126–57; Bettina Bradbury, *Working Families: Age, Gender, and Daily Survival in Industrializing Montreal* (Toronto: University of Toronto Press, 2007), 152–81; Meg Luxton, *More Than a Labour of Love: Three Generations of Women's Work in the Home* (Toronto: Women's Press, 1980).

6  Veronica Strong-Boag, *The Parliament of Women: The National Council of Women of Canada, 1893–1929*, National Museum of Man, Mercury Series (Ottawa, ON:University of Ottawa Press, 1976); Parr, *Domestic Goods*; Joan Sangster, "Consuming Issues: Women on the Left, Political Protest, and the Organization of Homemakers, 1920–1960," in *Framing Our Past: Canadian Women's History in the Twentieth Century*, ed. Sharon Anne Cook, Lorna R. McLean, and Kate O'Rourke (Montreal and Kingston: McGill-Queen's University Press, 2001), 240–7; Julie Guard, "Women Worth Watching: Radical Housewives in Cold War Canada," in *Whose National Security? Canadian State Surveillance and the Creation of Enemies*, ed. Gary Kinsman, Dieter K. Buse, and Mercedes Steedman (Toronto: Between the Lines, 2000), 73–90; Julie Guard, "A Mighty Power against the Cost of Living: Canadian Housewives Organize in the 1930s," *International Labor and Working-Class History* 77 (Spring 2010): 27–47; Julie Guard, "The Politics of Milk: Canadian Housewives Organize in the 1930s," in Iacovetta, Korinek, and Epp, *Edible Histories, Cultural Politics*, 271–85; Julie Guard, *Radical Housewives: Price Wars and Food Politics in Mid-Twentieth-Century Canada* (Toronto: University of Toronto Press, 2019); Magda Fahrni, "Counting the Costs of Living: Gender, Citizenship, and a Politics of Prices in 1940s Montreal," *Canadian Historical Review* 83, no. 4 (December 2002): 483–504.

7  Nicholas, *Modern Girl*; Bertram, "New Icelandic Ethnoscapes"; Laurie K. Bertram, "Fashioning Conflicts: Gender, Power, and Icelandic Immigrant Hair and Clothing in North America, 1874–1933," in *Sisters or Strangers? Immigrant, Ethnic, and Racialized Women in Canadian History*, 2nd ed., ed. Marlene Epp and Franca Iacovetta (Toronto: University of Toronto Press, 2016), 275–97; Donica Belisle, "Sexual Spectacles: Women in Canadian Department Store Magazines between 1920 and

1950," in *Writing Feminist History: Productive Pasts and New Directions*, ed. Catherine Carstairs and Nancy Janovicek (Vancouver: UBC Press, 2013), 135–58; Myra Rutherdale, "Packing and Unpacking: Northern Women Negotiate Fashion in Colonial Encounters during the Twentieth Century," in *Contesting Bodies and Nation in Canadian History*, ed. Jane Nicholas and Patrizia Gentile (Toronto: University of Toronto Press, 2013), 117–33; Katrina Srigley, "Clothing Stories: Consumption, Identity, and Desire in Depression-Era Toronto," *Journal of Women's History* 19, no. 1 (Spring 2007): 82–104.

8  For example, Joy Parr, *The Gender of Breadwinners: Women, Men, and Change in Two Industrial Towns, 1880–1950* (Toronto: University of Toronto Press, 1990); Suzanne Morton, *Ideal Surroundings: Domestic Life in a Working-Class Suburb in the 1920s* (Toronto: University of Toronto Press, 1995); Joan Sangster, *Earning Respect: The Lives of Working Women in Small-Town Ontario, 1920–1960* (Toronto: University of Toronto Press, 1995); Denyse Baillargeon, *Making Do: Women, Family, and Home in Montreal during the Great Depression*, trans. Yvonne Klein (Waterloo, ON: Wilfrid Laurier University Press, 1999).

9  World Wildlife Fund, *Canadian Living Planet Report, 2007* (Toronto: WWF, 2007), 8.

10  World Wildlife Fund, *Living Planet Report, 2016* (Toronto: WWF, 2016), 60–1.

11  Vanessa Timmer, Emmanuel Prinet, and Dagmar Timmer, *Sustainable Household Consumption: Key Considerations and Elements for a Canadian Strategy* (Toronto: Consumers Council of Canada, 2009), 7.

12  Timmer et al., *Sustainable Household Consumption*, 7.

13  Juliet B. Schor and Craig J. Thompson, "Introduction: Practising Plenitude," in *Sustainable Lifestyles and the Quest for Plenitude: Case Studies in the New Economy*, ed. Schor and Thompson (New Haven, CT: Yale University Press, 2014), loc. 111, Kindle.

14  See especially the essays in R.W. Sandwell, *Powering Up Canada: A History of Power, Fuel, and Energy from 1600* (Montreal and Kingston: McGill-Queen's University Press, 2016), including Steve Penfold, "Petroleum Liquids," and Colin A.M. Duncan and R.W. Sandwell, "Manufactured and Natural Gas."

15  Parr, *Domestic Goods*, 8.

16  Pierre Bourdieu, *Distinction: A Social Critique of the Judgement of Taste*, trans. Richard Nice (Cambridge, MA: Harvard University Press, 1984), 255, 176, 271.

17  Bourdieu, 179, 199.

18  Bourdieu, 7.

19  Bourdieu, 34.

20  Nira Yuval-Davis, *Politics of Belonging: Intersectional Contestations* (London: Sage, 2011), loc. 180, 263, Kindle.

21  Yuval-Davis, loc. 147, 459.

22  Rutherdale, "Packing," loc. 2397, Kindle.

23  Rutherdale, loc. 2452, 2393.

24  Rutherdale, loc. 2393.

25  As quoted in Rutherdale, loc. 2618.

26  Bertram, "New Icelandic Ethnoscapes," 13.

27  As quoted in Bertram, 123.

28  Bertram, 11–13, 31.

29  Bertram, 12–13.

30  Bertram, 43.

31  Iacovetta, "Recipes for Democracy?," 15.

32  This literature is vast. For their clarity and erudition, however, see particularly Elizabeth Kowaleski-Wallace, *Consuming Subjects: Women, Shopping, and Business in the Eighteenth Century* (New York: Columbia University Press, 1997); Kate Haulman, *The Politics of Fashion in Eighteenth-Century America* (Chapel Hill: North Carolina University Press, 2011); and Gail Reekie, *Temptations: Sex, Selling, and the Department Store* (Sydney, Australia: Allen & Unwin, 1993).

33  The essays in Victoria de Grazia and Ellen Furlough's edited collection *The Sex of Things: Gender and Consumption in Historical Perspective* (Berkeley and Los Angeles: University of California Press, 1996) offer an excellent introduction to both of these issues. See especially Victoria de Grazia, introduction, 11–24; Abigail Solomon-Godeau, "The Other Side of Venus: The Visual Economy of Feminine Display," 113–50; and Victoria de Grazia, "Empowering Women and Citizen-Consumers," 275–86.

34  For example, Louise A. Tilly and Joan W. Scott, *Women, Work, & Family* (New York and London: Routledge, 1987).

35  Jan de Vries, *The Industrious Revolution: Consumer Behaviour and the Household Economy, 1650 to the Present* (Cambridge: Cambridge University Press, 2008), loc. 8438, Kindle.

36  De Vries, loc. 4710.

37  Statistics Canada, *Historical Statistics of Canada*, "Section D: The Labour Force," table D8–85, accessed 29 September 2017, http://www.statcan.gc.ca.

38  Statistics Canada, "The Surge of Women in the Workforce," accessed 29 September 2017,http://www.statcan.gc.ca.

39  Ellen Willis, "Women and the Myth of Consumerism," *Ramparts* 8, no. 12 (June 1970): 13–16, accessed 30 September 2017, http://fair-use.org.

40  Nan Enstad, *Ladies of Labour, Girls of Adventure: Working Women, Popular Culture, and Labor Politics at the Turn of the Twentieth Century*

(New York: Columbia University Press, 1999); Kathy Peiss, *Hope in a Jar: The Making of America's Beauty Culture* (Philadelphia: University of Pennsylvania Press, 1998).

41 Nicholas, *Modern Girl*.

42 For example, Parr, *Gender of Breadwinners*; Andrée Levesque, *Making and Breaking the Rules: Women in Quebec, 1919–1939*, trans. Yvonne Klein (Toronto: McClelland & Stewart, 1994).

43 Frank Trentmann, "Crossing Divides: Consumption and Globalization in History," *Journal of Consumer Culture* 9, no. 2 (2009): 188.

44 Monographs in this field include Belisle, *Retail Nation*; Sharon Anne Cook, *Sex, Lies, and Cigarettes: Canadian Women, Smoking, and Visual Culture, 1880–2000* (Montreal and Kingston: McGill-Queen's University Press, 2012); Michael Dawson, *Selling British Columbia: Tourism and Consumer Culture, 1890–1970* (Vancouver: UBC Press, 2004); Valerie Korinek, *Roughing It in the Suburbs: Reading "Chatelaine" Magazine in the Fifties and Sixties* (Toronto: University of Toronto Press, 2000); Morton, *Ideal Surroundings*; Parr, *Domestic Goods*; Steve Penfold, *The Donut: A Canadian History* (Toronto: University of Toronto Press, 2008); Jarrett Rudy, *The Freedom to Smoke: Tobacco Consumption and Identity* (Montreal and Kingston: McGill-Queen's University Press, 2005); and Keith Walden, *Becoming Modern in Toronto: The Toronto Industrial Exhibition and the Shaping of a Late Victorian Culture* (Toronto: University of Toronto Press, 1997). Edited collections include Cheryl Krasnick Warsh and Dan Malleck, eds., *Consuming Modernity: Gendered Behaviour and Consumerism before the Baby Boom* (Vancouver: UBC Press, 2013); Franca Iacovetta, Valerie J. Korinek, and Marlene Epp, eds., *Edible Histories, Cultural Politics: Towards a Canadian Food History* (Toronto: University of Toronto Press, 2012).

45 This point is made especially well by Douglas McCalla in his book *Consumers in the Bush: Shopping in Rural Upper Canada* (Toronto: University of Toronto Press, 2015), loc 223 526, Kindle.

46 Lynn Hunt, *Writing History in the Global Era* (New York: Norton, 2014), loc. 111, Kindle. For an example of this conflation in practice, see Eric Hobsbawm, "Marx and History," *New Left Review* 1, no. 143 (January–February 1984): 39–50.

47 For example, Nils Gilman, *Mandarins of the Future: Modernization Theory in Cold War America* (Baltimore, MD: Johns Hopkins University Press, 2007).

48 Craig Clunas, "Things in Between: Splendour and Excess in Ming China," in *The Oxford Handbook of the History of Consumption*, ed. Frank Trentmann (Oxford: Oxford University Press, 2012), 47–63; S. Jonathan Wiesen, "National Socialism and Consumption," in *The Oxford Handbook of the History of Consumption*, ed. Trentmann, 433–50.

49 Trentmann, introduction to *The Oxford Handbook*, loc. 241, Kindle.

50 Trentmann, loc. 241, Kindle.

51 For example, Margaret Scammell, "The Internet and Civic Engagement: The Age of the Citizen-Consumer," *Political Communication* 17, no. 4 (2000): 351–5; Stewart Lockie, "Responsibility and Agency with Alternative Food Networks: Assembling the 'Citizen Consumer,'" *Agriculture and Human Values* 26, no. 3 (September 2009): 193–201; and Henry A. Giroux, "Schools for Sale: Public Education, Corporate Culture, and the Citizen-Consumer," *Educational Forum* 63, no. 2 (1999): 140–9.

52 James Davidson, "Citizen Consumers: The Athenian Democracy and the Origins of Western Consumption," in *The Oxford Handbook*, ed. Trentmann, 22–45.

53 The field is constantly expanding. See Lawrence Glickman, *Buying Power: A History of Consumer Activism in America* (Chicago: University of Chicago Press, 2009); Lizabeth Cohen, *A Consumers' Republic: The Politics of Mass Consumption in Postwar America* (New York: Vintage, 2001); Frank Trentmann, "Citizenship and Consumption," *Journal of Consumer Culture* 7, no. 2 (2007): 147–58; and Matthew Hilton, *Prosperity for All: Consumer Activism in an Era of Globalization* (Ithaca, NY: Cornell University Press, 2009).

54 On growth as a concept see Robert J. Gordon, *The Rise and Fall of American Growth: The U.S. Standard of Living since the Civil War* (Princeton, NJ: Princeton University Press, 2016).

55 As quoted in Donald Winch, "The Problematic Status of the Consumer in Orthodox Economic Thought," in *The Making of the Consumer: Knowledge, Power and Identity in the Modern World*, ed. Frank Trentmann (London: Berg, 2006), 31.

56 Hilton, *Prosperity for All*, 4.

57 Strong-Boag, *The Parliament of Women*, 243.

58 Parr, *Domestic Goods*; Ruth Frager, "Politicized Housewives in the Jewish Communist Movement of Toronto, 1923–1933," in *Beyond the Vote: Canadian Women and Politics*, ed. Joan Sangster and Linda Kealey (Toronto: University of Toronto Press, 1989), 258–75; Sangster, "Consuming Issues"; Guard, "Women Worth Watching"; Guard, "A Mighty Power against the Cost of Living," 27–47; Julie Guard, "The Politics of Milk," 271–85.

59 Fahrni, "Counting the Costs," 2.

60 Fahrni, 3.

61 Yuval-Davis, *The Politics of Belonging*, 47.

62 Yuval-Davis, 58.

63 Yuval-Davis, 47–8.

64 Yuval-Davis, 69.

65 The word *embodied* here points to the importance of race and gender in defining Canadian citizenship categories. It is borrowed from Yuval-Davis, who argues in *The Politics of Belonging* that the category of citizen "is embodied" and involves "concrete people who are differentially situated in terms of gender, class, ethnicity, sexuality, ability, stage in the life cycle, etc." See Yuval-Davis, 48.

66 Graham Broad, *A Small Price to Pay: Consumer Culture on the Canadian Home Front, 1939–45* (Vancouver: UBC Press, 2013); Parr, *Domestic Goods*; Ian Mosby, *Food Will Win the War: The Politics, Culture, and Science of Food on Canada's Home Front* (Vancouver: UBC Press, 2014).

67 Carolyn Goldstein, *Creating Consumers: Home Economists in Twentieth-Century America* (Chapel Hill: University of North Carolina Press, 2012).

68 Parr, *Domestic Goods*; Frager, "Politicized Housewives"; Sangster, "Consuming Issues"; Guard, "Women Worth Watching"; Guard, "A Mighty Power"; Guard, "The Politics of Milk"; Fahrni, "Counting the Costs."

69 Of particular importance are studies of consumer issues within Indigenous communities. More quantitative studies that track changes in commodity circulation over long periods are also required. Starting points include Monica Bodirsky and Jon Johnson, "Decolonizing Diet: Healing by Reclaiming Traditional Indigenous Foodways," *Cuizine* 1, no. 1 (2008): 1–11; Michael P. Milburn, "Indigenous Nutrition: Using Traditional Food Knowledge to Solve Contemporary Health Problems," *American Indian Quarterly* 28, no. 3/4 (Summer/Autumn 2004): 411–34; Ann M. Carlos and Frank D. Lewis, "Trade, Consumption, and the Native Economy: Lessons from York Factory, Hudson Bay," *Journal of Economic History* 61, no. 4 (December 2001): 1037–64; Nicholette Prince, "Influence of the Hudson's Bay Company on Carrier and Coast Salish Dress, 1830–1850," *Material History Review* 38 (Fall 1993): 15–26; Robert S. DuPlessis, "Was There a Consumer Revolution in Eighteenth-Century New France?," *French Colonial History* 1 (2002): 143–59; Frank D. Lewis and M.C. Urquhart, "Growth and the Standard of Living in a Pioneer Economy: Upper Canada, 1826–1851," *William and Mary Quarterly* 56, no. 1 (January 1999): 151–81; David-Thiery Ruddel, "Clothing, Society, and Consumer Trends in the Montreal Area, 1792–1835," in *New England / New France, 1600–1850*, ed. Peter Benes et al. (Boston: Boston University Press, 1989), 122–34; Eric Sager and Peter Baskerville, "Unemployment, Living Standards, and the Working-Class Family in Urban Canada in 1901," *History of the Family* 2, no. 3 (1997): 229–54; David Gagan and Rosemary Gagan, "Working-Class Standards of Living in Late-Victorian Urban Ontario: A Review of the Miscellaneous Evidence on the Quality

of Material Life," *Journal of the Canadian Historical Association* 1, no. 1
(1990): 171–93; Trevor J.O. Dick, "Consumer Behavior in the Nineteenth
Century and Ontario Workers, 1885–1889," *Journal of Economic History*
46, no. 2 (June 1986): 477–88; Dominique Bouchard, "La culture matérielle des canadiens au XVIIIe siècle: Analyse du niveau de vie des
artisans du fer," *Revue d'histoire de l'Amérique française* 47, no. 4 (Spring
1994): 479–98; J.C. Herbert Emery and Clint Levitt, "Cost of Living,
Real Wages and Real Incomes in Thirteen Canadian Cities, 1900–1950,"
*Canadian Journal of Economics* 35, no. 1 (February 2002): 115–37; Sylvie
Taschereau, "L'arme favorite de l'épicier indépendant: Éléments d'une
histoire sociale du crédit (Montréal, 1920–1940)," *Journal of the Canadian
Historical Association* 4, no. 1 (1993): 265–92; Bettina Liverant, "From
Budgeting to Buying: Canadian Consumerism in the Post War Era," *Past
Imperfect* 8 (1999–2000): 62–92.

## 1 Temperance and the Rise of Sober Consumer Culture

1  See *Boardwalk Empire*, season 1, episode 1, "Boardwalk Empire," directed
   by Martin Scorsese, written by Terence Winter, aired 19 September 2010
   on HBO.
2  Mariana Valverde, "'When the Mother of the Race Is Free': Race,
   Reproduction, and Sexuality in First-Wave Feminism," in *Gender
   Conflicts: New Essays in Women's History*, ed. Mariana Valverde and
   Franca Iacovetta (Toronto: University of Toronto Press, 1992), 3–26;
   Sharon Cook, *"Through Sunshine and Shadow": The Women's Christian
   Temperance Union, Evangelicalism, and Reform in Ontario, 1874–1930*
   (Montreal and Kingston: McGill-Queen's University Press, 1995);
   Wendy Mitchinson, "The WCTU: 'For God, Home and Native Land': A
   Study in Nineteenth-Century Feminism," in *A Not Unreasonable Claim:
   Women and Reform in Canada, 1880s–1920s*, ed. Linda Kealey (Toronto:
   Women's Press, 1979), 151–68; Lorna McLean, "'Deserving' Wives and
   'Drunken' Husbands: Wife Beating, Marital Conduct, and the Law in
   Ontario, 1850–1910," *Histoire sociale / Social History* 69 (2002): 59–81;
   Kathryn Harvey, "Amazons and Victims: Resisting Wife-Abuse in
   Working-Class Montreal, 1869–1879," *Journal of the Canadian Historical
   Association / Revue de la Société historique du Canada* 2, no. 1 (1991):
   131–48.
3  Erika Rappaport, "Sacred and Useful Pleasures: The Temperance Tea
   Party and the Creation of a Sober Consumer Culture in Early Industrial
   Britain," *Journal of British Studies* 52, no. 4 (October 2013): 990–1016.
4  Rappaport, 1009, 993, 1004.
5  Rappaport, 1009.

6  Mary Scott, "Historical Sketch of the Dominion W.C.T.U.," *Woman's Journal*, May 1893, 1.

7  Wendy Mitchinson, "Woman's Christian Temperance Union," *The Oxford Companion to Canadian History*, ed. Gerald Hallowell (Toronto: Oxford University Press, 2004), 667.

8  Cook, *"Through Sunshine and Shadow,"* 7, 10, 87.

9  Mrs. Lottie McAlister, "Editorial: Nation Building," *Canadian White Ribbon Tidings*, May 1909, 1404.

10  Cook, *"Through Sunshine and Shadow,"* 19, 55.

11  *The Woman's Journal* was edited first by Mrs. Chisholm of Ottawa, then Miss Mary Scott of Ottawa, and finally by Annie O. Rutherford of Toronto; see "Published Monthly," *Woman's Journal*, January 1885, 1; "The Woman's Journal," *Woman's Journal*, March 1890, 4; "The Womans Journal," *Woman's Journal*, 15 March 1901, 6; "The Womans Journal," *Woman's Journal*, February 1903, 2.

12  In its first few years *White Ribbon Bulletin* was edited by Mrs. Asa Gordon of Ottawa, but by 1920 Mrs. Gordon Wright of London (Ontario) had assumed the editor-in-chief position. Barrie resident Mrs. Blanche Read Johnston, a prolific contributor, was editor, and Mrs. B.S. Cleveland of Saskatoon, Saskatchewan, was associate editor; "Canada's White Ribbon Bulletin," *White Ribbon Bulletin*, June 1910, 3; "Canada's White Ribbon Bulletin," *White Ribbon Bulletin*, July 1920, 10.

13  "'Tidings' Our Official Paper," *Canadian White Ribbon Tidings*, November 1939, 190. Mrs. Lottie McAlister, a Methodist minister's wife who had grown up near Milton (Ontario) and had completed a business training course, was the most prolific contributor; between 1906 and her death in 1936 she devoted much time to the journal.

14  Other editors included London-based activists Mrs. Gordon Wright, Mrs. Frederic H Waycott, and Mrs. Flora Yorke Miller. In June 1931 Mrs. L.C. McKinney of Claresholm, Alberta, was listed as the *Tidings'* editor; however, by October of that year Mrs. F.C. Ward of Toronto had filled the position. See "Tidings' Publication Board," *Canadian White Ribbon Tidings*, June 1906, back page; "Canadian White Ribbon Tidings," *Canadian White Ribbon Tidings*, 15 May 1908, 1104; "Canadian White Ribbon Tidings," *Canadian White Ribbon Tidings*, 15 October 1907, 1034; "The Canadian White Ribbon Tidings," *Canadian White Ribbon Tidings*, June 1931, 1; "The Canadian White Ribbon Tidings," *Canadian White Ribbon Tidings*, October 1931, 1.

15  Cook, *"Through Sunshine and Shadow,"* 147.

16  See, for example, *Woman's Journal*, February 1886, front page.

17  See, for example, *White Ribbon Tidings*, February 1910, front cover.

18 Its March 1915 cover featured the quotation "The Lord Giveth the Word; The Women That Publish the Tidings Are a Great Host" (a paraphrase of Psalms 68:11): see cover, *Woman's Century*, March 1915.

19 "Cider the Devil's Kindling Tool," *White Ribbon Bulletin*, February 1913, 32.

20 Mrs. May R. Thornley, "An Emergency," *Canadian White Ribbon Tidings*, November 1926, 222.

21 "How the Liquor Traffic Benefits the Dominion," *Woman's Journal*, December 1893, 8.

22 Strong-Boag, *Parliament of Women*, 316–18, 365–6, 390–2.

23 Wm. E. Scott, Deputy Minister of Agriculture, British Columbia, "Patriotic Purchasing," *Canadian White Ribbon Tidings*, July 1916, 173.

24 Western Canadian ideologues were against economic nationalism, arguing that the Made-in-Canada campaign privileged central Canadian manufacturers at the expense of western farmers, who in turn relied upon free markets to buy and sell at reasonable prices. See, for example, Georgina Newhall, "Household Economics and Politics," *Woman's Century*, May 1917, 8–9.

25 Canadian Trade Commission, "Canadian Women Buy at Home," *Canadian White Ribbon Tidings*, April 1919, 94.

26 Craig Heron, *Booze: A Distilled History* (Toronto: Between the Lines, 2003), 59, 166.

27 "British Columbia Is Not Getting Rich," *Canadian White Ribbon Tidings*, October 1923, 202; "Manitoba's Liquor Money," *Canadian White Ribbon Tidings*, October 1923, front page; "Government Sale the Worst Solution," *Canadian White Ribbon Tidings*, October 1924, front page; "Paying the Public Debt Out of the Liquor Business," *Canadian White Ribbon Tidings*, July–August 1924, 149; "Manitoba," *Canadian White Ribbon Tidings*, July–August 1926, 162; "Liquor-Unemployment Doles," *Canadian White Ribbon Tidings*, May 1926, front page; "'Control' Means More Drinking in Que.," *Canadian White Ribbon Tidings*, May 1926, front page; "Our Home Heart Debased," *Canadian White Ribbon Tidings*, July–August 1927, front page. On the introduction of government control see Heron, *Booze*, 270.

28 "Liquor and National Prosperity," *Canadian White Ribbon Tidings*, October 1933, 206.

29 Dorothy E. Clarke, "Liquor and Progress," *Canadian White Ribbon Tidings*, June 1935, 135.

30 For example, Kenneth McNaught, *A Prophet in Politics: A Biography of J.S. Woodsworth* (Toronto: University of Toronto Press, 2001).

31 "Tarr's Bazaar," *Woman's Journal*, January 1885, 3; "Womans' Peculiar Ills," *Woman's Journal*, May 1899, 9; "T. Eaton & Co.," *Woman's Journal*,

December 1886, 3; "The Robert Simpson Co. Limited," *Woman's Journal*, 31 January 1898, 12.

32 Mary Vipond, *The Mass Media in Canada*, 3rd. ed. (Toronto: James Lorimer, 2000), 18–20.

33 Susan Porter Benson, *Counter Cultures: Saleswomen, Managers, and Customers in American Department Stores, 1890–1940* (Urbana and Chicago: University of Illinois Press, 1988), 131–43.

34 "Happenings," *Woman's Journal*, 15 November 1899, 1.

35 Archer Wallace, "Secret of a Great Merchant's Success," *Canadian White Ribbon Tidings*, March 1932, 70; reprinted from *The Canadian Baptist*.

36 "Honor Roll of Magazines Not Advertising Liquors," *Canadian White Ribbon Tidings*, 1 February 1911, 1839.

37 "The Canadian Home Journal," *Canadian White Ribbon Tidings*, May 1919, 110.

38 Happy Thought Soap advertisement, *Woman's Journal*, July 1898, back cover.

39 Editorial, *Canadian White Ribbon Tidings*, 15 January 1908, 1098.

40 Certainly, "With Our Advertisers" helped the Ontario WCTU maintain a publication that was independent of the national office. Shortly after the "With Our Advertisers" scheme had been discontinued, *Tidings* was transferred to the Dominion branch. "With Our Advertisers," *Canadian White Ribbon Tidings*, 1 August 1911, 1979.

41 A 1916 annual report indicates that the Ontario WCTU received income of $1,276.29 from advertisements, enabling the advertisement department, after expenses, to maintain a balance of $491.23; "Report 1915–1916," *Canadian White Ribbon Tidings*, 1 November 1916, 263.

42 "With Our Advertisers," *Canadian White Ribbon Tidings*, 1 May 1912, 2193.

43 "With Our Advertisers," May 1920, 112.

44 "With Our Advertisers," 1 November 1917, 262.

45 "What Are They to Me?," *Canadian White Ribbon Tidings*, September 1921, 213, reprinted from the *Galt Daily Reporter*.

46 Portrayals of shopping women as selfish and destructive during this period were common; see Donica Belisle, "Crazy for Bargains: Inventing the Irrational Female Shopper in Modernizing English Canada," *Canadian Historical Review*, December 2011, 581–606.

47 "The Saloon Bar," *Canadian White Ribbon Tidings*, September 1932, 187.

48 "White Ribbon," Chatham, New Brunswick, "Temperance Hotels," *Woman's Journal*, February 1891, 2.

49 "Local Option," *Canadian White Ribbon Tidings*, 1 March 1904.

50 For example, "King Edward Hotel of Toronto Reports Best Year in History," *Canadian White Ribbon Tidings*, April 1921, 93.

51 "Temperance Hotels," *Canadian White Ribbon Tidings*, 15 December 1905, 469.
52 "Public Accommodation in Local Option Districts," *Canadian White Ribbon Tidings*, 15 June 1907, 939.
53 "Hotels in Canada Revived When Dry," *Canadian White Ribbon Tidings*, 11 December 1919, 158; originally published in the *Toronto Globe*.
54 "Blenheim under Prohibition," *Canadian White Ribbon Tidings*, 1 July 1904, unpaginated.
55 "A Little Girl's Testimony," *Woman's Journal*, November 1885, unpaginated.
56 "A Successful Coffee House," *Woman's Journal*, July–August 1893, 2.
57 Steve Pincus, "'Coffee Politicians Does Create': Coffeehouses and Restoration Political Culture," *Journal of Modern History* 67, no. 4 (December 1995): 807–34.
58 Jessica Sewell, "Tea and Suffrage," *Food, Culture & Society* 11, no. 4 (December 2008): 500.
59 "Milk a True Elixir of Life," *Canadian White Ribbon Tidings*, 1 June 1917, 126.
60 Miss Laura Hughes, "Milk Bars!!!," *Canadian White Ribbon Tidings*, October 1937, 173.
61 Hughes, "Milk Bars!!!"
62 Steve Penfold, *The Donut: A Canadian History* (Toronto: University of Toronto Press, 2008).
63 Hughes, "Milk Bars!!!"
64 S.M.W., "Cornwall's New Drinking Fountain," *Woman's Journal*, October 1901, 5.
65 S.M.W., "Cornwall's New Drinking Fountain," 5.
66 "The Use of the Pure Juice of the Grape at the Lord's Table," *Canadian White Ribbon Tidings*, 15 July 1905, unpaginated.
67 "Modern Fashions," *Canadian White Ribbon Tidings*, January 1932, 14.
68 "Non-alcoholic Fruit Products," *Canadian White Ribbon Tidings*, May 1935, 114.
69 "Non-alcoholic Fruit Product," 114; also, "Fruit Drinks," *Canadian White Ribbon Tidings*, February 1937, 112.
70 "Temperance Recipes," *Woman's Journal*, January 1892, 7.
71 Mrs. Shortreed, "A Special Appeal," *Woman's Journal*, December 1885, 1.
72 R. Fulton Irwin, "Good Literature: For Whom?," *Canadian White Ribbon Tidings*, May 1909, 1398.
73 "Christ in the Comfort Bag," *Woman's Journal*, February 1901, 6.
74 "Christ in the Comfort Bag," 6; also, "Good Reading for the Comfort Bags," *Canadian White Ribbon Tidings*, 15 June 1906, 519.
75 "Help the Sailors," *Woman's Journal*, April 1890, 1.

76  "Sailor's Rest," *Woman's Journal*, June 1892, 2.
77  "Our Sailors," *Canadian White Ribbon Tidings*, October 1912, 1.
78  Olivia C. Whitman, "Work among Sailors," *Woman's Journal*, April 1982, 3.
79  Cook, "Wet Canteens," 319.
80  "Dominion," *White Ribbon Bulletin*, December 1914, 180.
81  Cook, "Wet Canteens," 324.
82  Editorial, *Canadian White Ribbon Tidings*, September 2015, 212.
83  "Our New War Programme," *Canadian White Ribbon Tidings*, October 1917, 227.
84  "Our Boys Are Thirsty," *Canadian White Ribbon Tidings*, October 1917, 229.
85  Front page, *Canadian White Ribbon Tidings*, December 1917, 1.
86  "Alcohol Is Costly," *Canadian White Ribbon Tidings*, June 1931, 148.
87  "How Some Women Earn Money," *Woman's Journal*, April 1890, 1.
88  H.B.B., "Undervalued Work of Wives," *Canadian White Ribbon Tidings*, 1 February 1910, 1583; republished from *The Women's Journal*.
89  "The Greedy Bottle," *Woman's Journal*, October 1898, 8; "The Greedy Bottle," *Canadian White Ribbon Tidings*, 15 April 1908, 1153; "New Shoes," *Canadian White Ribbon Tidings*, January 1932, 15.
90  "Most Popular Bar-Tenders in Montreal," *Canadian White Ribbon Tidings*, 1 July 1904, no page number; "Why Money Spent in Drink Is Worse Than Wasted," *Canadian White Ribbon Tidings*, June 1934, 139.
91  "Sing a Song of Whiskey," *Canadian White Ribbon Tidings*, November 1915, 217.
92  F.J. Blanchard, "The Rum Mill's Grist," *Canadian White Ribbon Tidings*, 1 July 1905, no page; F.J Blanchard, "The Rum Mill's Grist," *Canadian White Ribbon Tidings*, 15 July 1905, 398.
93  "The Price of a Drink," *White Ribbon Bulletin*, October 1911, 9.
94  For example, "The Home of the Drinker," *Canadian White Ribbon Tidings*, October 1931, 216; "Beer Bubbles," *Canadian White Ribbon Tidings*, May 1933, 114.
95  Critic, "The Price of a Drink," *White Ribbon Bulletin*, October 1911, 9; Mariana Valverde, *The Age of Light, Soap, and Water: Moral Reform in English Canada, 1885–1925*, 2nd ed. (Toronto: University of Toronto Press, 2008).
96  "The Home of the Drinker," *Canadian White Ribbon Tidings*, October 1931, 216; "The Drunkard's Bargain," *Woman's Journal*, June 1892, 1.
97  "Do You Want a Home?," *Woman's Journal*, September 1893, 1.
98  Editorial, *Woman's Century*, July 1919, 6.
99  "It Means Billions to Legitimate Business," *Canadian White Ribbon Tidings*, July–August 1929, 149.

100 "What Drink Costs," *Woman's Journal*, 1 March 1900, 10.
101 E. Ryerson Young, "Curly's New Suit," *Canadian White Ribbon Tidings*, April 1924, 93.
102 "Beer Money," *Woman's Journal*, August 1901, 10.
103 Goldstein, *Creating Consumers*, 21–61.
104 "Our Thrift Department," *Canadian White Ribbon Tidings*, April 1921, 93.
105 "Drinking Less and Riding More," *Canadian White Ribbon Tidings*, December 1926, 251.
106 Editorial, *White Ribbon Bulletin*, November 1910, 4.
107 Editorial, *Canadian White Ribbon Tidings*, 1 April 1916, 86.
108 "The Veranda as a Summer Living Room," *Canadian White Ribbon Tidings*, 15 July 1905, 975; "Furnishing the Spare Room," *Canadian White Ribbon Tidings*, 1 September 1910, 1739; "Care in Selecting Wall Paper," *Canadian White Ribbon Tidings*, 1 February 1910, 1596; "In the Guest Room," *Canadian White Ribbon Tidings*, 1 November 1911, 2054; "Pictures in the Home," *Canadian White Ribbon Tidings*, 1 October 1911, 2030; "The Christmas Table," *Canadian White Ribbon Tidings*, 1 December 1912, 2363; "Hanging Pictures," *Canadian White Ribbon Tidings*, January 1913, 20; "Colour Scheme for a Living Room," *Canadian White Ribbon Tidings*, 1 November 1913, 262; R.E. Dinnick, "Effective Lighting in the Farm Home," *Canadian White Ribbon Tidings*, 1 November 1916, 266; L.D. Stearns, "What Constitutes Home," *Canadian White Ribbon Tidings*, April 1920, 94.
109 "A Happy Home," *Canadian White Ribbon Tidings*, 15 August 1905, 630.
110 "The Furnishing of a Home in Relation to Health and Happiness," *Canadian White Ribbon Tidings*, January 1914, 310.
111 "A Happy Home," *Canadian White Ribbon Tidings*, 15 August 1905, 630.
112 "The Good Housekeeper," *Canadian White Ribbon Tidings*, 15 February 1899, 1.
113 "A Happy Home," *Canadian White Ribbon Tidings*, 15 August 1905, 630.
114 D. Stearns, "What Constitutes Home," *Canadian White Ribbon Tidings*, April 1920, 94.
115 Channing, "My Symphony," *White Ribbon Bulletin*, February 1910, 6.

## 2 Shopping for Victory

1 Robert Brown and Ramsay Cook, *Canada, 1896–1921: A Nation Transformed* (Toronto: McClelland & Stewart, 1976), 72.
2 As quoted in Brown and Cook, 275.
3 Stacey Barker, "'Save Today What Our Allies Need Tomorrow': Food Regulation in Canada during the First World War" (master's thesis, Department of History, Carleton University, 2003), 69.
4 Barker, 228.

5 Barker, 98–9.

6 Meg Jacobs, *Pocketbook Politics: Economic Citizenship in Twentieth-Century America* (Princeton, NJ: Princeton University Press, 2005), 60.

7 "An Act to Confer Certain Powers upon the Governor in Council and to Amend the Immigration Act," Early Canadiana Online, accessed 15 March 2012, http://canadiana.org; P.C. 1460, *Canada Gazette*, 16 June 1917, in RG 13, vol. 1934, file 1924/1917, Library and Archives Canada (hereafter cited as LAC).

8 P.C. 3211, *Canada Gazette*, 15 November 1917, in RG 13, vol. 1934, file 1924/1917, LAC.

9 Brown and Cook, *Canada*, 240.

10 Barker, "'Save Today,'" 170.

11 Also John Herd Thompson, *The Harvests of War: The Prairie West, 1914–1918* (Toronto: McClelland & Stewart, 1978), 158.

12 "Jottings from Billboard," *The Voice*, 28 September 1917, accessed 16 March 2012, http://manitobia.ca.

13 Barker, "Save Today," 161–2.

14 Order 45, *Canada Gazette*, 12 June 1918.

15 Mourad Djebabla, "Le gouvernement fédéral et la diète de guerre proposée et imposée aux Canadiens ou la Première Guerre Mondiale et la consommation 'patriotiquement responsible,' 1917–1918," *Association québécoise d'histoire politique*, Autumn 2011, 171–89.

16 W.J. Hanna to Sir, 12 December 1917, in RG13, A2, vol. 217, LAC.

17 Barker, "Save Today," 130; "War Gardens' Display at the Armories," *Woman's Century*, September 1918.

18 "Food Controller Looks to Housewives," *Woman's Century*, September 1917, 4.

19 Robert Rutherdale, *Hometown Horizons: Local Responses to Canada's Great War* (Vancouver: UBC Press, 2004), 207.

20 Food Service Pledge, 1917, as reproduced in "Food Controller Looks to Housewives," *Woman's Century*, September 1917.

21 "Vision Your Sons," *Toronto Daily Star*, 11 September 1917, 10.

22 Canada Food Board, "Daily Office Bulletin," 10 February 1918, in RG 13, A2, vol. 217, LAC.

23 Barker, "Save Today," 143.

24 Mrs. G.L. Foulkes, "What Food Saving Really Is," *Victoria Colonist*, 22 July 1917, 16.

25 Kathleen Kyle, "The Call to Women," *Everywoman's World*, September 1917, 26.

26 *Women's War Conference*, 2–4, 14–18, 46.

27 Kathleen Bowker, "Active National Service for Women," *Woman's Century*, August 1917, 10.

28 National Council of Women, *Woman's Century*, March 1918, 10.

29　"Woes of Food Controllers," *Woman's Century*, November 1917, 2.

30　Kathleen Kyle, "The Call to Women," *Woman's Century*, September 1917, 26.

31　Kathleen Bowker, "Active National Service for Women," *Woman's Century*, August 1917, 10.

32　Barker, "Save Today," 208.

33　As quoted in Barker, 132.

34　As quoted in Barker, 157–8.

35　"Conservation and Education Were Outstanding Topics at Quebec Convention," *Canadian Home Journal*, August 1918, 32.

36　See also Strong-Boag, *Parliament of Women*, vii.

37　"November Thirteen Chosen for Canvass," *Victoria Times*, 1 November 1917, 15.

38　"Food Control and Woman's Duty," *Woman's Century*, November 1917, 8.

39　"Woman's Century," *Woman's Century*, August 1917, 8; Violet McNaughton to the editors, *Woman's Century*, March 1915, 8.

40　Margaret Graham Horton, "Pledge Card for the Deserving Rich," *Woman's Century*, April 1918, 12, 14.

41　"Food Control: A Grasp of the Situation," *Woman's Century*, December 1917, 8.

42　"Red Cross Society to Observe Food," *Victoria Times*, 19 July 1918, 6; "Rotarians Pledged to Conservation," *Victoria Colonist*, 6 July 1917, 7.

43　Barker, "Save Today," 176–7.

44　"Women's Forum Discuss Food Conservation and Its Attendant Problems," *Vancouver Sun*, 19 September 1917, 5.

45　"Our Organized Women Move: Will Canada Follow?," *Woman's Century*, September 1917, 10.

46　Isabel M. Ross, "Educational Division: Canada Food Board," *Woman's Century*, May 1918, 4.

47　"Our Organized Women Move," *Woman's Century*, September 1917.

48　"Testing Time for the Civilian," *Montreal Gazette*, 3 May 1918, 7.

49　T. Moore, "Saskatchewan," *Woman's Century*, January 1918, 10.

50　Untitled, *Woman's Century*, August 1917, 7.

51　Editorial on food rations, *Woman's Century*, February 1918, 10.

52　"Saskatchewan," *Woman's Century*, April 1918, 30.

53　Dr. John McCollough, "The Best Foods to Buy during the War," *Woman's Century*, August 1915, 4.

54　Mrs. J. Campbell-MacIver, "Thrift and Production," *Woman's Century*, April 1916, 3.

55　"Canada Food Board Recipe Books," poster, 1918, Toronto Public Library, http://www.torontopubliclibrary.ca.

56  "Mrs. Buchanan of Ravenna," *Everywoman's World*, September 1917, 28b.
57  See Matthew Hilton, "The Legacy of Luxury: Moralities of Consumption since the 18th Century," *Journal of Consumer Culture* 4 (2004): 101–23.
58  "La vie en temps de guerre," *La Bonne Parole*, July–August 1917, 14.
59  Mrs. G.L. Foulkes, "What Food Saving Really Is," *Victoria Colonist*, 22 July 1917, 16.
60  M. Alberta Deards, "A War Suggestion for Women," *Woman's Century*, April 1917, 18.
61  Louise Morris, "Extravagances and the War," *Woman's Century*, January 1917, 4.
62  Brown and Cook, *Canada*, 296.
63  Joan Sangster, "Mobilizing Women for War," in *Canada and the First World War: Essays in Honour of Robert Craig Brown*, ed. David Clark MacKenzie (Toronto: University of Toronto Press, 2005), 158
64  Morris, "Extravagances and the War," *Woman's Century*, January 1917, 4.
65  E. Blakely, "Luxury and Womanhood," *Woman's Century*, January 1917, 15.
66  Louise-Amélie Gayrand, "Le feminisme et la guerre," *La Bonne Parole*, March 1917, 66.
67  "Food Control and Woman's Duty, or Is Canada's Womanhood behind Her English Sister?," *Woman's Century*, November 1917, 8.
68  W.J. Hanna, "The Women of Canada Must Face the Situation," *Woman's Century*, February 1918, 15.
69  "Food Control," *Woman's Century*, January 1918, 12.
70  Katherine M. Caldwell, "An Army of Savers," *Everywoman's World*, September 1917, 25.
71  "How to Conserve Wheat, Meal and Bacon," *Woman's Century*, September 1917, 12
72  Mrs. Edwin Long, "Let Us Conserve Our Available Strength," *Woman's Century*, September 1916, 18.
73  Mrs. Edwin Long, 18.
74  "Montreal Women's Club," *Woman's Century*, May 1916, 23; Mrs. J.A. Wilson, *Ottawa Free Press*, February 1916, 24; "Brantford," *Woman's Century*, July 1919, 16.
75  "Montreal Women's Club," *Woman's Century*, May 1916, 23.
76  "National Council," *Woman's Century*, June 1916, 5–6.
77  W.J. Hanna, "The Women of Canada Must Face the Situation," *Woman's Century*, February 1918, 15.
78  "Buy Fresh Fish," Canada Food Board, 1918, MIKAN no. 3635511, accessed 19 March 2012, http://data2.archives.ca.
79  "Waste Not – Want Not," Canada Food Board, 1918, MIKAN no. 2897697, accessed 19 March 2012, http://data2.archives.ca.

80 Sangster, "Mobilizing Women," 153.
81 "Remember We Must Feed Daddy Too," Canada Food Board, 1918, accessed 27 March 2012, www.archives.gov.on.ca.
82 Sarah Glassford and Amy Shaw, "Transformation in a Time of War?," introduction to *A Sisterhood of Suffering and Service: Women and Girls of Canada and Newfoundland during the First World War*, ed. Glassford and Shaw (Vancouver: UBC Press, 2012), 12–13.
83 Jacobs, *Pocketbook Politics*, 60.

### 3 Home Economics and the Training of the Consumer Citizenry

1 Goldstein, *Creating Consumers*.
2 Shirley Rebus, Arlene Smith, and Norma Bannerman, "Canadian Home Economics Association, 1939–1989," *Illinois Teacher of Home Economics* 33, no. 1 (1989): 2.
3 These are available at the Glenbow Museum in Calgary, Alberta.
4 Goldstein, *Creating Consumers*, 23.
5 Goldstein, 24, 25.
6 McCalla, *Consumers in the Bush*, 11.
7 McCalla, 226n5. McCalla singles out the following authors as having misrepresented the consumer habits of rural people in the eighteenth through twentieth centuries: Alvin Finkel, Margaret Conrad, Donica Belisle, Randy Widdis, Michael Bliss, Kenneth Norrie, Douglas Owram, and J.C. Emery. See McCalla, 226–7, notes 5–8.
8 McCalla, 162–85. Beatrice Craig makes a similar argument regarding rural New Brunswick in *Backwoods Consumers and Homespun Capitalists: The Rise of a Market Culture in Eastern Canada* (Toronto: University of Toronto Press, 2009).
9 Goldstein, *Creating Consumers*, 26.
10 Goldstein, 25.
11 Goldstein, 26.
12 Catherine Charron, "Le front domestique à la Fédération nationale Saint-Jean-Baptiste: Entre crise de la domesticité et promotion de l'enseignement ménager, 1900–1927," *Histoire sociale/Social History* 43, no. 86 (2010): 345–68.
13 Johanna Gudrun Wilson, "A History of Home Economics Education in Manitoba 1826–1966" (master's thesis, University of Manitoba, 1966), 17.
14 Edith Rowles Simpson, *Home Economics in Canada: Prologue to Change* Saskatoon: University of Saskatchewan: 1964), 20–1, 19.
15 Simpson, 18.
16 James Snell, *Macdonald Institute: Remembering the Past, Embracing the Future* (Toronto: Dundurn, 2003).

17 Snell, *Macdonald Institute*.

18 Simpson, *Home Economics*, 80–91; Snell, *Macdonald Institute*, 19; *The University of Alberta Calendar, 1922–23* (Edmonton: University of Alberta, 1922), 56–8; Conférence donnée aux Écoles Ménagères provinciales," *La revue culinaire*, 15 January 1933, 14, Collection Institut Notre-Dame du Bon-Conseil de Montréal, P783, Centre d'archives de Montréal (hereafter cited as CAM).

19 Sara Burke, "Dancing into Education: The First World War and the Roots of Change in Women's Higher Education," in *Cultures, Communities, and Conflict: Histories of Canadian Universities and War*, ed. E. Lisa Panayotidis and Paul James Stortz (Toronto: University of Toronto Press, 2012), 95–120.

20 Paul Axelrod, *Making a Middle Class: Student Life in English Canada during the Thirties* (Montreal and Kingston: McGill-Queen's University Press, 1990), 67.

21 Ruby Heap, "From the Science of Housekeeping to the Science of Nutrition: Pioneers in Canadian Nutrition and Dietetics at the University of Toronto's Faculty of Household Science, 1900–1950," in *Challenging Professions: Historical and Contemporary Perspectives on Women's Professional Work*, ed. Elizabeth Smyth, Sandra Acker, Paula Bourne, and Alison Prentice (Toronto: University of Toronto Press, 1999), 141–70.

22 Mary Wilson, "Certified Women: Professional Program Curriculum at the Macdonald Institute for Domestic Science in Guelph, Ontario, Canada, 1903–1920," *History of Intellectual Culture* 8, no. 1 (2008/09): 1; Marta Danylewycz, "Domestic Science Education in Ontario, 1900–1940," in *Gender and Education in Ontario: An Historical Reader*, ed. Ruby Heap and Alison Prentice (Toronto: Canadian Scholars' Press, 1991), 142. See also Marta Danylewycz, Nadia Fahmy-Eid, and Nicole Thivierge, "'L'enseignment ménager' et les 'Home Economics' au Québec et en Ontario au début du 20e siècle Une analyse comparée," in *An Imperfect Past: Education and Society in Canadian History*, ed. J. Donald Wilson (Vancouver: UBC Press, 1984), 67–119, Diana Pederson, "The Scientific Training of Mothers: The Campaign for Domestic Science in Ontario Schools, 1890–1913," in *Critical Issues in the History of Canadian Science, Technology and Medicine*, ed. Richard A. Jarrell and Arnold E. Roos (Ottawa, ON: HSTC Publications, 1983), 178–94; Barbara Riley, "Six Saucepans to One: Domestic Science vs. the Home in British Columbia, 1900–1930," in *Not Just Pin Money: Selected Essays on the History of Women's Work in British Columbia*, ed. Barbara K. Latham and Roberta J. Pazdro (Victoria, BC: Camosun College, 1984), 159–81; Robert Stamp, "Teaching Girls Their God Given Place in Life: The Introduction of

Home Economics in the Schools," *Atlantis* 2, no. 2 (Spring 1977): 18–34; and Sherene Razack, "Schools for Happiness: Instituts Familiaux and the Education of Ideal Wives and Mothers," in *Delivering Motherhood: Maternal Ideologies and Practices in the 19th and 20th Centuries*, ed. Katherine Arnup, Andrée Levesque, and Ruth Roach Pierson (New York: Routledge, 1990), 211–37.

23 Ellen H. Richards, preface to *Woman Who Spends* (Boston: Barrows & Whitcomb, 1904), 1.

24 Bertha M. Terrill, *Household Management* (Chicago: American School of Household Economics, 1905).

25 "MacDonald Institute, Ontario Agricultural College, Easter Examinations, 1905–1905," Guelph University Archives, RE1 MAC A0004.

26 *Les Écoles Ménagères Provinciales*, 1906, Collection Institut Notre-Dame du Bon-Conseil de Montréal, P783, S3, CAM.

27 House Furnishing Exam, March 1912, UA 28, box 45, folder 20, examination papers, University of Manitoba Archives.

28 Collection Institut Notre-Dame du Bon-Conseil de Montréal, P783, IFP 1447, CAM.

29 "Course of Instruction, Household Science," A 75–0008/014(a), University of Toronto Archives.

30 Finding aid for Edith Ewart Papers, Mount Allison University Archives.

31 "Courses of Instruction, Household Science," in *Curriculum for Matriculation, 1928–9*, University of Toronto (Toronto: University of Toronto Press, 1928), 16.

32 Harriet A.L. Clark Fonds (1146), file B1990-0043/005(02), University of Toronto Archives and Records Management.

33 *The University of Alberta Calendar, 1922–23* (Edmonton: University of Alberta, 1922), 56–8.

34 Collection Institut Notre-Dame du Bon-Conseil de Montréal, P783, S3.0, CAM.

35 "Ecole des Sciences Ménagères," [c. 1915], Division des archives, Université de Montréal.

36 Carol Anderson and Katharine Mallinson, *Lunch with Lady Eaton: Inside the Dining Rooms of the Nation* (Toronto: ECW Press, 2004), 99.

37 "Economy and Efficiency Test at Domestic Science Class," *Woman's Century*, December 1916, 23.

38 Unsigned letter to Mr. H.G. Wright, 16 June 1918, RE1 MAC A0004, Guelph University Archives.

39 Letter to Mr. Norris, The Nineteen Hundred Washer Co., 6 June 1921, RE1 MAC A0004, Guelph University Archives.

40 Gunns Limited to Miss Wilson, 31 March 1920; W.D. Shamrock and Company to MacDonald Institute, 11 March 1920; T. Eaton Company to

Dr. G.I. Christie, 19 October 1929, RE1 MAC A0004, Guelph University Archives.

41  "MacDonald Institute Easter Examinations, 1936–1937, Household Management," RE1 MAC A0004, Guelph University Archives; also Amy Sue Bix, "Equipped for Life: Gendered Technical Training and Consumerism in Home Economics, 1920–1980," *Technology and Culture* 43, no. 4 (October 2002): 733.

42  Conférence donnée aux Écoles Ménagères provinciales," *La revue culinaire*, 15 January 1933, 14, Collection Institut Notre-Dame du Bon-Conseil de Montréal, P783, CAM.

43  Olive R. Cruikshank to G.I. Christie, 25 October 1932, RE1 MAC A0004, Guelph University Archives.

44  Nova Scotia Home Economics Association, *Newsletter*, December 1931, accession 7918, catalogue 2, Mount Allison University Archives.

45  Heidi MacDonald, "Maritime Women, the Great Depression, and the Dominion-Provincial Youth Training Program, 1937–39," in *Making Up the State: Women in 20th Century Atlantic Canada*, ed. Janet Guildford and Suzanne Morton (Fredericton, NB: Acadiensis Press, 2010), 142.

46  *University of Toronto Calendar, 1936–7* (Toronto: University of Toronto Press, 1937).

47  In terms of classroom instruction, 1930s home economics curricula closely resembled those of the 1920s. The University of Alberta continued to offer junior and senior courses in sewing, home nursing, textiles, foods, and household management; at mid-decade, home furnishing and clothing design courses were added.

48  "Federated Women's Institutes Sponsor Home Economics Week," Home Economics Week scrapbook, file 67, M1670, Alberta Home Economics Association, Glenbow Museum and Archives, Calgary, Alberta (hereafter cited as Glenbow).

49  "Three Clubs Join to Hold Exhibition," Home Economics Week scrapbook, file 67, M1670, Alberta Home Economics Association, Glenbow.

50  "Three Clubs Join to Hold Exhibition."

51  Mabel Patrick, "Basis of Home-Making Should Be Scientific," *Edmonton Journal*, 1 April 1932, Home Economics Week scrapbook, file 67, M1670, Alberta Home Economics Association, Glenbow.

52  Grace Duggan, "Home Biggest Business in This Modern World," Home Economics Week scrapbook, file 67, M1670, Alberta Home Economics Association, Glenbow.

53  Frances Swyripa, *Wedded to the Cause: Ukrainian-Canadian Women and Ethnic Identity, 1891–1991* (Toronto: University of Toronto Press, 1993).

54  Erika Dyck, *Facing Eugenics: Reproduction, Sterilization, and the Politics of Choice* (Toronto: University of Toronto Press, 2013), 59.

55 Jennifer Kelly and Dan Cui, "Racialization and Work," in *Working People in Alberta: A History*, ed. Alvin Finkel (Edmonton: University of Alberta Press, 2012), 267–86.

56 Mabel Patrick, "Adequate Diets Are Very Cheap," *Edmonton Journal*, April 1932, Home Economics Week scrapbook, file 67, M1670, Alberta Home Economics Association, Glenbow.

57 M.L. de Zwart, "White Sauce and Chinese Chews: Recipes as Postcolonial Metaphors," in *Unsettled Pasts: Reconceiving the West through Women's History*, ed. S. Carter (Calgary, AB: University of Calgary Press, 2005), 133–4.

58 Hazel McIntyre, "Reward of Good Cookery Reaped in Healthy Living," *Edmonton Journal*, April 1933, Home Economics Week scrapbook, file 67, M1670, Alberta Home Economics Association, Glenbow.

59 Goldstein, *Creating Consumers*, 44.

60 McIntyre, "Reward of Good Cookery Reaped in Healthy Living."

61 Hazel McIntyre, "Reward of Good Cookery Reaped in Healthy Living," *Edmonton Journal* (April 1933), Home Economics Week Scrapbook, File 67, M1670, Alberta Home Economics Association, Glenbow Museum and Archives, Calgary, Alberta.

62 De Zwart, "White Sauce," 133.

63 Patrick, "Adequate Diets Are Very Cheap."

64 Margaret Doyle, "Success in Good Dressing Lies in Fundamentals," *Edmonton Journal*, April 1932, Home Economics Week scrapbook, file 67, M1670, Alberta Home Economics Association, Glenbow.

65 Nicholas, *The Modern Girl*, 4.

66 Doyle, "Success in Good Dressing Lies in Fundamentals."

67 Enstad, *Ladies of Labor*, 25, 26, 29, 30.

68 Goldstein, *Creating Consumers*, 8, 2.

## 4 Rural Consumer Citizens

1 Nerman, "Alberta Farm Family."

2 Miles Olson's *Unlearn, Rewild: Earth Skills, Ideas and Inspiration for the Future Primitive* (Gabriola Island, BC: New Society Publishers, 2012) is an example of twenty-first-century homesteading philosophy.

3 For example, Shannon Hayes, *Radical Homemakers: Reclaiming Domesticity from a Consumer Culture* (New York: Left to Write Press, 2010).

4 Ferris Jabr, "How to Really Eat like a Hunter-Gatherer: Why the Paleo Diet Is Half-Baked," *Scientific American*, 3 June 2013, accessed 29 April 2016, http://www.scientificamerican.com.

5 McCalla, *Consumers in the Bush*, 67–88.

6 Claire Medlrum, in comments to "Alberta Farm Family Eating like
   Pioneers for a Year," by Danielle Nerman, *CBC News*, 27 November
   2015, accessed 29 April 2016, http://www.cbc.ca; also see Belisle, *Retail
   Nation*, 13–44.
7 "DickStorm," in comments to Nerman, "Alberta Farm Family."
8 "Alberta Family Eating like Pioneers for a Year Hungry for Spring,"
   *CBC News*, 29 April 2016, http://www.cbc.ca.
9 Olson, *Unlearn, Rewild*, 1.
10 Studies referencing consumer habits in northern North America prior to
   urbanization include Anne Marie Lane Jonah and Elizabeth Tait, "Filles
   d'Acadie, Femmes de Louisbourg: Acadian Women and French Colonial
   Society in Eighteenth-Century Louisbourg," *French Colonial History*
   8 (2007): 23–51; DuPlessis, "Was There a Consumer Revolution?,"
   143–59; Prince, "Influence of the Hudson's Bay Company," 15–26;
   Bouchard, "La culture matérielle," 479–98; Carlos and Lewis, "Trade,
   Consumption, and the Native Economy," 1037–64; Craig, *Backwoods
   Consumers*; McCalla, *Consumers in the Bush*.
11 Craig, *Backwoods Consumers*; McCalla, *Consumers in the Bush*.
12 For example, Nicholas, *The Modern Girl*.
13 Bettina Liverant offers an insightful analysis of this tendency in
   *Buying Happiness: The Emergence of Consumer Consciousness in Canada*
   (Vancouver: UBC Press, 2018), 3–43.
14 Important exceptions are Rebecca Beauseart, "'Foreigners in Town':
   Leisure, Consumption, and Cosmopolitanism in Late-Nineteenth and
   Early-Twentieth Century Tillsonburg, ON," *Journal of the Canadian
   Historical Association* 23, no. 1 (2012): 215–47; and Bertram, "New
   Icelandic Ethnoscapes."
15 Four sets of print records comprise this chapter's primary source material:
   newspaper and magazine articles about the Women's Institutes; histories
   of the institutes written by institute members; annual reports printed by
   the provincial and national organizations; and monthly institute newsletters. This chapter's notes distinguish archival records from other materials by noting the reference number and physical location of the archival
   collection in question. Materials sourced from libraries, including digital
   collections, are recognizable by their lack of archival reference data.
16 Elizabeth Bailey Price, "Eighth Biennial Convention," *Institute News*
   (Manitoba), November 1933, 1, in Manitoba Women's Institute Fonds,
   P4593, Archives of Manitoba.
17 Linda Ambrose, *For Home and Country: The Centennial History of the Women's
   Institutes in Ontario* (Erin, ON: Boston Mills Press, 1996); Linda Ambrose,
   *Women's Institutes in Canada: The First One Hundred Years, 1897–1997*
   (Ottawa, ON: Federated Women's Institutes of Canada, 2000); Margaret

Kechnie, *Organizing Rural Women: The Federated Women's Institutes of Ontario, 1897–1919* (Montreal and Kingston: McGill-Queen's University Press, 2003); Shelly Bosetti, "The Rural Women's University: Women's Institutes in Alberta, 1909–1940" (master's thesis, University of Alberta, 1983).

18 "Institutes and Homemakers," *Institute News* (Manitoba), July 1930, 2, Manitoba Women's Institute Fonds, P4593, Archives of Manitoba.

19 Kechnie, *Organizing Rural Women*, 31, 91.

20 Mrs. K.S. Aitken, "Income Earning for Farm Women," *Ontario Women's Institute Report*, 1923, in Ontario Women's Institute Branch Fonds, RG 16–86, Archives of Ontario.

21 For example, Emily J. Guest, "Income Earning Features for Girls and Women on the Farm," *Ontario Women's Institute Report*, 1923, 73–5, in Ontario Women's Institute Branch Fonds, RG 16–86, Archives of Ontario. Also see Linda Ambrose and Margaret Kechnie, "Social Control or Social Feminism? Two Views of the Ontario Women's Institutes," *Agricultural History* 73, no. 2 (Spring 1999): 227.

22 Ambrose, *Women's Institutes in Canada*, 4.

23 Advisory Board of Women's Institutes, *Women's Institute Work in British Columbia* (Victoria, BC: William H. Cullen, 1912).

24 As quoted by Bosetti, "The Rural Women's University," 54.

25 "What Is Happening in the Institute Movement," *Institute News* (Manitoba), June 1939, 3, Manitoba Women's Institute Fonds, P4593, Archives of Manitoba.

26 "Institutes and Homemakers," *Institute News* (Manitoba), July 1930, 2, Manitoba Women's Institute Fonds, P4593.

27 "Women Will Do Their Share," *Institute News* (Manitoba), July 1931, 4, Manitoba Women's Institute Fonds, P4593.

28 M. Louise Haszard, "Report on Home Economics," *Institute News* (PEI.), July 1932, 1, PEI Women's Institute Fonds, ACC4433, Prince Edward Island Provincial Archives.

29 "Orange Pudding," *Institute News* (PEI), April 1929, 7, PEI Women's Institute Fonds, ACC4433.

30 "Tested Recipes," *Institute News* (PEI), April 1929, 7, PEI Women's Institute Fonds, ACC4433.

31 Mrs. T.L. Guild, "Home Economics," *Report of the Sixth Biennial Convention* (Federated Women's Institutes of Canada, 1929), PEI Women's Institute Fonds, ACC4433.

32 Margaret H. (Mrs. M.E.) Honey, "Report of Provincial Convener of Committee on Home Economics," *Quebec Women's Institutes Annual Report*, 1932, Quebec Women's Institute Fonds, P412, SI, SS#, 1999–09–003/2, Annual Reports, *Bibliothèque et Archives nationales du Québec*.

33 "Correct Cooking Makes Cheaper Cuts of Beef Equally Appetizing," clipping from Home Economics Week scrapbook, 1–8 April 1933, file

67, M1670, Alberta Home Economics Association, Glenbow; "Home Economics," *Home and Country* (Nova Scotia), January 1935, 1; "Home Economics Work Is Wide and Varied," *Report of the Tenth Biennial Convention* (Federated Women's Institutes of Canada, 1937), 16.

34 South Waterloo District Women's Institute, *Fifty Years of Achievement* (Waterloo, ON: Women's Institute, 1953), Women's Institute Records, box 49, Guelph University Archives; Dorothy M. (Mrs. G.S.) Walsh, "Outline of Provincial Convener of Committee on Home Economics," *Home and Country* (Quebec), March 1938, 4, Quebec Women's Institutes Fonds, P412, CAM.

35 "Wool Shop at Halifax," *Home and Country* (Nova Scotia), April 1936, 1, courtesy of the Women's Institutes of Nova Scotia (WINS).

36 Mr. B.W. Rowe, "A Romance of the Textile Industry," Quebec Women's Institutes Fonds, P412, CAM.

37 "Federated Women's Institutes," *Institute News* (Manitoba), May 1933, 1, Manitoba Women's Institute Fonds, P4593, Archives of Manitoba.

38 "Handicraft Exchange," *Home and Country* (Nova Scotia), July 1929, 1–2, courtesy of WINS.

39 Bosetti, "The Rural Women's University," 115; Marianne Otty, *Fifty Years of Women's Institutes in New Brunswick, Canada, 1911–1961: A History* (Fredericton, NB: Women's Institutes, 1961), 119.

40 For example, Marie Hulster, "The Use of Lacquer," *Institute News* (PEI), April 1930, 2, PEI Women's Institute Fonds, ACC4433, Prince Edward Island Provincial Archives.

41 "The Eighteenth Annual Convention of the Women's Institutes," *Institute News* (Manitoba), July 1928, 1–2, Manitoba Women's Institute Fonds, P4593, Archives of Manitoba.

42 Margaret H. (Mrs. M.E.) Honey, "Report of Provincial Convener of Committee on Home Economics," *Quebec Women's Institutes Annual Report*, 1934, Quebec Women's Institute Fonds, P412, CAM.

43 Mrs. J.M. Richardson, "The Telephone: Its Contribution to Rural Life," *Home and Country* (Quebec), December 1938, 4, Quebec Women's Institute Fonds, P412, CAM.

44 Parr, *Domestic Goods*, appendix 1, "Households Equipped with Major Domestic Appliances, Percentage, Canada (Percentage, U.S.)"; Dianne Dodd, "Women and Domestic Technology: Household Drudgery, 'Democratized Consumption,' and Patriarchy," in *Framing Our Past: Canadian Women's History in the Twentieth Century*, ed. Sharon Anne Cook, Lorna R. McLean, and Kate O'Rourke (Montreal and Kingston: McGill-Queen's University Press, 2001), 101–10.

45 Advisory Board of Women's Institutes, *Women's Institute Work in British Columbia* (Victoria, BC: William H. Cullen, 1912), 11.

46 "The Dish-Washing Machine," *Canadian Home Journal*, October 1910, 38.

47 Miss J. Babb, "Efficient Kitchens," 1921, Quebec Women's Institute Fonds, P412, CAM.

48 "The Nova Scotia Kitchen," *Home and Country* (Nova Scotia), October 1928, 2, courtesy of WINS.

49 "Home Management," *Institute News* (Manitoba), May 1931, 2, Manitoba Women's Institute Fonds, P4593, Archives of Manitoba.

50 "Report of the Women's Institute Convention," *Manitoba Agricultural Extension News*, February 1921, 4, Manitoba Women's Institute Fonds, P4593.

51 Untitled article on home economics, *Home and Country* (Nova Scotia), January 1925, 2, courtesy of WINS.

52 Untitled report, *Home and Country* (Nova Scotia), June 1930, 2, courtesy of WINS.

53 M. Elizabeth McCurdy, "How One Woman Practices Thrift," *Institute News* (PEI), May 1931, 2, PEI Women's Institute Fonds, ACC4433, Prince Edward Island Provincial Archives.

54 Dorothy M. (Mrs. G.S.) Walsh, "Home Economics," *Home and Country* (Quebec), March 1938, 4, Quebec Women's Institute Fonds, P412, CAM.

55 "Highlights of the Twentieth Annual Convention," *Institute News* (Manitoba), July 1930, 1.

56 For example, Margaret H. Honey, "Outline of Provincial Convenor of Home Economics," *Home and Country* (Quebec), October 1934, 2, Quebec Women's Institute Fonds, P412, CAM.

57 Eleanor G. McFadden, "Dyeing and Tinting," *Manitoba Agricultural Extension News*, April 1922, 25, Manitoba Women's Institute Fonds, P4593, Archives of Manitoba.

58 "Convention Notes," 1915, Quebec Women's Institute Fonds, P412, CAM.

59 Miss Myrtle Hayward, "With the Women's Institutes," *Manitoba Agricultural Extension News*, February 1922, 16, Manitoba Women's Institute Fonds, P4593, Archives of Manitoba.

60 Untitled article on bread wrapping, *Home and Country* (Nova Scotia), July 1923, 2, courtesy ofWINS.

61 "Report of the Women's Institute Convention," *Manitoba Agricultural Extension News*, March 1921, 5, Manitoba Women's Institute Fonds, P4593, Archives of Manitoba.

62 Mary A. Clarke, "Home Economics Work Is Wide and Varied," in *Report of Eleventh Biennial Convention* (Ottawa, ON: FWIC, 1939), 16.

63 Clarke, 16.

64 Clarke, 16.

65 Glickman, *Buying Power*, loc. 1950, Kindle.

66 Glickman, loc. 3941.

67 Glickman, loc. 3941.

68  As quoted in "Alberta Women Asked to Observe 'Shopper's Creed,'" newspaper clipping, April 1933, in Home Economics Week scrapbook, file 67, M1670, Alberta Home Economics Association, Glenbow; "Shopper's Creed," *Home and Country* (Quebec), October 1934, 2; "The Shoppers' Creed," *Home and Country*, March 1935, 1.

69  For example, Mrs. H.H. Pitts, "Report of the Standing Committee on Canadian Industries," in *Report of the Tenth Biennial Convention* (Ottawa, ON: FWIC, 1937), 40.

70  For example, "Report on Canadian Industries," *Institute News* (PEI), October 1929, 1, PEI Women's Institute Fonds, ACC4433, Prince Edward Island Provincial Archives; Mrs. Joseph N. McKinnon, "Report of the Standing Committee on Canadian Industries," in *Report of the Sixth Biennial Convention* (Ottawa, ON: FWIC, 1929).

71  "With the Women's Institutes," *Manitoba Agricultural Extension News*, March 1922, 10.

72  Belisle, *Retail Nation*, 13–44.

73  "Home Industries Suggestions," *Home and Country* (Nova Scotia), April 1926, 2, courtesy ofWINS.

74  Yuval-Davis, *The Politics of Belonging*, 69.

75  "Buy at Home," *Home and Country* (Nova Scotia), January 1925, 4, courtesy of WINS.

76  "W.I. Exhibit," *Home and Country* (Nova Scotia), April 1927, 4, courtesy of WINS.

77  Mrs. Joseph N. McKinnon, "Canadian Industries," in *Report of the Sixth Biennial Convention* (Ottawa, ON: FWIC, 1929); "Watch for the Label!" *Home and Country* (Nova Scotia), October 1928, 1, courtesy of WINS.

78  "Buy Nova Scotia Products," *Home and Country* (Nova Scotia), December 1933, 1, courtesy ofWINS.

79  "Victoria Board of Trade," *Home and Country* (Nova Scotia), January 1925, 1, courtesy of WINS.

80  "Married Women Teachers Target at W.I. Conference," September 1930, clippings file, Alberta Women's Institutes, City of Edmonton Archives.

81  Mrs. Joseph N. McKinnon, "Report of the Standing Committee on Canadian Industries," in *Report of the Sixth Biennial Convention* (Ottawa: FWIC, 1929).

82  "Women's Institution Booth at Exhibition," *Institute News* (PEI), October 1931, 1.

83  Untitled clipping in Home Economics Week scrapbook, 1–8 April 1933, file 67, M1670 Alberta Home Economics Association, Glenbow.

84  "Home Economics Show Opened by Mayor Monday," clipping in Home Economics Week scrapbook.

85  "Mayor at Tivoli," clipping in Home Economics Week scrapbook.

86  "Firms Display Wares at Tivoli on 102nd St.," clipping in Home Economics Week scrapbook.

87  "The Women's Institute," Blue Willow advertisement, in Home Economics Week scrapbook.

88  "Home Economics Work Is Observed throughout City," clipping in Home Economics Week scrapbook.

89  "Hear Miss Gillis," clipping in Home Economics Week scrapbook.

90  "Service and Table Setting Is Demonstrated"; "Fashion Show and Tea," clippings in Home Economics Week scrapbook.

91  "A Display of Interior Decorating," clipping in Home Economics Week scrapbook.

92  "How Good Are You at Dressmaking?," clipping in Home Economics Week scrapbook.

93  "Claims Girls Should Be Taught Household Economics at School," and "Home Economics Week," clippings in Home Economics Week scrapbook.

94  "Is Hostess at Store Luncheon" and "Economics Week Grand Success," in Home Economics Week scrapbook.

95  Mrs. J. MacGregor Smith, quoted in "Federated Women's Institutes Sponsor Home Economics Week," in Home Economics Week scrapbook.

96  "Club Women Arrange Home Economics Show," in Home Economics Week scrapbook.

97  Eva M. Bishop, "Handicraft," *Home and Country* (Nova Scotia), April 1937, 1, courtesy of the Women's Institutes of Nova Scotia.

98  As quoted in *Legacy: A History of Saskatchewan Homemakers' Clubs and Women's Institutes, 1911–1988* (Saskatoon, SK: Focus Publishing, 1988), 5.

99  Margaret H. (Mrs. M.E.) Honey, "Report of Provincial Convener of Committee on Home Economics," *Quebec Women's Institutes Annual Report*, 1932, 54–5, Quebec Women's Institute Fonds, P412, CAM.

100  Minnie C. Dawson, "A Community Canning Centre," *Canadian Home Journal*, February 1922, 57.

101  "Country Store," *Institute News* (Manitoba), May 1931, 2, Manitoba Women's Institute Fonds, P4593, Archives of Manitoba.

102  Myrtle Hayward, "With the Women's Institutes," *Manitoba Agricultural Extension News*, January 1922, 6, Manitoba Women's Institute Fonds, P4593, Archives of Manitoba.

103  "Buying and Selling at Home," *Institute News* (Manitoba), January 1933, 1.

104  "Western Ontario Convention," *Women's Institutes Leaflet* (Toronto: Ontario Department of Agriculture, 1919), 15–16.

105  "A Programme for the District of Haldimand," *Canadian Home Journal*, August 1915.

106  Mrs. C.W. Farron, "Co-operative and Individual Labour Saving," in *Ontario Women's Institute Report* (Toronto: Ontario Women's Institute, 1923), 55–6.

107 Veronica Strong-Boag, "Pulling in Double Harness or Hauling a Double Load: Women, Work and Feminism on the Canadian Prairie," *Journal of Canadian Studies* 21, no. 3 (Fall 1986): 32–52.

108 Ethel M. Chapman, "Labor Savers for Farm Women," *Farmers' Magazine*, 15 January 1921, 12.

109 Chapman, 12.

110 "Programme of the Sheffield Branch," 1916, Home and Country Fonds, MS A709, University of Guelph Archives.

111 Emily J. Guest, "Income Earning Features for Girls and Women on the Farm," in *Ontario Women's Institute Report*, 1923, 74, Ontario Women's Institute Branch Fonds, RG 16–86, Archives of Ontario.

112 Miss Myrtle Hayward, "With the Women's Institutes," *Manitoba Agricultural News*, December 1921, 12.

113 Lottie C. Duncan, "A Vacation for Rural Women," *Institute News* (Manitoba), May 1930, 1, Manitoba Women's Institute Fonds, P4593, Archives of Manitoba.

114 "A Time Budget," *Institute* News, April 1937, 6, PEI Women's Institute Fonds, ACC4433, Prince Edward Island Provincial Archives.

115 "Some Hints for Mothers and Farm Women," *Institute News* (PEI), April 1930, 1, PEI Women's Institute Fonds, ACC4433, Prince Edward Island Provincial Archives.

116 "Some Hints for Mothers and Farm Women," 1.

## 5 For Whom Do We Dress?

1 Kaitlyn Juvik, "Why I Organized a 'No Bra Day' at My High School," *Guardian*, 17 June 2016, https://www.theguardian.com; also Hanna Orenstein, "This High School Senior Got Called Out for Not Wearing a Bra to School," *Seventeen*, 3 June 2016, http://www.seventeen.com; "No Bra, No Problem," *Mic*, June 2016, https://www.facebook.com.

2 Canadian Press, "Manitoba Teenager Files Complaint, Calling School's Dress Code Sexist," *Philippine Canadian* Inquirer, 20 November 2015, http://www.canadianinquirer.net.

3 "Government Rejects Law Change on Bosses Forcing Women to Wear High Heels at Work," *The Independent*, 21 April 2017, http://www .independent.co.uk.

4 Earls Canada, "Earls' Dress Code Update," 7 December 2017, https:// earls.ca.

5 Prince, "Influence of the Hudson's Bay Company," 15–26; Jan Noel, "Defrocking Dad: Masculinity and Dress in Montreal, 1700–1867," in *Fashion: A Canadian Perspective*, ed. Alexandra Palmer (Toronto: University of Toronto Press, 2004), 68–89; Barbara M. Freeman, "Laced In and Let Down: Women's Fashion Features in the Toronto Daily Press,

1890–1900," in Palmer, *Fashion*, 291–314; Deborah Fulsang, "The Fashion of Writing, 1985–2000: Fashion-Themed Television's Impact on the Canadian Fashion Press," in Palmer, *Fashion*, 315–38.

6 Christina Bates, "Shop and Factory: The Ontario Millinery Trade in Transition, 1870–1930," in Palmer, *Fashion*, 113–38; M. Elaine MacKay, "Three Thousand Stitches: The Development of the Clothing Industry in Nineteenth-Century Halifax," in Palmer, *Fashion*, 166–81; Penny Tinkler and Cheryl Krasnick Warsh, "Feminine Modernity in Interwar Britain and North America: Corsets, Cars, and Cigarettes," *Journal of Women's History* 20, no. 3 (2008): 113–43; and Susan Turnbull Caton, "Fashion and War in Canada, 1939–1945," in Palmer, *Fashion*, 249–69.

7 Eileen O'Connor, "Constructing Medical Social Authority on Dress in Victorian Canada," *Canadian Bulletin of Medical History* 25, no. 2 (2008): 391–406; Barbara Kelcey, "Dress Reform in Nineteenth Century Canada," in Palmer, *Fashion*, 229–48; Bertram, "New Icelandic Ethnoscapes"; Bertram, "Fashioning Conflicts," 275–97; Srigley, "Clothing Stories," 82–104; Rutherdale, "Packing," loc. 2359–711, Kindle; Nicholas, *The Modern Girl*; Valverde, *The Age of Light*, esp. 149–85; Lindsay McMaster, *Working Girls in the West: Representations of Wage Earning Women* (Vancouver: UBC Press, 2008), esp. 57–100; Carolyn Strange, *Toronto's Girl Problem: The Perils and Pleasures of the City, 1880–1930* (Toronto: University of Toronto Press, 1995); and Walden, *Becoming Modern in Toronto*.

8 Bertram, "New Icelandic Ethnoscapes"; Bertram, "Fashioning Conflicts," 275–97; Srigley, "Clothing Stories"; Nicholas, *The Modern Girl*.

9 Kelcey, "Dress Reform."

10 Flora MacDonald Denison, "Reform in Woman's Dress," *Woman's Century*, September 1918, 45.

11 Bertram, "New Icelandic Ethnoscapes," 33.

12 Srigley, "Clothing Stories," 97.

13 Nicholas, *The Modern Girl*, 45.

14 Kitty Hardcastle, "Fashion Wise & Otherwise," *Woman's Century*, April 1921, 29.

15 Kitty Hardcastle, "What Spring Portends in Dress," *Woman's Century*, February 1921, 25.

16 Nicholas, *The Modern Girl*, 97.

17 See, for example, Faye Hammill and Michelle Smith, *Magazines, Travel, and Middlebrow Culture: Canadian Periodicals in English and French, 1925–1960* (Liverpool, UK: Liverpool University Press, 2015).

18 Kelcey, "Dress Reform," 242.

19 "Dress at the Women's Liberal Federation," *White Ribbon Bulletin*, November 1912, 3.

20 See for example Miss Myrtle Hayward, "With the Women's Institutes," *Manitoba Agricultural Extension News*, October 1922, 10.
21 Julie-Ann Bureau, "Coupe et couture," *La Bonne Fermière*, April 1933, 15.
22 Mrs. (G.S.) Dorothy M. Walsh, "Home Dressmaking," *Home and Country* (Quebec), June 1937, 1.
23 McCall's advertisement, *Woman's Century*, November 1921, 20.
24 Srigley, "Clothing Stories," 95.
25 "The Housewife's Morning Dress," *Canadian White Ribbon Tidings*, October 1911, 2032. See also "Personal Appearance," *Canadian White Ribbon Tidings*, 15 November 1907, 1072.
26 As quoted in Valverde, *The Age of Light*, 149.
27 Cecilia Williams MacKinnon, "Some Hints for Mothers and Farm Women," *Institute News* (Charlottetown), April 1930, 1.
28 MacKinnon, 1.
29 Although they did not dwell upon this conception of fashion, writers who took such tack demonstrated similarities with contemporary sociologists. In 1899 theorist Thorstein Veblen suggested that women's attire bore the weight of class signification, with bourgeois wives particularly responsible for dressing in ways that reflected their husbands' socio-economic worth. See Thorstein Veblen, *The Theory of the Leisure Class* (London: Allen & Unwin, 1957 [1899]).
30 Report on Victoria, BC, *Woman's Century*, July 1920, 26.
31 "Woman and the Clothes Problem," *Woman's Century*, December 1919, 23.
32 "Women Physicians Warn against Indecent Dressing," *Canadian White Ribbon Tidings*, July 1919, 1.
33 "Les modes actuelles," *La Bonne Parole*, March 1919, 12.
34 "Chronique des oeuvres," *La Bonne Parole*, December 1920, 3.
35 "Dress at the Women's Liberal Federation," *White Ribbon Bulletin*, November 1912, 3.
36 Flora MacDonald Denison, "Reform in Woman's Dress," *Woman's Century*, September 1918, 45; "Nos amis," *La Bonne Parole*, January 1914, 2.
37 Hattie Orchard, "Following Fashions," *Canadian Home Journal*, June 1911, 31–2.
38 Anne Anderson Perry, "Party Politics and the Federated Clubs," *Woman's Century*, May 1919, 9.
39 "Footwear and Health," *Woman's Century*, January 1920, 14.
40 V.E. Taplin, "A Food-Crippled People We Are," *Woman's Century*, November 1917, 20.
41 Hattie Orchard, "Following Fashions," *Canadian Home Journal*, June 1911, 31–2; Flora MacDonald Denison, "Reform in Woman's Dress," *Woman's Century*, September 1918, 45.
42 Denison, 45.

43 "Nos amis," *La Bonne Parole*, January 1914, 2; "Fashion," *Woman's Century*, June 1916, 22; "L'economie domestique," *La Bonne Fermière*, July 1925, 80.

44 "Fashion," *Woman's Century*, June 1916, 22.

45 "L'economie domestique," *La Bonne Fermière*, July 1925, 80.

46 "Old Clothes," *Woman's Century*, December 1919, 11.

47 "The Tyranny of Style," *Woman's Century*, May 1919, 37.

48 Eleanor G. McFadden, "Lines in Dress," *Manitoba Agricultural Extension News*, October 1922, 10.

49 "Grace and Beauty," *Woman's Century*, February 1920, 26.

50 Madame XXX, "La réaction," *La Bonne Parole*, May 1914, 3.

51 Flora MacDonald Denison, "Reform in Woman's Dress," *Woman's Century*, September 1918, 45.

52 Madame XXX, "Psychologie d'une mode," *La Bonne Parole*, April 1914, 3.

53 "Who Is to Blame for Extravagance in Dress?," *Woman's Century*, March 1920, 58.

54 Constance Lynd [Emily Kirby], "Men – Women – Dress – Morals," *Woman's Century*, July 1920, 10–11.

55 "La femme belge" in "Chronique Internationale," *La Bonne Parole*, April 1920, 12.

56 "Glints and Gleanings," *Woman's Century*, May 1921, 16.

57 "Glints and Gleanings," 16.

58 "Appel aux magasins contre l'inconvenance des modes actuelles," *La Bonne Fermière*, July 1921, 72–3.

59 M.C. Forest, OP, "Les modes et la morale," *La Bonne Parole*, November 1928, 8.

60 Mme Georges Morel, "Création d'un élégant costume de bain," *La Bonne Parole*, March 1935, 11.

61 "Le L.C.F.," *La Bonne Parole*, May 1935, 16.

62 See, for example, "Footwear and Health," *Woman's Century*, January 1920, 14.

63 "Old Clothes," *Woman's Century*, December 1919, 11.

64 M. Alberta Deards, "A War Suggestion for Women," *Woman's Century*, July 1916, 16.

65 E. Blakeley, "Luxury and Womanhood," *Woman's Century*, January 1918, 15.

66 "Twelve Old Dresses," *Canadian White Ribbon Tidings*, August 1915, 199.

67 Woman's Citizens' League of Hamilton, "Report," *Woman's Century*, July 1920, 20.

68 "Canadian Housewife," *Woman's Century*, July 1920, 20.

69 "Recommendations for a Return to a Simpler Mode of Life," *Woman's Century*, January 1921, 14.

70 As quoted in "Home-Making," *Canadian Home Journal*, October 1910, 39.

71  Noel, "Defrocking Dad."

72  Srigley, "Clothing Stories," 86.

73  Srigley, 94.

74  Srigley, 89.

75  Kitty Hardcastle, "Fashionwise and Otherwise," *Woman's Century*, January 1921, 16.

76  Hattie Orchard, "Ontario Women's Institutes," *Canadian Home Journal*, June 1911, 32.

77  "With the Women's Institutes," *Manitoba Agricultural Extension News*, October 1922, 10.

78  "Grace and Beauty: True Patriotism," *Woman's Century*, February 1920, 26–7.

79  Bourdieu, *Distinction*, 176.

80  Enstad, *Ladies of Labor*, 17–47.

81  "Grace and Beauty: True Patriotism," *Woman's Century*, February 1920, 26–7.

82  Valverde, "'When the Mother of the Race Is Free,'" 4–5.

83  These sentiments will be explored more fully in the next section. See also Mariana Valverde, "The Love of Finery: Fashion and the Fallen Woman in Nineteenth-Century Social Discourse," *Victorian Studies* 32, no. 2 (Winter 1989): 168–88.

84  Appel aux magasins contre l'inconvenance des modes actuelles," *La Bonne Fermière*, July 1921, 72–3.

85  Linda Scott, *Fresh Lipstick: Redressing Fashion and Feminism* (New York: Palgrave Macmillan, 2005), 329–31.

## 6 Challenging Capitalism?

1  Sheila Rowbotham, "Consumer Power: Women's Contribution to Alternatives and Resistance to the Market in the United States, 1880–1940," in *Women and Market Societies: Crisis and Opportunity*, ed. B. Einhorn and E.J. Yeo (London: Edward Elgar Publishing, 1995), 11–12.

2  Marie-Emmanuelle Chessel, "Women and the Ethics of Consumption in France at the Turn of the Twentieth Century: The Ligue Sociale d'Acheteurs," in *The Making of the Consumer: Knowledge, Power and Identity in the Modern World*, ed. Frank Trentmann (Oxford: Berg, 2006), 81. See also Jacobs, *Pocketbook Politics*; Katherine Kish Sklar, "The Consumers' White Label Campaign of the National Consumers' Leagues, 1898–1918," in *Getting and Spending: European and American Consumer Societies in the Twentieth Century*, ed. Susan Strasser, Charles McGovern, and Matthias Judt (New York: Cambridge University Press, 1998), 17–36; Karen Hunt, "The Politics of Food and Women's Neighborhood Activism in First World War Britain," *International Labor and Working-Class History*

77 (Spring 2010): 8–26; Matthew Hilton, "The Female Consumer and the Politics of Consumption in Twentieth-Century Britain," *Historical Journal* 45, no. 1 (March 2002): 103–28; Judith Smart, "The Politics of the Small Purse: The Mobilization of Housewives in Interwar Australia," *International Labor and Working-Class History* 77 (Spring 2010): 48–68; Annelise Orleck, "'We Are That Mythical Thing Called the Public': Militant Housewives during the Great Depression," *Feminist Studies* 19, no. 1 (Spring 1993): 147–72; Dana Frank, "Housewives, Socialists, and the Politics of Food: The 1917 New York Cost-of-Living Protests," *Feminist Studies* 11, no. 2 (Summer 1985): 255–85; and Lawrence Glickman, "'Make Lisle the Style': The Politics of Fashion in the Japanese Silk Boycott, 1937–1940," *Journal of Social History* 38, no. 3 (Spring 2005): 573–608.

3 For movements focusing on price activism, see Jacobs, *Pocketbook Politics*; Hunt, "The Politics of Food"; Smart, "The Politics of the Small Purse"; Orleck, "'We Are That Mythical Thing'"; and Frank, "Housewives, Socialists, and the Politics of Food." For movements focusing on social activism, see Sklar, "The Consumers' White Label Campaign"; Hilton, "The Female Consumer"; and Glickman, "'Make Lisle the Style.'"

4 Ian MacPherson, "'In These Pioneer Days': George Keen and Leadership through Sacrifice and Determination," in *Canadian Co-operatives in the Year 2000: Memory, Mutual Aid, and the Millennium*, ed. Brett Fairbairn, Ian MacPherson, and Nora Russell (Saskatoon, SK: Centre for the Study of Co-operatives, 2000), 48.

5 MacPherson, "'In These Pioneer Days,'" 51.

6 Rusty Neal, *Brotherhood Economics: Women and Co-operatives in Nova Scotia* (Sydney, NS: Cape Breton University Press, 1998).

7 Dana Frank, *Purchasing Power: Consumer Organizing, Gender, and the Seattle Labor Movement, 1919–1929* (Cambridge: Cambridge University Press, 1994), 40–65, 108–38, 212–46; Tracey Deutsch, *Building a Housewives' Paradise: Gender, Politics, and American Grocery Stores in the Twentieth Century* (Chapel Hill: University of North Carolina Press, 2010), 105–32.

8 For research on consumer activism in later periods, see especially Parr, *Domestic Goods*, 84–100; and Fahrni, "Counting the Costs," 1–13.

9 Georgina M. Taylor, "'Let Us Co-operate': Violet McNaughton and the Co-operative Ideal," in *Canadian Co-operatives in the Year 2000: Memory, Mutual Aid, and the Millennium*, ed. Brett Fairbairn, Ian MacPherson, and Nora Russell, 57–78 (Saskatoon, SK: Centre for the Study of Co-operatives, 2000), 67; MacPherson, "'In These Pioneer Days,'" 51.

10 Ian MacPherson, *Each for All: A History of the Co-operative Movement in English Canada, 1900–1945* (Toronto: Macmillan, 1979), 110.

11 Neal, *Brotherhood Economics*, 63.
12 Neal, 67.
13 MacPherson, "'In These Pioneer Days,'" 48.
14 Neal, *Brotherhood Economics*, 25.
15 Neal, 25.
16 A.L. Hollis, "The Woman with the Basket," *Western Producer*, 24 November 1927, 15.
17 As quoted in Neal, *Brotherhood Economics*, 60–1.
18 As quoted in Neal, 58.
19 *History of the Saskatchewan Women's Co-operative Guild* (Regina: Saskatchewan Women's Co-operative Guild, 1955), 9.
20 Margaret Hobbs, "The Women's Pages of *The Western Producer*, 1925–1939: Violet McNaughton and Interwar Feminism in Canada," *Women's and Social Movements Online*, September 2009, 1.
21 Taylor, "'Let Us Co-operate,'" 57–78.
22 Violet McNaughton, "Consumers' Co-operation Is Immediate Field of Action for Western Farm Women," *Western Producer*, 24 November 1927, 17.
23 Mrs. John [Violet] McNaughton, "Club Purchasing Popular in West," *Grain Growers' Guide*, 25 February 1914, 22.
24 Taylor, "'Let Us Co-operate,'" 64.
25 "The Co-operative Outlook," *Western Producer*, 29 June 1939, 13.
26 McNaughton, "Consumers' Co-operation Is Immediate Field of Action," 17.
27 Neal, *Brotherhood Economics*, 65.
28 Statistics Canada, "Cities, Towns, and Villages in Canada," table no. A-11, in *Eighth Census of Canada, 1941*, accessed 26 June 2014, https://ia600709.us.archive.org.
29 Neal, *Brotherhood Economics*, 69.
30 Neal, 65–7.
31 Also in Neal, 63.
32 R. James Sacouman, "Underdevelopment and the Structural Origins of Antigonish Movement Co-operatives in Eastern Nova Scotia," *Acadiensis* 7, no. 1 (Autumn 1977): 71.
33 Sacouman, 67.
34 As quoted in Santo Dodaro and Leonard Pluta, *The Big Picture: The Antigonish Movement of Eastern Nova Scotia* (Montreal and Kingston: McGill-Queen's University Press, 2012), 40, 49.
35 Neal, *Brotherhood Economics*, 141–60; Dodaro and Pluta, *The Big Picture*, 99.
36 Neal, *Brotherhood Economics*, 76.
37 St Francis Xavier Extension Department, *What Can the Women Do?* (Antigonish, NS: St Francis Xavier University, 1942), 1.

38  Dodaro and Pluta, *The Big Picture*, 94.
39  Ida Gallant Delaney, *Shopping-Basket Economics* (Antigonish, NS: St Francis Xavier University, c. 1942), 38.
40  Delaney, 5.
41  Delaney, 8.
42  Delaney, 13–14.
43  Delaney, 9.
44  Delaney, 11.
45  Delaney, 38.
46  Delaney, 28.
47  Delaney, 35.
48  Delaney, 21.
49  Delaney, 35.
50  Advisory Board of Women's Institutes, *Women's Institute Work in British Columbia*. (Victoria, BC: William H. Cullen, 1912), 30–1.
51  "Farm Women's Clubs," *Grain Growers' Guide*, 14 April 1915, 24.
52  Emily Jackson, "Raising Money for the Poor," *Grain Growers' Guide*, 31 March 1915, 29.
53  David I. Macleod, "Food Prices, Politics, and Policy in the Progressive Era," *Journal of the Gilded Age and Progressive Era* 8, no. 3 (July 2009): 379.
54  "Canadian National Housewives' League," *Toronto Daily Star*, 14 February 1914, 19.
55  "Women Started Boycott on the High Price of Eggs," *Toronto Daily Star*, 16 December 1913, 1.
56  "Women Started Boycott on the High Price of Eggs," 1.
57  "Second League Sale," *Toronto Daily Star*, 28 January 1914, 10.
58  "Housewives' League Censure Aldermen," *Toronto Daily Star*, 19 May 1914, 2.
59  "Housewives' League to Meet Commission," *Toronto Daily Star*, 17 February 1914, 10.
60  "Housewives' League to Meet Commission," 10.
61  "Women Create Demand for the Impure Food," *Toronto Daily Star*, 24 February 1914, 10.
62  "Too Many Consumers, Too Few Producers," *Toronto Daily Star*, 16 February 1914, 12.
63  "Co-operation to Help Housewife Fight High Cost," *Toronto Daily Star*, 13 January 1914, 5.
64  "Women's Meetings," *Toronto Daily Star*, 23 June 1914, 12.
65  Janice Williams Rutherford, *Selling Mrs. Consumer: Christine Frederick and the Rise of Household Efficiency* (Athens: University of Georgia Press, 2003).
66  "Housewives League to Meet Commission," *Toronto Daily Star*, 17 February 1914, 10.

67  "Women Explain Why Cost of Living Is So High," *Toronto Daily Star*, 18 April 1914, 24.

68  "Second Housewives' League Sale," *Toronto Daily Star*, 28 January 1914, 10.

69  "Women Create Demand for the Impure Food," *Toronto Daily Star*, 24 February 1914, 10.

70  "Second Housewives' League Sale," *Toronto Daily Star*, 28 January 1914, 10.

71  "Women Broke Doors at League Sale Rush," *Toronto Daily Star*, 4 February 1914, 5.

72  "Forming Base of Supplies," *Toronto Daily Star*, 28 January 1914, 10.

73  "Housewives' League Censure Aldermen," *Toronto Daily Star*, 19 May 1914, 2.

74  "Housewives' League Censure Aldermen," 2.

75  "Housewives' League Asks for Markets," *Toronto Daily Star*, 30 March 2014, 10.

76  "Would Donate Land to Start Curb Market," *Toronto Daily Star*, 8 July 1914, 13.

77  "Housewives' League Censure Aldermen," *Toronto Daily Star*, 19 May 1914, 2.

78  "Lack of Rain, Not War, Sent Butter Sky High," *Toronto Daily Star*, 21 August 1914, 7; "Toronto Steaks Not Well Trimmed Now," *Toronto Daily Star*, 23 August 1914, 10.

79  "Read Punch, Watch Wasted Bread Crusts," *Toronto Daily Star*, 22 September 1914, 8.

80  "Toronto Housewives' League," *Toronto Daily Star*, 11 February 1914, 12.

81  "Women Started Boycott on the High Price of Eggs," *Toronto Daily Star*, 13 December 1916, 1.

82  "Another Housekeeper," and "The High Prices of Food," *Toronto Daily Star*, 2 October 1916, 6.

83  "Housewives' League Hands Jolt to High Cost of Living," *Toronto Daily Star*, 26 January 1914, 7.

84  "To Grow Vegetables in Toronto's Gardens," *Toronto Daily Star*, 17 March 1914, 10.

85  "Housewives Know All Mr. Flavelle Can Say," *Toronto Daily Star*, 19 February 1914, 3.

86  "Housewives Know All Mr. Flavelle Can Say," 3.

87  Mrs. Wilson, "Household League of Ottawa," *Woman's Century*, March 1915, 14.

88  "Housewives' League Well Under Way Now," *Montreal Daily Mail*, 27 February 1914, 4.

89  See, for example, "Housewives' League Doing Pioneer Work," *Montreal Daily Mail*, 29 January 1917, 10.

90  "English Branch of Housewives' Club," *Quebec Telegraph*, 31 May 1917, 3.

91  "Housewives Order 30 or 40 Tons Butter," *Globe*, 18 October 1917, 3.

92 "Notre courier," *La Bonne Parole*, November 1917, 13.

93 Marie Louise Bousquet, "Le coin du travail," *La Bonne Parole*, April 1918, 12.

94 "The Housewives' League," *Maritime Merchant*, 30 July 1914, 24.

95 "Peterborough Local Council," *Woman's Century*, March 1915, 3.

96 Georgina A. Newhall, "An Adventure in Economics," *Saturday Night*, 14 February 1914, 41.

97 Newhall, 41, 45.

98 Newhall, 42.

99 "To Bring Producers and Consumers Closer," *Vancouver Sun*, 21 July 1915, 5.

100 "Farm Women's Clubs," *Grain Growers' Guide*, 1 September 1915, 22.

101 "Farm Women's Clubs," *Grain Growers' Guide*, 14 April 1915, 24.

102 "Farm Women's Clubs," *Grain Growers' Guide*, 2 June 1915, 19; "Farm Women's Clubs," *Grain Growers' Guide*, 31 March 1915, 29.

103 "Quebec: A Hit at the High Cost of Living," *Woman's Century*, April 1920, 32.

104 For example, Georgina Newhall, "Canadian Housewife," *Woman's Century*, March 1918, 15.

105 Landon Storrs, *Civilizing Capitalism: The National Consumers' League, Women's Activism, and Labor Standards in the New Deal Era* (Chapel Hill: University of North Carolina Press, 2000), 2–3.

106 "Consumers' League Will Continue Effort," *Toronto Daily Star*, 29 May 1920, 12.

107 "Women Plan to Extend the Potato Boycott," *Toronto Daily Star*, 1 May 1920, 10.

108 Mrs. T.L. Guild, "Home Economics," in *Report of the Sixth Biennial Convention* (Ottawa, ON: FWIC, 1929).

109 "Consumers' League Conducts Stall at the Public Market," *Calgary Herald*, 1921, clipping in Annie Gale Fonds, file "Newspaper clippings," Glenbow.

110 "Chez les femmes d'affaires," *La Bonne Parole*, November 1937, 12.

111 Soeur Marie Gérin-Lajoie, "Les Fruits de la coopération," *La Bonne Parole*, October 1938, 1–3.

112 Jeanne Lapointe, "Au comité central d'étude: Le coopératisme et ses avantages," *La Bonne Parole*, February 1939, 10–1.

113 Mrs. Georgina Newhall, "Home Economics," *Woman's Century*, June 1916, 2.

114 Georgina Newhall, "The Canadian Housewife," *Woman's Century*, August 1917, 9.

115 Newhall, "The Canadian Housewife," 9.

116 Georgina Newhall, "An Organization for Consumers," *Woman's Century*, February 1917, 5.

117 Georgina Newhall, "The Associated Consumers," *Woman's Century*, March 1917, 7.
118 Georgina Newhall, "A Lost Society," *Woman's Century*, June 1919, 20.

## Conclusion

1 As quoted in (Mrs. M.E.) Margaret H. Honey, "Report of Provincial Convener of Committee on Home Economics," *Quebec Women's Institutes Annual Report*, 1932, 54–5, Quebec Women's Institute Fonds, P412, SI, 1999-09-003/2, annual reports, *Bibliothèque et Archives nationales du Québec*.
2 Glickman, *Buying Power*, loc. 3908–4114, Kindle.
3 "Federated Women's Institutes Sponsor Home Economics Week," Home Economics Week scrapbook, file 67, M1670, Alberta Home Economics Association, Glenbow.
4 A particularly powerful lament of the intrusion of commerce into the late-twentieth-century public sphere is Naomi Klein's *No Logo: Taking Aim at the Brand Bullies* (Toronto: Vintage, 2000). Also see Susan Delacourt, *Shopping for Votes: How Politicians Choose Us and We Choose Them* (Madeira Park, BC: Douglas & McIntyre, 2013). The latter book offers a strong and convincing analysis of marketing within the last fifty years of Canadian election campaigns. At the same time it does overstate the case that citizenship and consumption merged in Canada after the Second World War. Delacourt writes that the "partnership between consumerism and the citizenry has been building since the early years of the twentieth century" (4).
5 *Oxford English Living Dictionaries*, accessed 23 January 2018, https://en.oxforddictionaries.com, s.v. "prosumer."
6 For example, Michele Micheletti, Andreas Follesdal, and Dietlind Stolle, eds., *Politics, Products, and Markets: Exploring Political Consumerism Past and Present* (New Brunswick, NJ: Transaction Publishers, 2004).
7 Glickman, *Buying Power*, 155–253. Also see Wendy Wiedenhoft Murphy, "Boycotts, Buycotts, and Legislation: Tactical Lessons from Workers and Consumers during the Progressive Era," in *Shopping for Change: Consumer Activism and the Possibilities of Purchasing Power*, ed. Louis Hyman and Joseph Tohill (Toronto: Between the Lines, 2017), 29–40; and Mark Robbins, "Making a Middle-Class 'Public': Middle-Class Consumer Activism in Post–First World War America," in *Shopping for Change*, ed. Hyman and Tohill, 53–64.
8 Sangster, "Consuming Issues," 240–7; Parr, *Domestic Goods*; Guard, "Women Worth Watching, 73–90; Guard, "A Mighty Power," 27–47; Guard, "The Politics of Milk," 271–85.

9  Glickman, *Buying Power*, 310; Trentmann, "Citizenship and Consumption," 147–8.

10 Kate Soper, "Re-thinking the 'Good Life': The Citizenship Dimension of Consumer Disaffection with Consumerism," *Journal of Consumer Culture* 7, no. 2 (2007): 206.

11 Cohen, *A Consumers' Republic*, loc. 546, Kindle.

12 MacIver, "Women and the Cost of Living," *Woman's Century*, January 1917, 5.

13 For example, Lara Campbell, "'Respectable Citizens of Canada': Gender, Maternalism, and the Welfare State in the Great Depression," in *Maternalism Reconsidered: Motherhood, Welfare and Social Policy in the Twentieth Century*, ed. Marian van der Klein et al. (New York: Berghahn Books, 2012), 103.

14 Joan Sangster, introduction to "Part Four: Women's Activism and the State," in *Framing Our Past: Canadian Women's History in the Twentieth Century*, ed. Sharon Anne Cook, Lorna R. McLean, and Kate O'Rourke (Montreal and Kingston: McGill-Queen's University Press, 2001), 201, 203.

15 Mrs. Drummond, 1894, as quoted in N.E.S. Griffiths, *The Splendid Vision: Centennial History of the National Council of Women of Canada, 1893 to 1993* (Ottawa, ON: Carleton University Press, 1993), 51.

16 Valverde, "'When the Mother of the Race Is Free,'" 3–26; Carol Bacchi, *Liberation Deferred? The Ideas of the English-Canadian Suffragists* (Toronto: University of Toronto Press, 1983).

17 Cecily Devereux, "New Woman, New World: Maternal Feminism and the New Imperialism in the White Settler Colonies," *Women's Studies International Forum* 27, no. 2 (1999): 178; Cecily Devereux, *Growing a Race: Nellie L. McClung and the Fiction of Eugenic Feminism* (Montreal and Kingston: McGill-Queen's University Press, 2005); Valverde, "'When the Mother of the Race Is Free'"; Jennifer Henderson, *Settler Feminism and Race Making in Canada* (Toronto: University of Toronto Press, 2003).

18 Devereux, *Growing a Race*, 27–8; 42–3; Devereux, "New Woman," 177, 180; Valverde, "'When the Mother of the Race Is Free,'" 3–26.

19 "Grace and Beauty: True Patriotism," *Woman's Century*, February 1920, 26–7.

20 Valverde, "'When the Mother of the Race Is Free,'" 5.

21 M.C. Forest, OP, "Les modes et la morale," *La Bonne Parole*, November 1928, 8.

22 Bourdieu, *Distinction*, 6.

# Bibliography

## Primary Sources

Advisory Board of Women's Institutes. *Women's Institute Work in British Columbia*. Victoria, BC: William H. Cullen, 1912.

*Calendar of the University of Alberta, 1933–34*. Edmonton: University of Alberta, 1933.

*Calendar of the University of Alberta, 1935–36*. Edmonton: University of Alberta, 1935.

Delaney, Ida Gallant. *Shopping-Basket Economics*. Antigonish, NS: St Francis Xavier University, c. 1942.

Federated Women's Institutes. *Report of the Eleventh Biennial Convention*. Ottawa, ON: Federated Women's Institutes, 1939.

– *Report of the Sixth Biennial Convention*. Ottawa, ON: Federated Women's Institutes, 1929.

– *Report of the Tenth Biennial Convention*. Ottawa, ON: Federated Women's Institutes, 1937.

*History of the Saskatchewan Women's Co-operative Guild*. Regina: Saskatchewan Women's Co-operative Guild, 1955.

Ontario Women's Institutes. *1923 Convention Report*. Ontario: Ontario Women's Institutes, 1923.

– *Report of the Ontario Women's Institutes, 1922*. Ontario: Ontario Women's Institutes, 1922.

Richardson, Ellen H. *Woman Who Spends*. Boston: Barrows & Whitcomb, 1904.

St Francis Xavier Extension Department. *What Can the Women Do?* Antigonish, NS: St Francis Xavier University, 1942.

*The University of Alberta Calendar, 1922–23*. Edmonton: University of Alberta, 1922.

*University of Toronto Calendar, 1936–7*. Toronto: University of Toronto Press, 1937.

Webb, Catherine. *The Woman with the Basket: The History of the Women's Co-operative Guild, 1883–1927*. Manchester, UK: Co-operative Wholesale Society's Printing Works, 1927.

"Western Ontario Convention." In *Women's Institutes Leaflet*, 15–16. Toronto: Ontario Department of Agriculture, 1919.

### Secondary Sources

"Alberta Family Eating like Pioneers for a Year Hungry for Spring." *CBC News*. 29 April 2016. Last accessed 29 April 2016. http://www.cbc.ca.

Ambrose, Linda. *For Home and Country: The Centennial History of the Women's Institutes in Ontario*. Erin, ON: Boston Mills Press, 1996.

– *Women's Institutes in Canada: The First One Hundred Years, 1897–1997*. Ottawa, ON: Federated Women's Institutes of Canada, 2000.

Ambrose, Linda, and Margaret Kechnie. "Social Control or Social Feminism? Two Views of the Ontario Women's Institutes." *Agricultural History* 73, no. 2 (Spring 1999): 222–37.

Anderson, Carol, and Katharine Mallinson. *Lunch with Lady Eaton: Inside the Dining Rooms of the Nation*. Toronto: ECW Press, 2004.

Axelrod, Paul. *Making a Middle Class: Student Life in English Canada during the Thirties*. Montreal and Kingston: McGill-Queen's University Press, 1990.

Bacchi, Carol. *Liberation Deferred? The Ideas of the English-Canadian Suffragists*. Toronto: University of Toronto Press, 1983.

Baillargeon, Denyse. *Making Do: Women, Family, and Home in Montreal during the Great Depression*. Translated by Yvonne Klein. Waterloo, ON: Wilfrid Laurier University Press, 1999.

Barker, Stacey. "'Save Today What Our Allies Need Tomorrow': Food Regulation in Canada during the First World War." Master's thesis, Department of History, Carleton University, 2003.

Bates, Christina. "Shop and Factory: The Ontario Millinery Trade in Transition, 1870–1930." In Palmer, *Fashion*, 113–38.

Beauseart, Rebecca. "'Foreigners in Town': Leisure, Consumption, and Cosmopolitanism in Late-Nineteenth and Early-Twentieth Century Tillsonburg, ON." *Journal of the Canadian Historical Association* 23, no. 1 (2012): 215–47.

Belisle, Donica. "Crazy for Bargains: Inventing the Irrational Female Shopper in Modernizing English Canada." *Canadian Historical Review*, December 2011, 581–606.

– *Retail Nation: Department Stores and the Making of Modern Canada*. Vancouver: UBC Press, 2011.

– "Sexual Spectacles: Women in Canadian Department Store Magazines between 1920 and 1950." In *Writing Feminist History: Productive Pasts and*

*New Directions*, edited by Catherine Carstairs and Nancy Janovicek, 135–58. Vancouver: UBC Press, 2013.

Belisle, Donica, and Kiera Mitchell. "Mary Quayle Innis: Faculty Wives' Contributions and the Making of Academic Celebrity." *Canadian Historical Review* 99, no. 3 (Fall 2018): 456–86.

Benson, Susan Porter. *Counter Cultures: Saleswomen, Managers, and Customers in American Department Stores, 1890–1940*. Urbana and Chicago: University of Illinois Press, 1988.

Bertram, Laurie K. "Fashioning Conflicts: Gender, Power, and Icelandic Immigrant Hair and Clothing in North America, 1874–1933." In *Sisters or Strangers? Immigrant, Ethnic, and Racialized Women in Canadian History*, 2nd ed., edited by Marlene Epp and Franca Iacovetta, 275–97. Toronto: University of Toronto Press, 2016.

– "New Icelandic Ethnoscapes: Material, Visual, and Oral Terrains of Cultural Expression in Icelandic-Canadian History, 1875–Present." PhD diss., Department of History, University of Toronto, 2010.

Bix, Amy Sue. "Equipped for Life: Gendered Technical Training and Consumerism in Home Economics, 1920–1980." *Technology and Culture* 43, no. 4 (October 2002): 728–54.

Bodirsky, Monica, and Jon Johnson. "Decolonizing Diet: Healing by Reclaiming Traditional Indigenous Foodways." *Cuizine* 1, no. 1 (2008): 1–11.

Bosetti, Shelly. "The Rural Women's University: Women's Institutes in Alberta, 1909–1940." Master's thesis, University of Alberta, 1983.

Bouchard, Dominique. "La culture matérielle des canadiens au XVIIIe siècle: Analyse du niveau de vie des artisans du fer." *Revue d'histoire de l'Amérique française* 47, no. 4 (Spring 1994): 479–98.

Bourdieu, Pierre. *Distinction: A Social Critique of the Judgement of Taste*. Translated by Richard Nice. Cambridge, MA: Harvard University Press, 1984.

Bradbury, Bettina. *Working Families: Age, Gender, and Daily Survival in Industrializing Montreal*. Toronto: University of Toronto Press, 2007.

Broad, Graham. *A Small Price to Pay: Consumer Culture on the Canadian Home Front, 1939–45*. Vancouver: UBC Press, 2013.

Brown, Robert, and Ramsay Cook. *Canada, 1896–1921: A Nation Transformed*. Toronto: McClelland & Stewart, 1976.

Burke, Sara. "Dancing into Education: The First World War and the Roots of Change in Women's Higher Education." In *Cultures, Communities, and Conflict: Histories of Canadian Universities and War*, edited by E. Lisa Panayotidis and Paul James Stortz, 95–120. Toronto: University of Toronto Press, 2012.

Campbell, Lara. "'Respectable Citizens of Canada': Gender, Maternalism, and the Welfare State in the Great Depression." In *Maternalism*

*Reconsidered: Motherhood, Welfare and Social Policy in the Twentieth Century*, edited by Marian van der Klein, Rebecca Jo Plant, Nichole Sanders, and Lori R. Weintraub, 99–120. New York: Berghahn Books, 2012.

Canadian Press. "Manitoba Teenager Files Complaint, Calling School's Dress Code Sexist." *Philippine Canadian Inquirer*, 20 November 2015. http:// www.canadianinquirer.net.

Carlos, Ann M., and Frank D. Lewis. "Trade, Consumption, and the Native Economy: Lessons from York Factory, Hudson Bay." *Journal of Economic History* 61, no. 4 (December 2001): 1037–64.

Caton, Susan Turnbull. "Fashion and War in Canada, 1939–1945." In Palmer, *Fashion*, 249–69.

Charron, Catherine. "Le front domestique à la Fédération nationale Saint-Jean-Baptiste: Entre crise de la domesticité et promotion de l'enseignement ménager, 1900–1927." *Histoire sociale / Social History* 43, no. 86 (2010): 346–68.

Chessel, Marie-Emmanuelle. "Women and the Ethics of Consumption in France at the Turn of the Twentieth Century: The Ligue Sociale d'Acheteurs." In *The Making of the Consumer: Knowledge, Power and Identity in the Modern World*, edited by Frank Trentmann, 81–98. Oxford: Berg, 2006.

Clunas, Craig. "Things in Between: Splendour and Excess in Ming China." In *The Oxford Handbook of the History of Consumption*, edited by Frank Trentmann, 47–63. Oxford: Oxford University Press, 2012.

Cohen, Lizabeth. *A Consumers' Republic: The Politics of Mass Consumption in Postwar America*. New York: Vintage, 2001.

Cook, Sharon Anne. *Sex, Lies, and Cigarettes: Canadian Women, Smoking, and Visual Culture, 1880–2000*. Montreal and Kingston: McGill-Queen's University Press, 2012.

– *"Through Sunshine and Shadow": The Women's Christian Temperance Union, Evangelicalism, and Reform in Ontario, 1874–1930*. Montreal and Kingston: McGill-Queen's University Press, 1995.

Cook, Tim. "Wet Canteens and Worrying Mothers: Alcohol, Soldiers, and Temperance Groups in the Great War." *Histoire sociale / Social History* 35, no. 70 (2002): 311–30.

"Courses of Instruction, Household Science." In *Curriculum for Matriculation, 1928–9*, University of Toronto. Toronto: University of Toronto Press, 1928.

Craig, Beatrice. *Backwoods Consumers and Homespun Capitalists: The Rise of a Market Culture in Eastern Canada*. Toronto: University of Toronto Press, 2009.

Danylewycz, Marta. "Domestic Science Education in Ontario, 1900–1940." In *Gender and Education in Ontario: An Historical Reader*, edited by Ruby Heap and Alison Prentice, 129–47. Toronto: Canadian Scholars' Press, 1991.

Danylewycz, Marta, Nadia Fahmy-Eid, and Nicole Thivierge. "'L'enseignment ménager' et les 'Home Economics' au Québec et en Ontario au début du 20e siècle: Une analyse comparée." In *An Imperfect Past: Education and Society in Canadian History*, edited by J. Donald Wilson, 67–119. Vancouver: UBC Press, 1984.

Davidson, James. "Citizen Consumers: The Athenian Democracy and the Origins of Western Consumption." In *The Oxford Handbook of the History of Consumption*, edited by Frank Trentmann, 22–45. Oxford: Oxford University Press, 2012.

Dawson, Michael. *Selling British Columbia: Tourism and Consumer Culture, 1890–1970*. Vancouver: UBC Press, 2004.

Delacourt, Susan. *Shopping for Votes: How Politicians Choose Us and We Choose Them*. Madeira Park, BC: Douglas & McIntyre, 2013.

Deutsch, Tracey. *Building a Housewives' Paradise: Gender, Politics, and American Grocery Stores in the Twentieth Century*. Chapel Hill: University of North Carolina Press, 2010.

Devereux, Cecily. *Growing a Race: Nellie McClung and the Fiction of Eugenic Feminism*. Montreal and Kingston: McGill-Queen's University Press, 2005.

– "New Woman, New World: Maternal Feminism and the New Imperialism in the White Settler Colonies." *Women's Studies International Forum* 22, no. 2 (1999): 175–84.

De Zwart, M.L. "White Sauce and Chinese Chews: Recipes as Postcolonial Metaphors." In *Unsettled Pasts: Reconceiving the West through Women's History*, edited by S. Carter, 129–49. Calgary, AB: University of Calgary Press, 2005.

Dick, Trevor J.O. "Consumer Behavior in the Nineteenth Century and Ontario Workers, 1885–1889." *Journal of Economic History* 46, no. 2 (June 1986): 477–88.

"DickStorm." In comments to "Alberta Farm Family," by Danielle Nerman.

Djebabla, Mourad. "Le gouvernement fédéral et la diète de guerre proposée et imposée aux Canadiens ou la Première Guerre Mondiale et la consommation 'patriotiquement responsible,' 1917–1918." *Association québécoise d'histoire politique*, Autumn 2011, 171–89.

Dodaro, Santo, and Leonard Pluta. *The Big Picture: The Antigonish Movement of Eastern Nova Scotia*. Montreal and Kingston: McGill-Queen's University Press, 2012.

Dodd, Dianne. "Women and Domestic Technology: Household Drudgery, 'Democratized Consumption,' and Patriarchy." In *Framing Our Past: Canadian Women's History in the Twentieth Century*, edited by Sharon Anne Cook, Lorna R. McLean, and Kate O'Rourke, 101–10. Montreal and Kingston: McGill-Queen's University Press, 2001.

DuPlessis, Robert S. "Was There a Consumer Revolution in Eighteenth-Century New France?" *French Colonial History* 1 (2002): 143–59.

Dyck, Erika. *Facing Eugenics: Reproduction, Sterilization, and the Politics of Choice*. Toronto: University of Toronto Press, 2013.

Earls Canada. "Earls Dress Code Update." 7 December 2017. https://earls.ca/news/earls-dress-code-update.

Early Canadiana Online. "An Act to Confer Certain Powers upon the Governor in Council and to Amend the Immigration Act." Accessed 15 March 2012, http://canadiana.org.

Emery, J.C. Herbert, and Clint Levitt. "Cost of Living, Real Wages and Real Incomes in Thirteen Canadian Cities, 1900–1950." *Canadian Journal of Economics* 35, no. 1 (February 2002): 115–37.

Enstad, Nan. *Ladies of Labour, Girls of Adventure: Working Women, Popular Culture, and Labor Politics at the Turn of the Twentieth Century*. New York: Columbia University Press, 1999.

Fahrni, Magda. "Counting the Costs of Living: Gender, Citizenship, and a Politics of Prices in 1940s Montreal." *Canadian Historical Review* 83, no. 4 (December 2002): 483–504.

Frager, Ruth. "Politicized Housewives in the Jewish Communist Movement of Toronto, 1923–1933." In *Beyond the Vote: Canadian Women and Politics*, edited by Joan Sangster and Linda Kealey, 258–75. Toronto: University of Toronto Press, 1989.

Frank, Dana. "Housewives, Socialists, and the Politics of Food: The 1917 New York Cost-of-Living Protests." *Feminist Studies* 11, no. 2 (Summer 1985): 255–85.

– *Purchasing Power: Consumer Organizing, Gender, and the Seattle Labor Movement, 1919–1929*. Cambridge: Cambridge University Press, 1994.

Freeman, Barbara M. "Laced In and Let Down: Women's Fashion Features in the Toronto Daily Press, 1890–1900." In Palmer, *Fashion*, 291–314.

Fulsang, Deborah. "The Fashion of Writing, 1985–2000: Fashion-Themed Television's Impact on the Canadian Fashion Press." In Palmer, *Fashion*, 315–38.

Gagan, David, and Rosemary Gagan. "Working-Class Standards of Living in Late-Victorian Urban Ontario: A Review of the Miscellaneous Evidence on the Quality of Material Life." *Journal of the Canadian Historical Association* 1, no. 1 (1990): 171–93.

Gilman, Nils. *Mandarins of the Future: Modernization Theory in Cold War America*. Baltimore, MD: Johns Hopkins University Press, 2007.

Giroux, Henry A. "Schools for Sale: Public Education, Corporate Culture, and the Citizen-Consumer." *Educational Forum* 63, no. 2 (1999): 140–9.

Glassford, Sarah, and Amy Shaw. "Transformation in a Time of War?" Introduction to *A Sisterhood of Suffering and Service: Women and Girls of*

*Canada and Newfoundland during the First World War*, edited by Sarah Glassford and Amy Shaw, 12–13. Vancouver: UBC Press, 2012.

Glickman, Lawrence. *Buying Power: A History of Consumer Activism in America*. Chicago: University of Chicago Press, 2009.

– "'Make Lisle the Style': The Politics of Fashion in the Japanese Silk Boycott, 1937–1940." *Journal of Social History* 38, no. 3 (Spring 2005): 573–608.

Goldstein, Carolyn M. *Creating Consumers: Home Economists in Twentieth-Century America*. Chapel Hill: University of North Carolina Press, 2012.

Gordon, Robert J. *The Rise and Fall of American Growth: The U.S. Standard of Living since the Civil War*. Princeton, NJ: Princeton University Press, 2016.

"Government Rejects Law Change on Bosses Forcing Women to Wear High Heels at Work." *The Independent*, 21 April 2017. http://www.independent .co.uk.

Grazia, Victoria de, and Ellen Furlough, eds. *The Sex of Things: Gender and Consumption in Historical Perspective*. Berkeley and Los Angeles: University of California Press, 1996.

Guard, Julie. "A Mighty Power against the Cost of Living: Canadian Housewives Organize in the 1930s." *International Labor and Working-Class History* 77, no. 1 (Spring 2010): 27–47.

– "The Politics of Milk: Canadian Housewives Organize in the 1930s." In *Edible Histories, Cultural Politics: Towards a Canadian Food History*, edited by Franca Iacovetta, Valerie J. Korinek, and Marlene Epp, 271–85. Toronto: University of Toronto Press, 2012.

– *Radical Housewives: Price Wars and Food Politics in Mid-Twentieth-Century Canada*. Toronto: University of Toronto Press, 2019.

– "Women Worth Watching: Radical Housewives in Cold War Canada." In *Whose National Security? Canadian State Surveillance and the Creation of Enemies*, edited by Gary Kinsman, Dieter K. Buse, and Mercedes Steedman, 73–90. Toronto: Between the Lines, 2000.

Hammill, Faye, and Michelle Smith, *Magazines, Travel, and Middlebrow Culture: Canadian Periodicals in English and French, 1925–1960*. Liverpool, UK. Liverpool University Press, 2015.

Harvey, Kathryn. "Amazons and Victims: Resisting Wife-Abuse in Working-Class Montreal, 1869–1879." *Journal of the Canadian Historical Association / Revue de la Société historique du Canada* 2, no. 1 (1991): 131–48.

Haulman, Kate. *The Politics of Fashion in Eighteenth-Century America*. Chapel Hill: North Carolina University Press, 2011.

Hayes, Shannon. *Radical Homemakers: Reclaiming Domesticity from a Consumer Culture*. New York: Left to Write Press, 2010.

Heap, Ruby. "From the Science of Housekeeping to the Science of Nutrition: Pioneers in Canadian Nutrition and Dietetics at the University of

Toronto's Faculty of Household Science, 1900–1950." In *Challenging Professions: Historical and Contemporary Perspectives on Women's Professional Work*, edited by Elizabeth Smyth, Sandra Acker, Paula Bourne, and Alison Prentice, 141–70. Toronto: University of Toronto Press, 1999.

Henderson, Jennifer. *Settler Feminism and Race Making in Canada*. Toronto: University of Toronto Press, 2003.

Heron, Craig. *Booze: A Distilled History*. Toronto: Between the Lines, 2003.

Hilton, Matthew. "The Female Consumer and the Politics of Consumption in Twentieth-Century Britain." *Historical Journal* 45, no. 1 (March 2002): 103–28.

– "The Legacy of Luxury: Moralities of Consumption since the 18th Century." *Journal of Consumer Culture* 4 (2004): 101–23.

– *Prosperity for All: Consumer Activism in an Era of Globalization*. Ithaca, NY: Cornell University Press, 2009.

Hobbs, Margaret. "The Women's Pages of *The Western Producer*, 1925–1939: Violet McNaughton and Interwar Feminism in Canada." *Women's and Social Movements Online*, September 2009, 1.

Hobsbawm, Eric. "Marx and History." *New Left Review* 1, no. 143 (January–February 1984): 39–50.

Hunt, Karen. "The Politics of Food and Women's Neighborhood Activism in First World War Britain." *International Labor and Working-Class History* 77 (Spring 2010): 8–26.

Hunt, Lynn. *Writing History in the Global Era*. New York: Norton, 2014. Kindle.

Iacovetta, Franca. "Recipes for Democracy? Gender, Family, and Making Female Citizens in Cold War Canada." *Canadian Woman Studies* 12, no. 20 (2000): 12–27.

Iacovetta, Franca, Valerie J. Korinek, and Marlene Epp, eds. *Edible Histories, Cultural Politics: Towards a Canadian Food History*. Toronto: University of Toronto Press, 2012.

Jabr, Ferris. "How to Really Eat like a Hunter-Gatherer: Why the Paleo Diet Is Half-Baked." *Scientific American*, 3 June 2013. Accessed 29 April 2016. http://www.scientificamerican.com.

Jacobs, Meg. *Pocketbook Politics: Economic Citizenship in Twentieth-Century America*. Princeton, NJ: Princeton University Press, 2005.

Jonah, Anne Marie Lane, and Elizabeth Tait. "Filles d'Acadie, Femmes de Louisbourg: Acadian Women and French Colonial Society in Eighteenth-Century Louisbourg." *French Colonial History* 8 (2007): 23–51.

Juvik, Kaitlyn. "Why I Organized a 'No Bra Day' at My High School." *Guardian*, 17 June 2016. https://www.theguardian.com.

Kechnie, Margaret. *Organizing Rural Women: The Federated Women's Institutes of Ontario, 1897–1919*. Montreal and Kingston: McGill-Queen's University Press, 2003.

Kelcey, Barbara. "Dress Reform in Nineteenth Century Canada." In Palmer, *Fashion*, 229–48.

Kelly, Jennifer, and Dan Cui. "Racialization and Work." In *Working People in Alberta: A History*, edited by Alvin Finkel, 267–86. Edmonton: University of Alberta Press, 2012.

Klein, Naomi. *No Logo: Taking Aim at the Brand Bullies*. Toronto: Vintage, 2000.

Korinek, Valerie. *Roughing It in the Suburbs: Reading "Chatelaine" Magazine in the Fifties and Sixties*. Toronto: University of Toronto Press, 2000.

Kowaleski-Wallace, Elizabeth. *Consuming Subjects: Women, Shopping, and Business in the Eighteenth Century*. New York: Columbia University Press, 1997.

Krasnick Warsh, Cheryl, and Dan Malleck, eds. *Consuming Modernity: Gendered Behaviour and Consumerism before the Baby Boom*. Vancouver: UBC Press, 2013.

*Legacy: A History of Saskatchewan Homemakers' Clubs and Women's Institutes, 1911–1988*. Saskatoon, SK: Focus Publishing, 1988.

Levesque, Andrée. *Making and Breaking the Rules: Women in Quebec, 1919–1939*. Translated by Yvonne Klein. Toronto: McClelland & Stewart, 1994.

Lewis, Frank D., and M.C. Urquhart. "Growth and the Standard of Living in a Pioneer Economy: Upper Canada, 1826–1851." *William and Mary Quarterly* 56, no. 1 (January 1999): 151–81.

Liverant, Bettina. *Buying Happiness: The Emergence of Consumer Consciousness in Canada*. Vancouver: UBC Press, 2018.

– "From Budgeting to Buying: Canadian Consumerism in the Post War Era." *Past Imperfect* 8 (1999–2000): 62–92.

Lockie, Stewart. "Responsibility and Agency with Alternative Food Networks: Assembling the 'Citizen Consumer.'" *Agriculture and Human Values* 26, no. 3 (September 2009): 193–201.

Luxton, Meg. *More Than a Labour of Love: Three Generations of Women's Work in the Home*. Toronto: Women's Press, 1980.

MacDonald, Heidi. "Maritime Women, the Great Depression, and the Dominion-Provincial Youth Training Program, 1937–39." In *Making Up the State: Women in 20th Century Atlantic Canada*, edited by Janet Guildford and Suzanne Morton, 131–50. Fredericton, NB: Acadiensis Press, 2010.

MacKay, M. Elaine. "Three Thousand Stitches: The Development of the Clothing Industry in Nineteenth-Century Halifax." In Palmer, *Fashion*, 166–81.

Macleod, David I. "Food Prices, Politics, and Policy in the Progressive Era." *Journal of the Gilded Age and Progressive Era* 8, no. 3 (July 2009): 365–406.

MacPherson, Ian. *Each for All: A History of the Co-operative Movement in English Canada, 1900–1945*. Toronto: Macmillan, 1979.

– "'In These Pioneer Days': George Keen and Leadership through Sacrifice and Determination." In *Canadian Co-operatives in the Year 2000: Memory,*

*Mutual Aid, and the Millennium,* edited by Brett Fairbairn, Ian MacPherson, and Nora Russell, 40–56. Saskatoon, SK: Centre for the Study of Co-operatives, 2000.

Manitoba Culture, Heritage, and Recreation. *The Women's Institutes of Manitoba.* Winnipeg, MB: Historic Resources Branch, 1985.

McCalla, Douglas. *Consumers in the Bush: Shopping in Rural Upper Canada.* Toronto: University of Toronto Press, 2015.

McLean, Lorna. "'Deserving' Wives and 'Drunken' Husbands: Wife Beating, Marital Conduct, and the Law in Ontario, 1850–1910." *Histoire sociale / Social History* 69 (2002): 59–81.

McMaster, Lindsay. *Working Girls in the West: Representations of Wage Earning Women.* Vancouver: UBC Press, 2008.

McNaught, Kenneth. *A Prophet in Politics: A Biography of J.S. Woodsworth.* Toronto: University of Toronto Press, 2001.

Medlrum, Claire. Comment to Nerman, "Alberta Farm Family."

Micheletti, Michele, Andreas Follesdal, and Dietlind Stolle, eds. *Politics, Products, and Markets: Exploring Political Consumerism Past and Present.* New Brunswick, NJ: Transaction Publishers, 2004.

Milburn, Michael P. "Indigenous Nutrition: Using Traditional Food Knowledge to Solve Contemporary Health Problems." *American Indian Quarterly* 28, no. 3/4 (Summer/Autumn 2004): 411–34.

Mitchinson, Wendy. "The WCTU: 'For God, Home and Native Land': A Study in Nineteenth-Century Feminism." In *A Not Unreasonable Claim: Women and Reform in Canada, 1880s–1920s,* edited by Linda Kealey, 151–68. Toronto: Women's Press, 1979.

– "Woman's Christian Temperance Union." In *The Oxford Companion to Canadian History,* edited by Gerald Hallowell, 667. Toronto: Oxford University Press, 2004.

Morton, Suzanne. *Ideal Surroundings: Domestic Life in a Working-Class Suburb in the 1920s.* Toronto: University of Toronto Press, 1995.

Mosby, Ian. *Food Will Win the War: The Politics, Culture, and Science of Food on Canada's Home Front.* Vancouver: UBC Press, 2014.

Neal, Rusty. *Brotherhood Economics: Women and Co-operatives in Nova Scotia.* Sydney, NS: Cape Breton University Press, 1998.

Nerman, Danielle. "Alberta Farm Family Eating like Pioneers for a Year." *CBC News,* 27 November 2015. Accessed 29 April 2016. http://www.cbc.ca.

Nicholas, Jane. *The Modern Girl: Feminine Modernities, the Body, and Commodities in the 1920s.* Toronto: University of Toronto Press, 2015.

"No Bra, No Problem." *Mic,* June 2016. https://www.facebook.com.

Noel, Jan. "Defrocking Dad: Masculinity and Dress in Montreal, 1700–1867." In Palmer, *Fashion,* 68–89.

Norman, Alison. "'Fit for the Table of the Most Fastidious Epicure': Culinary Colonialism in the Contact Zone." In *Edible Histories, Cultural Politics: Towards a Canadian Food History*, edited by Franca Iacovetta, Valerie J. Korinek, and Marlene Epp, 31–51. Toronto: University of Toronto Press, 2012.

O'Connor, Eileen. "Constructing Medical Social Authority on Dress in Victorian Canada." *Canadian Bulletin of Medical History* 25, no. 2 (2008): 391–406.

O'Donnell, Lorraine. "Le voyage virtuel: Les consommatrices, le monde de l'étranger et Eaton à Montréal, 1880–1980." *Revue d'histoire de l'Amérique français* 58, no. 4 (Spring 2005): 535–68.

Olson, Miles. *Unlearn, Rewild: Earth Skills, Ideas and Inspiration for the Future Primitive.* Gabriola Island, BC: New Society Publishers, 2012.

Orenstein, Hanna. "This High School Senior Got Called Out for Not Wearing a Bra to School." *Seventeen*, 3 June 2016. http://www.seventeen.com.

Orleck, Annelise. "'We Are That Mythical Thing Called the Public': Militant Housewives during the Great Depression." *Feminist Studies* 19, no. 1 (Spring 1993): 147–72.

Otty, Marianne. *Fifty Years of Women's Institutes in New Brunswick, Canada, 1911–1961: A History.* Fredericton, NB: Women's Institutes, 1961.

*Oxford English Living Dictionaries.* "Prosumer." Accessed 23 January 2018. https://en.oxforddictionaries.com.

Palmer, Alexandra, ed. *Fashion: A Canadian Perspective.* Toronto: University of Toronto Press, 2004.

Parr, Joy. *Domestic Goods: The Material, the Moral, and the Economic in the Postwar Years.* Toronto: University of Toronto Press, 1999.

– *The Gender of Breadwinners: Women, Men, and Change in Two Industrial Towns, 1880–1950.* Toronto: University of Toronto Press, 1990.

Pederson, Diana. "The Scientific Training of Mothers: The Campaign for Domestic Science in Ontario Schools, 1890–1913." In *Critical Issues in the History of Canadian Science, Technology, and Medicine,* edited by Richard A. Jarrell and Arnold E. Roos, 178–94. Ottawa, ON: HSTC Publications, 1983.

Peiss, Kathy. *Hope in a Jar: The Making of America's Beauty Culture.* Philadelphia: University of Pennsylvania Press, 1998.

Penfold, Steve. *The Donut: A Canadian History.* Toronto: University of Toronto Press, 2008.

Pincus, Steve. "'Coffee Politicians Does Create': Coffeehouses and Restoration Political Culture." *Journal of Modern History* 67, no. 4 (December 1995): 807–34.

Prince, Nicholette. "Influence of the Hudson's Bay Company on Carrier and Coast Salish Dress, 1830–1850." *Material History Review* 38 (Fall 1993): 15–26.

Rappaport, Erika. "Sacred and Useful Pleasures: The Temperance Tea Party and the Creation of a Sober Consumer Culture in Early Industrial Britain." *Journal of British Studies* 52, no. 4 (October 2013): 990–1016.

Razack, Sherene. "Schools for Happiness: Instituts Familiaux and the Education of Ideal Wives and Mothers." In *Delivering Motherhood: Maternal Ideologies and Practices in the 19th and 20th Centuries*, edited by Katherine Arnup, Andrée Levesque, and Ruth Roach Pierson, 211–37. New York: Routledge, 1990.

Rebus, Shirley, Arlene Smith, and Norma Bannerman. "Canadian Home Economics Association, 1939–1989." *Illinois Teacher of Home Economics* 33, no. 1 (1989): 2.

Reekie, Gail. *Temptations: Sex, Selling, and the Department Store*. Sydney, Australia: Allen & Unwin, 1993.

Riley, Barbara. "Six Saucepans to One: Domestic Science vs. the Home in British Columbia, 1900–1930." In *Not Just Pin Money: Selected Essays on the History of Women's Work in British Columbia*, edited by Barbara K. Latham and Roberta J. Pazdro, 159–81. Victoria, BC: Camosun College, 1984.

Robbins, Mark. "Making a Middle-Class 'Public': Middle-Class Consumer Activism in Post–First World War America." In *Shopping for Change: Consumer Activism and the Possibilities of Purchasing Power*, edited by Louis Hyman and Joseph Tohill, 53–64. Toronto: Between the Lines, 2017.

Rowbotham, Sheila. "Consumer Power: Women's Contribution to Alternatives and Resistance to the Market in the United States, 1880–1940." In *Women and Market Societies: Crisis and Opportunity*, edited by B. Einhorn and E.J. Yeo, 11–29. London: Edward Elgar Publishing, 1995.

Ruddel, David-Thiery. "Clothing, Society, and Consumer Trends in the Montreal Area, 1792–1835." In *New England / New France, 1600–1850*, edited by Peter Benes, Jane Montague Benes, and Ross W. Beales, 122–34. Boston: Boston University Press, 1989.

Rudy, Jarrett. *The Freedom to Smoke: Tobacco Consumption and Identity*. Montreal and Kingston: McGill-Queen's University Press, 2005.

Rutherdale, Myra. "Packing and Unpacking: Northern Women Negotiate Fashion in Colonial Encounters during the Twentieth Century." In *Contesting Bodies and Nation in Canadian History*, edited by Jane Nicholas and Patrizia Gentile, 117–33. Toronto: University of Toronto Press, 2013.

Rutherdale, Robert. *Hometown Horizons: Local Responses to Canada's Great War*. Vancouver: UBC Press, 2004.

Rutherford, Janice Williams. *Selling Mrs. Consumer: Christine Frederick and the Rise of Household Efficiency*. Athens: University of Georgia Press, 2003.

Sacouman, R. James. "Underdevelopment and the Structural Origins of Antigonish Movement Co-operatives in Eastern Nova Scotia." *Acadiensis* 7, no. 1 (Autumn 1977): 66–85.

Sager, Eric, and Peter Baskerville. "Unemployment, Living Standards, and the Working-Class Family in Urban Canada in 1901." *History of the Family* 2, no. 3 (1997): 229–54.

Sandwell, R.W. *Powering Up Canada: A History of Power, Fuel, and Energy from 1600.* Montreal and Kingston: McGill-Queen's University Press, 2016.

Sangster, Joan. "Consuming Issues: Women on the Left, Political Protest, and the Organization of Homemakers, 1920–1960." In *Framing Our Past: Canadian Women's History in the Twentieth Century*, edited by Sharon Anne Cook, Lorna R. McLean, and Kate O'Rourke, 240–7. Montreal and Kingston: McGill-Queen's University Press, 2001.

– *Earning Respect: The Lives of Working Women in Small-Town Ontario, 1920–1960.* Toronto: University of Toronto Press, 1995.

– Introduction to "Part Four: Women's Activism and the State." In *Framing Our Past: Canadian Women's History in the Twentieth Century*, edited by Sharon Anne Cook, Lorna R. McLean, and Kate O'Rourke, 201–11. Montreal and Kingston: McGill-Queen's University Press, 2001.

– "Mobilizing Women for War." In *Canada and the First World War: Essays in Honour of Robert Craig Brown*, edited by David Clark MacKenzie, 157–93. Toronto: University of Toronto Press, 2005.

Scammell, Margaret. "The Internet and Civic Engagement: The Age of the Citizen-Consumer." *Political Communication* 17, no. 4 (2000): 351–5.

Schor, Juliet B., and Craig J. Thompson. "Introduction: Practising Plenitude." In *Sustainable Lifestyles and the Quest for Plenitude: Case Studies in the New Economy*, edited by Schor and Thompson, location 111. New Haven, CT: Yale University Press, 2014. Kindle.

Scorsese, Martin, dir. *Boardwalk Empire.* Season 1, episode 1, "Boardwalk Empire." Written by Terence Winter. Aired 19 September 2010 on HBO.

Scott, Linda. *Fresh Lipstick: Redressing Fashion and Feminism* New York: Palgrave Macmillan, 2005.

Sewell, Jessica. "Tea and Suffrage." *Food, Culture & Society* 11, no. 4 (December 2008): 500.

Simpson, Edith Rowles. *Home Economics in Canada: Prologue to Change.* Saskatoon, SK: University of Saskatchewan, 1964.

Sklar, Katherine K. "The Consumers' White Label Campaign of the National Consumers' Leagues, 1898–1918." In *Getting and Spending: European and American Consumer Societies in the Twentieth Century*, edited by Susan Strasser, Charles McGovern, and Matthias Judt, 17–36. New York: Cambridge University Press, 1998.

Smart, Judith. "The Politics of the Small Purse: The Mobilization of Housewives in Interwar Australia." *International Labor and Working-Class History* 77 (Spring 2010): 48–68.

Snell, James. *Macdonald Institute: Remembering the Past, Embracing the Future.* Toronto: Dundurn, 2003.

Soper, Kate. "Re-thinking the 'Good Life': The Citizenship Dimension of Consumer Disaffection with Consumerism." *Journal of Consumer Culture* 7, no. 2 (2007): 205–29.

Srigley, Katrina. "Clothing Stories: Consumption, Identity, and Desire in Depression-Era Toronto." *Journal of Women's History* 19, no. 1 (Spring 2007): 82–104.

Stamp, Robert. "Teaching Girls Their God Given Place in Life: The Introduction of Home Economics in the Schools." *Atlantis* 2, no. 2 (Spring 1977): 18–34.

Statistics Canada. "Cities, Towns, and Villages in Canada." Table no. A-11. In *Eighth Census of Canada, 1941.* Accessed 26 June 2014. https://archive.org /details/1941981941P7NOA111941ef.

– *Historical Statistics of Canada.* "Section D: The Labour Force," table D8-85. Accessed 29 September 2017. http://www.statcan.gc.ca.

– "The Surge of Women in the Workforce." Accessed 29 September 2017. http://www.statcan.gc.ca.

Storrs, Landon. *Civilizing Capitalism: The National Consumers' League, Women's Activism, and Labor Standards in the New Deal Era.* Chapel Hill: University of North Carolina Press, 2000.

Strange, Carolyn. *Toronto's Girl Problem: The Perils and Pleasures of the City, 1880–1930.* Toronto: University of Toronto Press, 1995.

Strong-Boag, Veronica. *The New Day Recalled: Lives of Girls and Women in English Canada, 1919–1939.* Toronto: Copp Clark Pitman, 1988.

– *The Parliament of Women: The National Council of Women of Canada, 1893– 1929.* National Museum of Man, Mercury Series. Ottawa, ON: University of Ottawa Press, 1976.

– "Pulling in Double Harness or Hauling a Double Load: Women, Work and Feminism on the Canadian Prairie." *Journal of Canadian Studies* 21, no. 3 (Fall 1986): 32–52.

Swyripa, Frances. *Wedded to the Cause: Ukrainian-Canadian Women and Ethnic Identity, 1891–1991.* Toronto: University of Toronto Press, 1993.

Taschereau, Sylvie. "L'arme favorite de l'épicier indépendant: Éléments d'une histoire sociale du crédit (Montréal, 1920–1940)." *Journal of the Canadian Historical Association* 4, no. 1 (1993): 265–92.

Taylor, Georgina M. "'Let Us Co-operate': Violet McNaughton and the Co-operative Ideal." In *Canadian Co-operatives in the Year 2000: Memory, Mutual Aid, and the Millennium,* edited by Brett Fairbairn, Ian MacPherson, and Nora Russell, 57–78. Saskatoon, SK: Centre for the Study of Co-operatives, 2000.

Terrill, Bertha M. *Household Management.* Chicago: American School of Household Economics, 1905.

Thompson, John Herd. *The Harvests of War: The Prairie West, 1914–1918*. Toronto: McClelland & Stewart, 1978.

Thorstein, Veblen. *The Theory of the Leisure Class*. London: Allen & Unwin, 1957 [1899].

Tilly, Louise A., and Joan W. Scott. *Women, Work, & Family*. New York and London: Routledge, 1987.

Timmer, Vanessa, Emmanuel Prinet, and Dagmar Timmer. *Sustainable Household Consumption: Key Considerations and Elements for a Canadian Strategy*. Toronto: Consumers Council of Canada, 2009.

Tinkler, Penny, and Cheryl Krasnick Warsh. "Feminine Modernity in Interwar Britain and North America: Corsets, Cars, and Cigarettes." *Journal of Women's History* 20, no. 3 (2008): 113–43.

Trentmann, Frank. "Citizenship and Consumption." *Journal of Consumer Culture* 7, no. 2 (2007): 147–58.

– "Crossing Divides: Consumption and Globalization in History." *Journal of Consumer Culture* 9, no. 2 (2009): 187–220.

– Introduction to *The Oxford Handbook of the History of Consumption*, edited by Trentmann, 1–22. New York: Oxford University Press, 2012.

–, ed. *The Oxford Handbook of the History of Consumption*. New York: Oxford University Press, 2012.

Valverde, Mariana. *The Age of Light, Soap, and Water: Moral Reform in English Canada, 1885–1925*. 2nd ed. Toronto: University of Toronto Press, 2008.

– "The Love of Finery: Fashion and the Fallen Woman in Nineteenth-Century Social Discourse." *Victorian Studies* 32, no. 2 (Winter 1989): 168–88.

– "'When the Mother of the Race Is Free': Race, Reproduction, and Sexuality in First-Wave Feminism." In *Gender Conflicts: New Essays in Women's History*, edited by Franca Iacovetta and Mariana Valverde, 3–26. Toronto: University of Toronto Press, 1992.

Vipond, Mary. *The Mass Media in Canada*. 3rd ed. Toronto: James Lorimer, 2000.

Vries, Jan de. *The Industrious Revolution: Consumer Behaviour and the Household Economy, 1650 to the Present*. Cambridge: Cambridge University Press, 2008. Kindle.

Walden, Keith. *Becoming Modern in Toronto: The Toronto Industrial Exhibition and the Shaping of a Late Victorian Culture*. Toronto: University of Toronto Press, 1997.

Wiedenhoft Murphy, Wendy. "Boycotts, Buycotts, and Legislation: Tactical Lessons from Workers and Consumers during the Progressive Era." In *Shopping for Change: Consumer Activism and the Possibilities of Purchasing Power*, edited by Louis Hyman and Joseph Tohill, 29–40. Toronto: Between the Lines, 2017.

Wiesen, S. Jonathan. "National Socialism and Consumption." In *The Oxford Handbook of the History of Consumption*, edited by Trentmann, 433–50. Oxford: Oxford University Press, 2012.

Willis, Ellen. "Women and the Myth of Consumerism." *Ramparts* 8, no. 12 (June 1970): 13–16. Accessed 30 September 2017. http://fair-use.org.

Wilson, Johanna Gudrun. "A History of Home Economics Education in Manitoba 1826–1966." Master's thesis, University of Manitoba, 1966.

Wilson, Mary. "Certified Women: Professional Program Curriculum at the Macdonald Institute for Domestic Science in Guelph, Ontario, Canada, 1903–1920." *History of Intellectual Culture* 8, no. 1 (2008/09): 1–17.

Winch, Donald. "The Problematic Status of the Consumer in Orthodox Economic Thought." In *The Making of the Consumer: Knowledge, Power and Identity in the Modern World*, edited by Frank Trentmann, 31–52. London: Berg, 2006.

Women's Auxiliary of the Win-the-War League. *Win-the-War Suggestions and Recipes* [1918]. In *Ontario and the First World War, 1914–1918: A Collection of Documents*, edited by Barbara M. Wilson, 138. Toronto: University of Toronto Press, 1977.

World Wildlife Fund. *Canadian Living Planet Report, 2007*. Toronto: World Wildlife Fund, 2007.

– *Living Planet Report, 2016*. Toronto: World Wildlife Fund, 2016.

Yuval-Davis, Nira. *The Politics of Belonging: Intersectional Contestations*. London: Sage, 2011.

# Index

Page numbers in italics refer to illustrations.

Acadia University, 77
advertising: and collective buying, 151; and conservation, 48; for department stores, 86; false, 182; fashion, 129; and Mrs. Consumer, 157, *159*; in support of temperance, 23; in WCTU journals, 23, 24, 25, 203nn40–1
aesthetics, 7, 143
Alberta: buy-at-home campaigns, 112, 114, *115*, 186; collective buying, 163, 173–4, 175; consumer citizenship, 116; consumer protection, 109; home economics education, 75, 77, 82, 92, 94, 110, 188; population, 91–2; and rural consumers, 98, 102, 105, 106; temperance, 22. *See also* Home Economics Weeks
Alberta Home Economics Association, 75, 88, 89
Alberta Sheep Breeders' Association, 109
alcohol and alcoholism: activism against, 18, 25, 27, 34, 186; alternatives to, 19, 27, 29, 30, 31–2, 35; and department stores,

23; effect on Canadian economy, 21–2; and family hardships, 36–9, 41; and food control, 58; and masculine spaces, 27–8. *See also* temperance
Ambrose, Linda, 100, 101
American General Federation of Women's Clubs, 110
American School of Household Economics, 79
appliances: availability, 75–6, 106; brand name, 84; in home economics education, 84–5, 87, 92; sewing machines, 105; as social improvement, 40, 75–6, 123, 158; stoves, 24, 84. *See also* labour-saving devices
assimilation, 8–9, 91–2, 94
Association des employées de manufacture, 132–3

Bacchi, Carol, 190
Barker, Stacey, 45
BC Consumers' League, 174–5
beachwear, 135, 138, *139*
beef: collective buying, 153, 170; conservation, 52, 53; and home

economics education, 80; prices, 46, 59, 170; substitutions, 47, 52, 59, 67, *68*; war-marked, 45
belonging, 3, 8, 9, 10, 13–14, 16
Bertram, Laurie K., 9, 126, 127
Beynon, Francis Marion, 54, 151
Birks Jewellers, 83
Blakely, E., 63, 140
*Bonne Fermière, La*, 134, 137
*Bonne Parole, La*: and collective buying, 173, 176; on fashion, 132–3, 134, 135, 137–8, *139*; and wartime, 60, 63
Borden, Robert, 43, 45, 46
Bourdieu, Pierre, 6–7, 8, 143, 191, 192
boycotts and buycotts, 13, 98, 163, 164, 169, 177, 186
brand-name goods: consumer protection, 109; endorsed by women's movements, 23, 24, 114; in home economics education, 74, 84, 88, 96; in recipes, 24, 25, 104
bread: appliances, 84; and collective buying, 172; conservation campaigns, 48, 52, 60; and consumer citizenship, 108–9; in non-English diets, 92; prices, 46; production, 75, 157; substitutions, 59; and temperance, 18, 36, 37
British Canadian Co-operative, 153–4
British Columbia: buy-at-home campaigns, 112; collective buying, 163, 174–5; and consumer protection, 109; and dress codes, 131; fruit prices, 104; pledge-card campaigns, 48, 49; women's movements, 20, 102, 163
British Imperial Association, 165
British Women's Co-operative Guild, 152
Brown, Robert, 62

budgeting: and collective buying, 148, 161; in home economics education, 73, 74, 79, 80, 82, 90–1; and low-income buyers, 44, 94, 141, 150, 164, 185; and pooled incomes, 120; of rural consumers, 105, 108, 109, 183; "The Shopper's Creed" (poem), 110; and temperance, 38; of time, 120–1; in wartime, 44, 46, 60
butter: boycotts, 163; collective buying, 170, 172, 176; and food control, 47, 58; and home economics education, 86; prices, 46, 166; and rural consumers, 102, 104, 112; substitutions, 13; and temperance, 18; war-marked, 45
buy-at-home campaigns, 112–13, *113*, 114, *115*, 186

Calgary Consumers' League, 173–4, 176
Canada: consumption and the environment, 5–6, 17; in First World War, 14, 21, 44, 45–52; food exports, 45; government inspections, 108–9; inflation, 46; labour force, 10; Wartime Elections Act, 50. *See also* conservation in wartime
Canada Food Board: dissolution, 59; and food prices, 46–7, 187; publications, 60, *61*, 67, *68*, *69*, 70, *71*; vigilance committee, 57
Canadian Business Women's Club, 165
Canadian Clubs, 55, 67
Canadian Consumers' Bureau, 109
*Canadian Co-operator*, 151
Canadian Expeditionary Force, 34, 117

*Canadian Food Bulletin*, 53
*Canadian Home Journal*, 24, 128
Canadian Household Economic
   Association (CHEA), 163, 164,
   168–9
*Canadian White Ribbon Tidings*:
   about, 20, 201nn13–14; "Curly's
   New Suit" (poem), 39; Honor Roll
   of Magazines, 23; on provocative
   clothing, 132; readers' letters, 24;
   "The Rum Mill's Grist" (story),
   37; on unpatriotic shopping, 26;
   on wet canteens, 34–5; "What
   Are They to Me" (article), 25, 26;
   "With Our Advertisers" section,
   24, 25, 203nn40–1
canning: community centre, 117;
   factories, 176; and sugar prices,
   175; in wartime, 65, 66, 67, 69,
   117. *See also* preserving
Canuck bread mixers, 84
capitalism: and collective buying,
   149, 150, 162, 178, 185; and home
   economics education, 73, 74, 83,
   89, 97; and rural consumers, 99;
   support of, 19, 21, 186–7. *See also*
   Women's Christian Temperance
   Union
catalogues, 98–9, 134, 137
Catholics: beachwear, 138, *139*; on
   fashion, 125, 132–3, 135, 137
CBC News, 98–9
Cercles de fermières, 104, 127, 128–9,
   135, 137, 144–5
CHEA. *See* Canadian Household
   Economic Association
children: affected by alcoholism,
   33, 35, 36, 37–9, 181; and
   co-operatives, 154, *167*; and
   department stores, 3; and fashion,

183; opportunities for, 42; and
   temperance, 19, 27
citizenship theory, 14
classes: belonging, 8; and clothing,
   94–6, 127, 141, 142, 143–4, 146,
   191; conservation disconnects,
   53, 54–5, 59; in co-operatives,
   149–50, 162, 164–5, 179; different
   aesthetics of, 7, 192; and luxuries,
   62–3, 141; and nationhood, 5;
   and rural consumers, 103; social
   improvement, 39–40; values in
   home economics education, 80,
   81–2, 88, 94, 95, 96–7
clothing: and happiness, 130; and
   Indigenous peoples, 8–9; lack
   caused by alcoholism, 37; and
   pledge-card campaigns, 54;
   production, 75, 107; for rural
   consumers, 121, 122; and social
   status, 142; and thrift, 141; for
   wives and children, 38–9. *See also*
   fashion
cocktails, 31
coffee: as alternative to alcohol,
   18, 19, 27, 29, 33, 34–5; rural
   consumers, 98, 99, 112, 114
Coffee House (Chicago), 29–30
coffee houses, 27
Cohen, Lizabeth, 188
Collective Buyers' Association, 175
collective buying, 148–79; aims,
   148–9; difficulties, 16, 149–50,
   166–7, 177–9; and gender, 149,
   150–62, *155*, *159*; interwar, 154,
   175–8; vs. individual buying,
   148; women's movements, 148,
   162–75, *167*, 176, 178, 179. *See
   also* co-operatives; Housewives'
   Leagues

comforts, 39, 42, 62, 138, 182

Communist Party, 187

community building, 102, 103, 117, 118, 122

conservation in wartime: and class, 52–5; criticism of tactics, 55; food regulations, 58–9; government promotion of, 47–52, *68*, *69*, 70, 71; and moral values, 60, 61–4, 183; pledge-card campaigns, 48–50, *49*, 53–4, 70, 72, 187; programs by women's groups, 67, 117; self-regulation by women, 56–7, 62, 70, *71*; use of military metaphors, 64–5, *65*; vigilante surveillance, 57–8, 72; in women's publications, 59–60, 61–7

consumer activism, 109–10, 122, 181, 186, 187

consumer citizenship: consumers vs. citizens, 187; and homemakers, 114; partnerships, 187–8; predominant frames, 14, 180; promotion of, 89; by rural consumers, 99–100, 108–16; shaped in home economics education, 73, 74, 97; studies, 12–13, 231n4; in wartime, 13, 14, 15, 44, 60, 65, 70–2

consumer culture: effects of industrialization and urbanization, 75–6; family oriented, 42; ideal of white bourgeois woman, 5, 74, 94, 96–7, 143; studies, 6, 11; values, 41; women's economic independence, 19, 29, 30, 35–6, 41, 42, 120. *See also* collective buying; fashion; home economics education; rural consumers; temperance; wartime consumer culture

consumer goods, 41, 42, 75, 80

consumer identity: in magazines, 25, *26*; Mrs. Consumer, 157–8, *159*, 160, 161

consumerism, defined, 158, 160

consumer knowledge, sharing of, 103–8

consumer protection, 109–10, 170–1, 184

Consumers Council of Canada, 5

*Consumers' Digest*, 110

Consumers' League, 175–6, 177

Consumers' National Federation, 110

consumption: and citizenship, 187, 188; concept, 12; drawbacks, 182–3; and the environment, 5–6, 17; and gender roles, 4–5, 10–11, 189; and periodization, 11–12; politicized, 185–6; role in home economics theory, 79; significance, 3–5, 6, 17, 181–2, 231n4; standards in home economics education, 80–1, 97; statistics, 5; vs. production, 73, 74, 75, 78–9, 97; and women's liberation, 181–2

consumptive labour, 158

conversion themes, 32–5

conviviality, 18–19, 27, 28

Cook, Ramsay, 62

Cook, Sharon Anne, 20

Cook, Tim, 34

cooking skills and tools: and English Canadian customs, 9–10, 91; home economics education, 74, 77, 84, 92–3, 96, 97, 104; "Reward of Good Cookery Reaped in Healthy Living" (article), 92–3; in wartime, 66, 67, 70, 72

Co-operative Associations Act, 153

Co-operative Commonwealth Federation, 187

co-operatives: alternatives to, 161,
178; class biases, 149–50, 164;
"CO-OP" label, 160; difficulties,
16, 149–50, 162, 179; leadership,
149, 150, 178–9; membership, 149,
150–1; publications, 151, 157–8;
types, 150–1, 152–3, 154; women's
preferences, 149, 160–1, 178–9,
185; women's role, 148–9, 151–2,
154, 155, 156–7, 160. See also
Housewives' Leagues
co-operative stores, 149, 152, 153,
154, 160–1, 171, 179
Co-operative Union of Canada, 154
Co-operative Wholesale Society, 151
Copeland, Donalda McKillop, 8
Cost of Living Inquiry, 165
"Country Store" events, 118, 122
Craig, Beatrice, 99
creativity: and consumption, 3,
184; and fashion, 125, 128, 129;
and homemaking, 41; and rural
consumers, 106, 116–17; in
wartime, 59, 70. See also interior
decorating; thrift
"Curly's New Suit" (poem), 39

Davidson, James, 12
Delacourt, Susan, 231n4
Delancy, Ida, 156, 157–8, 159, 160,
161, 178
Denison, Flora MacDonald, 126, 134
department stores: advertising, 23;
and collective buying, 153, 177; and
everyday life, 3; in home economics
education, 81, 83, 85–6, 86, 87,
88, 96; Home Economics Weeks,
114–16; and rural consumers, 111,
120; studies, 6; tea rooms, 30; and
temperance, 23, 186

Devereux, Cecily, 190
De Zwart, M.L., 92, 94
diets, 91–2, 93–4
Distinction (Bourdieu), 6
domestic sciences. See home
economics education
Dominion-Provincial Youth
Training Program, 87
dress codes, 124–5, 131, 137, 143, 191
dressmaking, 116, 128–9
Duggan, Grace, 89–91
Dupuis Frères, 85–6, 86

Eastern Europeans, 91
Eaton's department store: and
collective buying, 111, 153; in
everyday life, 3; and home
economics education, 83, 84,
87; in Home Economics Weeks,
88, 115–16; studies, 6; and
temperance, 23, 186, 188
École Ménagère Provinciale
(Montreal): home economics,
74–5, 77, 79–80, 81, 85–6, 86; and
product advertisements, 83
Edmonton Creche Society, 88
Edmonton Journal, 89, 94
Edmonton Junior League, 88
education, 37–8, 78, 158, 164, 171.
See also fashion; home economics
education; rural consumers
eggs: boycotts, 169; collective buying,
172, 176; consumer protection, 108;
and diets, 92; and home economics
education, 93; prices, 47, 163, 166,
169; and rural consumers, 102, 104,
120; in wartime, 47
elegance, 41, 143, 144, 146, 191
employment, 10, 21, 82, 83, 85, 142,
186, 190

Enstad, Nan, 11, 95–6, 143
environment, and consumption,
5–6, 17
E.T. Wright (company) kitchen
appliances, 84
evangelicalism, 19, 20. *See also*
Women's Christian Temperance
Union
*Everywoman's World*, 50, 52, 60, 64–5,
65, 129

Fahrni, Magda, 13
family hardships, and alcoholism,
36–9, 41
Farm Women's Vacation Week, 120
fashion, 124–47; attractions of, 16,
127–30, 181; during conservation,
60–2, 63–4, 138, 183; costs, 134–5,
145; dress codes, 124–5, 131, 191;
as enslaving, 16, 134, 135, 136, 182;
and feminism, 145, 146; as form
of communication, 130–3, 223n29;
in home economics education, 74,
94–6, 97; and identity construction,
8–9, 16; influence of, 134; and
male gaze, 11, 131–2, 136, 145–6;
mastering the art, 126, 141–5; moral
issues, 125, 135–6, 138, 140, 145,
183–4, 191; and nationalism, 25,
143–4; physically restrictive, 124,
126, 134, 145, 182; and selfishness,
25, 26, 64, 66, 138, 140; solutions to
difficulties, 136–41, 139; studies,
125–6; "Success in Good Dressing
Lies in Fundamentals" (article),
94–5; trends, 126, 127; in
wartime, 138, 140; and women's
organizations, 126–7
Federated Women's Institutes of
Canada (FWIC), 114, 115, 117, 180

Fédération nationale Saint-
Jean-Baptiste (FNSJB): collective
buying, 176–7; on conservation,
56, 60; and consumer citizenship,
15; on fashion, 137, 138, 139;
ideology, 127; and Women's War
Conference, 51
feminine spaces, 29–30
feminists: and citizenship, 14; and
consumption, 10; economic
independence, 35, 42; and
fashion, 6, 124–5, 126, 145, 146;
maternalism, 42, 127, 189–90.
*See also* Women's Christian
Temperance Union
field trips, 83, 86–7, 96
fish: as food substitute, 33, 43, 47, 52,
67, 68; and rural consumers, 112
flour: brands in recipes, 25;
collective buying, 172;
conservation, 52, 53, 58, 64;
prices, 46; substitutions, 33, 43,
47; and temperance, 23
food: and alcoholism, 37, 39; bulk
buying, 97, 174; distribution,
165, 167–8; Euro-Canadian,
97; inspections, 108–9; prices,
13, 46–7, 148, 163–5, 166, 187;
profiteering, 164, 166, 169, 170–1;
quality, 166; and rural consumers,
104–5; substitutes in wartime, 43,
47, 59, 66; vendor's conditions,
164; war-marked for export, 43,
45–6. *See also specific foods*
food control: and class disconnects,
55; government campaigns in
wartime, 44–52; media responses
to, 52, 53; women's responses
to, 44, 52, 58. *See also* conservation
in wartime

food controllers, 45, 52, 56–7, 58
Frager, Ruth, 13
Frederick, Christine, 165
French Canadians: and
    conservation, 63–4; and fashion,
    125, 127, 133, 137, 142, 144–6; and
    home economics, 85–6, *86*
*Fresh Lipstick* (Scott), 145
fruit, 104–5, 107, 166, 174–5, 176
fruit drinks, 27, 31
fuel, 21, 43, 46, 55, 183

*Galt Daily Reporter*, 25, *26*
gender: and collective buying,
    149, 150–62, *155*, *159*; labour
    divisions, 10–11, 39–40; roles in
    consumption, 4–5, 10–11, 189
George, Lloyd, 50
Gérin-Lajoie, Antoinette, 83, 85, 86, *86*
Glickman, Lawrence, 109, 186
*Globe, The*, 52
Goldstein, Carolyn M., 75, 76, 93
groceries, rural access to, 98–9
Guard, Julie, 13, 187
guilds, 151–2, 153–4, 178, 185

Hanna, William J., 45–6, 47, 57, 58
Happy Thought Soap, 24
Henderson, Jennifer, 190
Hilton, Matthew, 13
home economics education, 73–97;
    and academics, 74, 78, 89–95, 97;
    appliances, 84–5, 87, 92; archives,
    74–5; "Basis of Home-Making
    Should Be Scientific" (article), 89–
    90; on branded goods, 74, 84, 96;
    budgeting, 73, 74, 79, 80, 82, 90–1;
    on consumption standards, 80–1,
    97; consumption vs. production,
    73, 74, 78–9, 90, 97, 157–8; on

cooking skills and tools, 74, 92–3,
    96; on correct diets, 91–2, 93–4; in
    the countryside, 103, 104; courses,
    15, 73, 79–80, 87–8, 96, 213n47; on
    dress, 74, 94–6; history, 73, 75–8;
    "Home Biggest Business in This
    Modern World" (article), 90–1;
    and Home Economics Week, 74,
    88–9, 116, 188; importance of,
    89–91, 97; interior decorating, 74,
    81–2; labour-saving devices, 84–5;
    links to industry, 74, 83–8, *86*, 96;
    practice houses, 87; promotion of
    white cultural values, 9–10, 94, 97,
    191; and sense of superiority, 91,
    96; shaping the modern consumer
    citizen, 16, 73, 74, 97, 164, 187; in
    universities, 77–8
Home Economics Weeks, 74, 88–9,
    113–16, *115*, 188
home economists, 39, 74, 77, 160
home furnishings, 38, 40, 41, 80,
    81–2, 88, 96, 107
Homemakers Clubs, 109–10
homemaking, 4, 40–1, 102–3
home ownership, 38, 82
homesteading movement, 98–9
Hoodless, Adelaide, 101, 102
Horton, Margaret Graham, 54
hotels, 27, 28–9, 45
Housewives' Leagues: aims,
    164, 170, 172, 173; collective
    buying, 163–70, *167*, 171, 177,
    185; difficulties, 16, 169, 185;
    on distribution channels, 165,
    167–8; farmers' markets, 168, 169,
    173–4, 176, 185; guest speakers,
    165; lobbying and outreach, 165,
    174; membership, 167, 170; sales,
    165–7, *167*, 170, 178

housing, and alcoholism, 37, 38, 182
Hudson's Bay Company, 88, 115–16
Hunt, Lynn, 11

Iacovetta, Franca, 10
ice cream, 27, 33, 58
Icelandic Canadians, 9, 127
identity construction, 8–9
immigrants, 9, 10, 76, 91–2
Imperial Orders of the Daughters of the Empire, 51
income earning, as rural concern, 101, 103
Indigenous peoples, 8–9
inflation: and collective buying, 150, 185; in wartime, 46, 47, 52, 55, 62, 169, 182
Ingersoll Cream Cheese, 24
Institute News, 102
interior decorating, 74, 80, 81–2, 105–6, 116
intersectionality, 7

Jacobs, Meg, 72

Kechnie, Margaret, 100
Keen, George, 151, 152, 154
Kelcey, Barbara, 126
Kirby, Emily, 136–7
kitchens, 10, 40, 81, 84, 92, 106–7. See also appliances
Kiwanis Club, 88, 114

labour, gendered division of, 10–11, 39–40
labour-saving devices: in home economics education, 84–5; and rural consumers, 16, 106, 119, 121, 122, 123, 158; and women's liberation, 181

Ladies' Home Journal, 24, 129
League of Loyal Nova Scotians, 112
Ligue des ménagères, 172
Lillian Massey School of Domestic Science and Art, 77, 80
linens, 75, 80, 81, 85–6, 86
Local Councils of Women: collective buying, 175; frugality committee, 67; and Housewives' Leagues, 171, 173; and moral values, 60; pledge-card campaigns, 50, 53; surveillance of conservation, 57–8
lumber camps, 32
luxuries: and class conflict, 141; and criticism of women, 140; and temperance, 39, 42; vs. elegance, 41; in wartime, 57, 62, 63, 64, 183
Lynd, Constance, 136–7

MacDonald Institute (Guelph): field trips, 86–7; home economics education, 74–5, 77, 79, 80, 84, 85; testing recipes, 104
MacGregor Smith, Mrs. J., 114, 115, 116, 180
Macphail, Agnes, 151
MacPherson, Ian, 148, 149, 151
"Made in Canada" campaign, 21, 202n24
magazines, 23–4; and fashion, 128, 129, 134; in home economics education, 81–2, 92; and rural consumers, 120; and temperance, 41
mail-order houses, 111
male gaze, 11, 131–2, 133, 136–7, 145–6
Manitoba: collective buying, 153, 163, 175; consumer protection, 109; Farm Women's Vacation Week, 120; and fashion, 124, 127, 143;

home economics education, 75, 77, 80, 81; and rural consumers, 102, 107, 108, 111, 118; and thrift, 183; WCTUs, 20; WIs, 102

Manitoba Agricultural College, 74–5, 80, 81, 120, 135

manufacturing, 22, 45, 58, 90, 93

margarine, 13, 33, 43, 46–7, 58

markets, 104, 148, 166, 168, 169, 173–4, 176, 185

masculine spaces, 27, 29, 32

maternalism, 12, 127, 189–90

McCalla, Douglas, 76, 98, 99, 210n7

McCall's sewing patterns, 129

McClary Stove Company, 84

McClung, Nellie, 51, 151

McGill University, 77

McIntyre, Hazel, 89, 92–4

McLean's, 52

McNaughton, Violet, 54, 152–3

media, 32–5, 52. See also advertising; and specific journals

men: and alcohol, 28, 41, 181; consumer habits, 19, 32–5; in the countryside, 102; economic power, 42, 177, 188; masculine spaces, 27–8, 29, 32; role in co-operatives, 148–9, 150–1, 156, 157; in wartime, 50, 62, 63, 64, 66, 70, 140; women's superiority over, 190. See also male gaze

Methodists, 13, 39, 106–7

milk and milk bars, 27, 30–1, 97, 163, 165

Modern Girl, The (Nicholas), 95

modernity: in attire, 95, 126, 127, 130, 133; bourgeois nature of, 88, 96; and consumption, 9–10, 11–12, 160; in the countryside, 99, 102, 120; and evangelicalism, 20; and

home economics training, 80, 82, 90, 91; and rural consumers, 158

Moffat Stoves, 24, 84

Montreal Plain Clothes League, 60–1

Montreal Women's Club, 67

moral values: and appeals to retailers, 137; conservation in wartime, 60, 61–4, 183; and dress, 96, 97, 132–3, 135–6, 137–8, 146

Mount Allison University, 74–5, 77, 81

Mrs. Consumer, 157–8, 159, 160, 161

National Consumers' League, 173, 175

National Council of Women (NCW): collective buying, 162; on conservation, 52, 56; and consumer citizenship, 13, 15; on fashion, 134, 135, 138; ideology, 127, Old Clothes League, 135; publications, 20; and Women's War Conference, 51

National Dry Goods Association of the United States, 38

National Housewives' League, 163, 164, 169

nationalism: and fashion, 26, 140, 142, 143–4; and home economics, 9–10, "Made in Canada" campaign, 21, 202n24; and racism, 144; unpatriotic shopping, 25, 26, 203n46

NCW. See National Council of Women

Neal, Rusty, 149, 151, 154, 156

needlework, 105, 106, 116, 117, 128–9

New Brunswick, 20, 28, 74, 87, 106

Newhall, Georgina, 173, 174, 177–8

Nicholas, Jane, 95, 126, 127

Nineteen Hundred Washer Company, 84

"NoBraNoProblem" (hashtag), 124

Noel, Jan, 142

Nova Scotia: buy-at-home
   campaigns, 112, *113*, 186;
   collective buying, 173;
   co-operatives, 149, 153–4, *155*,
   156, 160–2, 178; frugality, 105;
   rural consumers, 102, 158

Olson, Miles, 99
Ontario: collective buying, 163, 164,
   165, 166, 169, 172; conservation,
   50, 52, 54, 66, 117; and fashion, 126,
   127, 129, 130, 134, 141–2, 143; home
   economics education, 74, 77, 81,
   84, 86, 87–8, 119; and male gaze,
   132; rural consumers, 106, 119–20;
   temperance, 23, 28–9, 31, 32; in
   wartime, 51, 67, 188; WIs, 100,
   118. *See also* department stores;
   Housewives' Leagues; Women's
   Christian Temperance Union
Organization of Resources
   Committee, 48
Ottawa Household League, 171–2
*Oxford Handbook of the History of
   Consumption* (Trentmann), 12

Parlby, Irene, 51, 151
Parr, Joy, 6, 13, 187
pastry bars, 31
Patrick, Mabel, 89–91, 94
patriotic consumerism, 66, 67, 72,
   111, 186, 187
Peiss, Kathy, 11
periodization, 11–12
Phaneuf, Florine, 138, *139*
*Politics of Belonging* (Yuval-Davis), 7
pork: collective buying, 170;
   conservation, 52, 53; prices, 46;
   substitutions, 47, 59, 67, *68*;
   war-marked, 45

potatoes, 170, 172, 174, 175–6, 177
poultry, 47, 86, 100, 104, 166, 168
Poverty Balls, 118, 122
practice houses, 87
preserving, 47, 65, *69*, 75. *See also*
   canning
Prince Edward Island: buy-at-home
   campaigns, 113; conservation, 52;
   and fashion, 121, 130; and rural
   consumers, 104, 107, 113, 120;
   temperance, 30; and WCTUs, 20
producerist consumerism, 16, 105,
   117, 122–3, 184
prohibition, 18, 21–2, 24, 27, 38, 182.
   *See also* temperance
prosumers, 184
Protestants, 62, 125, 144
Purity Flour, 23, 25, 186, 188

Quebec: buy-at-home campaigns,
   112–13; collective buying,
   163, 172–3, 175, 176–7, 185;
   conservation, 48, 53, 57, 67;
   consumer citizenship, 13, 108;
   fashion, 60, 126, 129, 133, 137–8,
   *139*; food prices, 105; and home
   economics education, 74, 77, 79,
   83, 85–6, 108; Home Economics
   Weeks, 113–14; rural consumers,
   110–11, 117; technologies, 106;
   temperance, 24; and WCTUs, 20
Quebec Homemakers Clubs, 53
*Quebec Telegraph*, 172

racism: in consumer practices, 5, 8,
   190; consumption studies, 12; and
   dress, 8–9, 144, 145, 146, 191; in
   home economics education, 94;
   and nationalism, 144
radios, and rural consumers, 106

Rappaport, Erika, 18
reading rooms, for sailors, 33
recipe books, 60, *61*, 66–7
recipes: and collective buying,
    171; and conservation, 60, 72;
    and cooking skills and tools,
    92–3; non-Canadian, 94; and rural
    consumers, 104; using brands, 24,
    26, 104; without alcohol, 32
Red Cross, 55, 62, 138
Red Rose Tea, 23, 24, 186, 187–8
respite, 27, 30, 119, 120–1, 181
restaurants, 29–30
*Revue Culinaire, La*, 86, *86*
Richardson, Ellen H., 78, 79
rights, 13–14, 108–10, 122
Rotary Clubs, 55
"Rum Mill's Grist, The" (story), 37
rural consumers, 98–123; access to
    groceries, 98–9; catalogues, 98–9,
    134, 137; collective buying, 163;
    as consumer citizens, 99–100,
    122, 123; frugality vs. entitlement,
    100, 116–22, 123, 182; and labour-
    saving devices, 16, 106, 119, 121,
    122, 123, 158; movements, 98,
    100–3, 110; producerist, 16, 105,
    117, 122–3, 184; respite, 119, 120–1;
    responsibilities, 110–16, *113*,
    *115*; rights, 108–10, 122; sharing
    consumer knowledge, 101, 103–8,
    117, 122, 158; studies, 76, 99. *See
    also* Women's Institutes
Rutherdale, Myra, 8
Rutherdale, Robert, 48
Ruzicka family, 98

sailors, and alcohol, 31, 33–4
Saint John Home Service School, 87
saloons, 27–8, 29, 31, 33, 41

Sangster, Joan, 13, 63, 70, 187, 189
Saskatchewan: activism, 54, 109,
    152; collective buying, 175;
    conservation, 58; and co-operation,
    152; Co-operative Associations
    Act, 153; co-operatives, 152, 153,
    154, 178; fruit prices, 104; and
    home economics education, 77;
    Homemakers Clubs, 109, 110;
    rural consumers, 102, 105, 117; and
    temperance, 27–8
Saskatchewan Equal Franchise
    Board, 58
Saskatchewan Grain Growers'
    Association, 152, 175
*Saturday Evening Post*, 24
schoolchildren, and dress codes,
    124, 131
Schor, Juliet B., 5
Scott, Linda, 145, 146
selfishness, and fashion, 25, 26, 64,
    66, 138, 140
sewing machines, 105
sexism, and fashion, 124, 125, 137
Sheila Rowbotham, 148
"Shopper's Creed, The" (poem),
    110–11
*Shopping-Basket Economics*
    (Delaney), 157–8, 162
*Shopping for Votes* (Delacourt), 231n4
Shortt, Elizabeth, 51
Shredded Wheat, 23, 24, 25
simplicity: and conservation, 51, 63;
    in fashion, 126, 143, 144, 145; in
    interior decorating, 82
Simpson's department store, 3, 23,
    87, 111, 186
"Sing a Song of Whiskey" (song), 36
Smith, Adam, 13
soap making, 75, 79

social decline, 76, 77
social status: and consumer culture,
    5, 6–7; and fashion, 142, 146–7,
    223n29; intersectionality, 7
socio-economic divides, 101, 102–3
soldiers, and alcohol, 34–5
Soper, Kate, 187
sophistication, 11, 142–3, 144, 146, 191
Srigley, Katrina, 126, 127, 129, 142
Stevens, H.H., 180
St Francis Xavier University, 87, 154,
    155–7, 156, 159
St Lawrence Market, 168
St Lawrence Sugar, 26, 83
stores, and cleanliness, 161, 162,
    170, 172
stoves, 24, 84
Strong-Boag, Veronica, 13, 119
sugar: brands in recipes, 25;
    conservation, 47, 52, 58; and
    home economics, 83; regulated
    supply, 175; substitutions, 59; and
    temperance, 18, 32; war-marked, 45
superiority: and clothing, 142,
    143, 191; in home economics
    education, 9–10, 91, 93, 96, 191;
    and imperial feminism, 190;
    racial and ethnic, 5, 7, 190–1, 192;
    and standards of taste, 7–10, 143,
    144–5, 191, 192
sustainability, 5–6, 17
Syndicat economique des
    ménagères, 172–3

T. Eaton Company. See Eaton's
    department store
tea, 24, 29, 30, 34, 67, 98, 112, 114
tea parties, 18–19
tea rooms, 27, 30
telephones, and rural consumers, 106

temperance, 18–42; and access
    to commodities, 35–41, 181–2;
    advertising in support of, 23; on
    alternatives to alcohol, 27, 30,
    31–2, 35; anti-saloon campaign,
    27–8; celebrations of, 18–19; dry
    establishments, 27–31; economic
    benefits, 21–2; hotels, 28; reform
    of sojourning men, 32–5; support
    of businesses, 22–5, 186, 187–8;
    in United Kingdom, 18. See also
    Women's Christian Temperance
    Union
textiles: commercially produced, 76,
    116; and fashion, 76, 107, 129, 143;
    in home economics education,
    82, 83, 87, 88, 96; and rural
    consumers, 105, 106; wool, 109
Thimble and Trinket Fund, 34
Thompson, Craig J., 5
Thomson, Henry B., 46, 47
Thorp, Nicola, 124–5
thrift: campaigns, 48, 50, 51, 53,
    54–5, 59, 64; and clothing,
    141; and food prices, 52; and
    homesteading movement, 99;
    linked with morality, 64, 65, 183;
    and moral values, 60, 62–4; of rural
    consumers, 103, 107–8, 118, 122;
    theme in publications, 59, 63; vs.
    entitlement, 116–22; in wartime,
    183; and working classes, 44, 53,
    55, 171
tin, 54, 55
tobacco, 19, 23, 24, 28, 30, 38
Toronto Daily Star: advertising, 48,
    49; collective buying, 166, 167;
    and fashion, 130; on food prices,
    153, 168, 169
Touchette, Kayla, 124

Trentmann, Frank, 11, 12
Triscuits, 24
Truro School of Domestic Science, 77

Ukrainian Canadians, 91
United Farmers of Alberta, 163, 175
United Kingdom: co-operative
    guilds, 148, 151–2; dress codes,
    124–5; and First World War, 43,
    44–5, 48; temperance, 18
United States: consumer activism,
    16, 109–10, 163, 186; co-operatives,
    148, 149, 153; food-administration
    office, 45; home economics
    education, 15, 73, 75, 77, 96
Université de Montréal, 83
University of Alberta: home
    economics, 75, 77, 92, 94, 213n47;
    and Home Economics Week, 88, 89
University of Manitoba, 75, 80, 81
University of Saskatchewan, 77
University of Toronto, 74–5, 77,
    81–2, 87
Unlearn, Rewild (Olson), 99

vacuum cleaners, 40, 106, 119, 181
Valverde, Mariana, 144, 190
Veblen, Thorstein, 223n29
Victory Loans, 43
Voice, The (Winnipeg), 46

Wanamaker's of Philadelphia, 23
War Measures Act, 45
wartime consumer culture, 43–72;
    collective buying, 163, 169, 177;
    consumer citizenship, 14, 15,
    70–2; fashion, 138, 140; food
    control, 13, 44–7, 185; government
    campaigns, 47–52, 183. See also
    conservation in wartime

Wartime Elections Act, 50
water and water fountains, 27, 31
WCTU. See Women's Christian
    Temperance Union
Wealth of Nations, The (Smith), 13
Western Canada Livestock Union, 109
wet canteens, 27, 34
White Ribbon Bulletin, 20, 128, 133,
    201n12
Willis, Ellen, 10–11
Wilson, Lockie, 165
Win-the-War League, 56, 66
WIs. See Women's Institutes
Woman's Century: about, 20, 54,
    59, 202n18; "The Best Foods to
    Buy during the War" (article),
    59; and branded goods, 84;
    and class disconnect, 54; on
    conservation, 51, 53, 54, 56–7,
    59–60, 64; "Extravagances and
    the War" (article), 62; on fashion,
    60–1, 129, 131, 134–5, 137, 141;
    "Fashion Wise & Otherwise"
    (column), 128; on food prices,
    52; on food regulations,
    58; "Grace and Beauty"
    (article), 143–4; "Luxury and
    Womanhood" (article), 63, 140;
    military metaphors, 64; "Pledge
    Card for the Deserving Rich"
    (article), 54
Woman's Citizens' League, 141
Woman Who Spends (Richardson),
    78, 79
women: communicating
    respectability, 41, 42; and
    conservation campaigns, 50,
    59; as consumer citizens, 4, 180,
    187; economic independence, 19,
    29, 30, 35–6, 41, 42, 120; ideal as

white bourgeois, 5, 74, 94, 96–7,
143; labour force, 10; patriotism,
21, 43, 44, 50, 59, 62, 65, 66, 70, 71;
in public sphere, 29; right to vote,
50; social identities, 4, 189–90;
support of state's agenda, 51–2,
72; university enrolment, 78
women's bodies, 140, 146, 147
Women's Christian Temperance
Union (WCTU), 18–42; aims and
ideals, 15, 19–20, 22, 23, 42; on
alternatives to alcohol, 27, 30,
31–2, 35; anti-saloon campaign,
27–8; on conservation, 56; on
drinkers and their families, 37;
on dry establishments, 27–31; on
economic benefits of prohibition,
21–2; evangelicalism, 20; history,
19–20, 101; membership, 19, 127;
mother-and-child-focused vision,
19, 35–41, 42; in popular media,
18; publications, 20, 21, 23–5,
201nn11–14, 203nn40–1; reform
of sojourning men, 32–5; support
of businesses, 22–5, 42, 186; and
Women's War Conference, 51
Women's Grain Growers
Associations, 152, 163, 175
women's groups: and class-based
divisions, 59; conservation
programs, 56, 67, 72; criticism

of food controllers, 56; and
government conferences, 51;
publication themes, 59–60, 62–7.
See also specific organizations
Women's Institutes (WIs): about,
100–3, 127; collective buying,
162–3; and consumer citizenship,
15; and Home Economics Week,
88; on income earning, 101, 103;
Institute News, 102; membership,
100, 102–3, 123; sharing consumer
knowledge, 101, 103–8, 184; "The
Shopper's Creed" (poem), 110
Women's Institutes of Nova Scotia
(WINS), 105, 106–7, 111–12, 113, 117
Women's Journal, 20, 23, 24, 201n11
Women's Liberal Federation, 128
women's liberation, and consumption,
181–2
Women's War Conference, 51, 188
wool, 109, 184
working classes: diets, 94; and fashion,
127, 141; and social decline, 76; and
thrift, 44, 53, 55; training in home
economics, 77
World Wildlife Fund, 5

Young Women's Christian
Association (YWCA), 15, 56, 77,
169
Yuval-Davis, Nira, 7, 8, 14, 112

# STUDIES IN GENDER AND HISTORY

General Editors: Franca Iacovetta and Karen Dubinsky

1 Suzanne Morton, *Ideal Surroundings: Domestic Life in a Working-Class Suburb in the 1920s*

2 Joan Sangster, *Earning Respect: The Lives of Working Women in Small-Town Ontario, 1920–1960*

3 Carolyn Strange, *Toronto's Girl Problem: The Perils and Pleasures of the City, 1880–1930*

4 Sara Z. Burke, *Seeking the Highest Good: Social Service and Gender at the University of Toronto, 1888–1937*

5 Lynne Marks, *Revivals and Roller Rinks: Religion, Leisure, and Identity in Late-Nineteenth-Century Small-Town Ontario*

6 Cecilia Morgan, *Public Men and Virtuous Women: The Gendered Languages of Religion and Politics in Upper Canada, 1791–1850*

7 Mary Louise Adams, *The Trouble with Normal: Postwar Youth and the Making of Heterosexuality*

8 Linda Kealey, *Enlisting Women for the Cause: Women, Labour, and the Left in Canada, 1890–1920*

9 Christina Burr, *Spreading the Light: Work and Labour Reform in Late-Nineteenth-Century Toronto*

10 Mona Gleason, *Normalizing the Ideal: Psychology, Schooling, and the Family in Postwar Canada*

11 Deborah Gorham, *Vera Brittain: A Feminist Life*

12 Marlene Epp, *Women without Men: Mennonite Refugees of the Second World War*

13 Shirley Tillotson, *The Public at Play: Gender and the Politics of Recreation in Postwar Ontario*

14 Veronica Strong-Boag and Carole Gerson, *Paddling Her Own Canoe. The Times and Texts of E. Pauline Johnson (Tekahionwake)*

15 Stephen Heathorn, *For Home, Country, and Race: Constructing Gender, Class, and Englishness in the Elementary School, 1880–1914*

16 Valerie J. Korinek, *Roughing It in the Suburbs: Reading* Chatelaine *Magazine in the Fifties and Sixties*

17 Adele Perry, *On the Edge of Empire: Gender, Race, and the Making of British Columbia, 1849–1871*

18 Robert A. Campbell, *Sit Down and Drink Your Beer: Regulating Vancouver's Beer Parlours, 1925–1954*

19 Wendy Mitchinson, *Giving Birth in Canada, 1900–1950*

20 Roberta Hamilton, *Setting the Agenda: Jean Royce and the Shaping of Queen's University*

21 Donna Gabaccia and Franca Iacovetta, eds., *Women, Gender, and Transnational Lives: Italian Workers of the World*

22 Linda Reeder, *Widows in White: Migration and the Transformation of Rural Women, Sicily, 1880–1920*

23 Terry Crowley, *Marriage of Minds: Isabel and Oscar Skelton Re-inventing Canada*

24 Marlene Epp, Franca Iacovetta, and Frances Swyripa, eds., *Sisters or Strangers? Immigrant, Ethnic, and Racialized Women in Canadian History*

25 John G. Reid, *Viola Florence Barnes, 1885–1979: A Historian's Biography*

26 Catherine Carstairs, *Jailed for Possession: Illegal Drug Use Regulation and Power in Canada, 1920–1961*

27 Magda Fahrni, *Household Politics: Montreal Families and Postwar Reconstruction*

28 Tamara Myers, *Caught: Montreal Girls and the Law, 1869–1945*

29 Jennifer A. Stephen, *Pick One Intelligent Girl: Employability, Domesticity, and the Gendering of Canada's Welfare State, 1939–1947*

30 Lisa Chilton, *Agents of Empire: British Female Migration to Canada and Australia, 1860s–1930*

31 Esyllt W. Jones, *Influenza 1918: Disease, Death, and Struggle in Winnipeg*

32 Elise Chenier, *Strangers in Our Midst: Sexual Deviancy in Postwar Ontario*

33 Lara Campbell, *Respectable Citizens: Gender, Family, and Unemployment in the Great Depression, Ontario, 1929–1939*

34 Katrina Srigley, *Breadwinning Daughters: Young Working Women in a Depression-Era City, 1929–1939*

35 Maureen Moynagh with Nancy Forestell, eds., *Documenting First Wave Feminisms, Volume I: Transnational Collaborations and Crosscurrents*

36 Mona Oikawa, *Cartographies of Violence: Women, Memory, and the Subject(s) of the "Internment"*

37 Karen Flynn, *Moving beyond Borders: A History of Black Canadian and Caribbean Women in the Diaspora*

38 Karen Balcom, *The Traffic in Babies: Cross Border Adoption and Baby-Selling between the United States and Canada, 1930–1972*

39 Nancy M. Forestell with Maureen Moynagh, eds., *Documenting First Wave Feminisms, Volume II: Canada – National and Transnational Contexts*

40 Patrizia Gentile and Jane Nicholas, eds., *Contesting Bodies and Nation in Canadian History*

41 Suzanne Morton, *Wisdom, Justice, and Charity: Canadian Social Welfare through the Life of Jane B. Wisdom, 1884–1975*

42 Jane Nicholas, *The Modern Girl: Feminine Modernities, the Body, and Commodities in the 1920s*

43 Pauline A. Phipps, *Constance Maynard's Passions: Religion, Sexuality, and an English Educational Pioneer, 1849–1935*

44 Marlene Epp and Franca Iacovetta, eds., *Sisters or Strangers? Immigrant, Ethnic, and Racialized Women in Canadian History, second edition*

45 Rhonda L. Hinther, *Perogies and Politics: Radical Ukrainians in Canada, 1891–1991*

46 Valerie J. Korinek, *Prairie Fairies: A History of Queer Communities and People in Western Canada, 1930–1985*

47 Julie Guard, *Radical Housewives: Price Wars and Food Politics in Mid-Twentieth Canada*

48 Nancy Janovicek and Carmen Nielson, *Reading Canadian Women's and Gender History*

49 L.K. Bertram, *The Viking Immigrants: Icelandic North Americans*

50 Donica Belisle, *Purchasing Power: Women and the Rise of Canadian Consumer Culture*